The Empty Room

Surviving the Loss of
a Brother or Sister at Any Age

Elizabeth DeVita-Raeburn

SCRIBNER
New York London Toronto Sydney

SCRIBNER
1230 Avenue of the Americas
New York, NY 10020

For information regarding special discounts for bulk purchases,
please contact Simon & Schuster Special Sales at 1-800-456-6798
or business@simonandschuster.com.

Designed by Kyoko Watanabe
Text set in Aldine

Manufactured in the United States of America

1 3 5 7 9 10 8 6 4 2

Library of Congress Cataloging-in-Publication Data

DeVita-Raeburn, Elizabeth.
The empty room: surviving the loss of a brother or sister/
Elizabeth DeVita-Raeburn.
p. cm.
Includes bibliographical references.
1. Bereavement—Psychological aspects.
2. Brothers and sisters—Death—Psychological aspects. I. Title.

BF575.G7D48 2004
155.9'37'0855dc22
2003066786

ISBN 0-7432-0151-5

For Ted

CONTENTS

The Empty Room

INTRODUCTION

The movie *The Big Chill* begins with the death of a character you never meet, except for a few shots of his body being dressed for burial. As it turns out, this faceless individual is instrumental to the plot. His funeral brings his old circle of friends together, to relive the past and renegotiate the present in the wake of his absence. Each person must reconsider who he or she is, individually and within the group, because of his death. You never meet the man who has died, but you feel his absence, which is actually a presence of sorts. Director Lawrence Kasdan got something right here, something that resonates, about the aftermath of loss.

The death of someone you love forces you to reconsider who you are. It forces you to belong to a club to which no one wants to be a member, and to which just about everyone, save those who die young, eventually belongs. In her 1978 book, *Illness as Metaphor,* the writer and critic Susan Sontag writes: "Illness is the night-side of life, a more onerous citizenship. Everyone who is born holds dual citizenship, in the kingdom of the well and in the kingdom of the sick." It's the same way with death. Or rather, being a survivor. Suddenly, ready or not, your membership is activated. It's your turn, it's your journey. What now?

This book is about my journey and the journey of those who

have lost a brother or sister. In 1980, when I was fourteen, my only sibling, my older brother, Ted, died from a rare immune deficiency disease after an eight-year illness, during which he'd had to live in a sterile "bubble" room at The National Institutes of Health in Bethesda, Maryland. His illness spanned a good portion of my childhood, long enough that it had become normal to me. I was devastated when he died. My life, my very identity, was shattered. But I wouldn't understand that for years. And I wouldn't fully explore my loss until I came to write this book.

The story of this book began eleven years after Ted's death. At the time, I was working as an editorial assistant at *The Washington Post,* answering phones, organizing supplies, begging to write small stories, and puzzling over what to do with my life. I'd gotten the job because my father, an oncologist, knew a patient who worked there. Journalism, while not my ambition, was deemed an acceptable form of writing by my parents, because it meant a paycheck. Except what I was doing wasn't really journalism. It was more like standing with my nose pressed against the window. And part of me was still toying with the idea of going to medical school.

I'd worked in medical research labs from the time I was fifteen until I was nineteen, labs run by one of my brother's former doctors. I was comfortable in the hospital; it felt like home. I knew sickness, death. They were, if not old friends, familiar companions. And a life outside the hospital, not engaged in crisis-saturated life-and-death issues, seemed meaningless. But the idea of being in the hospital for the rest of my life, confronted with a part of my life I also wanted to get past, also made me feel slightly hysterical. Trapped. What I really wanted was to be happy, to be normal. But I had no idea how to make that happen.

The line between what I felt I should do and what I wanted was hopelessly blurred. I frequently did things to pull the rug out from under myself, just to see if answers would become dislodged in the settling dust. Plus, though I craved normalcy, I was much more comfortable with stress and crisis. I found everyday sameness—

breakfast, lunch, dinner, work, bills, the gym—unnerving. I struggled with the most mundane tasks. I struggled with relationships. I struggled with an eating disorder. I drank too much. I alternated among bravado, exhibitionism, insecurity, and my "invisible woman" routine. I could make myself so quiet that people missed me in rooms and backed into me in elevators. I observed a lot. I molded my reactions, my behavior, to those around me. I was a chameleon, an actress. I had no idea who I was.

By the time I was twenty-five and working at the *Post,* I was old enough to sense that I was both tough and fragile, but not old enough, or wise enough, yet, to know where and how. I abruptly quit my job (the pull-the-rug-out-from-under-myself routine) and called a veteran science writer I knew of. My latest plan was to combine writing with science; I could help people without sentencing myself to a future in the hospital. Calling someone you want a job from, and offering to buy them coffee, is the kind of advice that people give but never act on themselves. But I didn't know any better. Luckily for me, the woman I contacted was amused, and willing to meet.

I don't know how the subject of our brothers came up. She knew of mine because she was a reporter. In the pre-AIDS days of my brother's illness, before newspapers and magazines were rife with science and health stories, and before health and talk shows regularly trotted out people with rare medical afflictions, my brother's story had been big news. His story, and that of another boy, were combined for an unauthorized 1976 made-for-TV movie called *The Boy in the Plastic Bubble.* My family regularly got calls from newspapers, from the mainstream to the worst of the tabloids, wanting to write about Ted. *The National Enquirer* sent a photographer to his funeral. Though we don't get calls anymore, he and this other boy are still strange, abstract figures in American pop culture. Variations of the phrase "boy in the plastic bubble" have appeared in a Paul Simon song, on an episode of *Seinfeld,* in a movie satire of the first movie, and as the name of a board game.

This journalist told me she had a brother who died at an age close to my brother's—seventeen—of cystic fibrosis. Children with the disease have a better survival rate these days, but when her brother was sick, most didn't live to see their twenties. I don't remember exactly what she told me, or what I said in response. I only remember the eerie sense of resonance. All that time, I had thought I was the only one. I thought losing a sibling was my own strange story. I began to wonder if my struggles had been set in motion by my brother's illness and death. What struck me most, however, was that this woman treated the story of my brother as if it were mine to tell. As if, in fact, it had happened to me, too, and in a unique way. This was novel. Usually people asked me how my parents had gotten through it. She was the first to ask about me. Until then, I had not really been a figure in my own life story.

I began to change that day. Slowly, I started consciously to claim ownership of the events in my own life, events that, I was beginning to understand, had had a profound impact on every aspect of who I was. I began to let myself think that what had happened was not only my brother's famous story, or my parents' overwhelming tragedy, but my story, my loss, my tragedy, too. Separate. I began to unearth my feelings, long suppressed, about the loss of my only sibling, the older brother I'd adored. I began to see that my brother's illness and death, that my role as the healthy, surviving sibling, wasn't just some bizarre anomaly amid the rest of society's shared normalcy. I realized that I might be part of a group whose largely uncharted experience has had no name, no movement, no language. Sibling loss.

Our relationships with our brothers and sisters are key to understanding ourselves. Where they end and where we begin is often so seamless, the loss of a sibling can be a crippling blow to our understanding of who we are, and how we function and relate to others. I suspect that this holds true even in cases in which people have distant or troubled relationships with their brothers and sisters. "Closeness" is not, as we often presume, a prerequisite for connection, and the story of "intimate" relationships is not always a happy one. I've come to think of siblings as an actor might think of a backstory—the imagined background of a character he's going to play. Those of us in the audience may never get a glimmer of a character's imagined history, but it's there all the same, informing that character's identity, behavior, and choices. Those of us who have siblings all have a "backstory."

It is, therefore, all the more perplexing to me that the loss of a sibling has long been considered less significant than other losses. It's only in the last twenty years that it has been recognized as a trauma approaching that of the loss of a parent or child. Still, except for the efforts of a handful of experts—many of whom have lost a sibling themselves, and have been compelled to do research to answer their own questions—this idea is not universally accepted. Though an estimated 25 percent of Americans have lost a sibling, sibling loss is overshadowed by the parents' loss of their child. In the case of adult siblings, it is overshadowed by the losses of the surviving spouses and children.

In greeting card stores across the country I have found, as often as not, bereavement cards for the loss of a parent, child, or pet, but not for that of a sibling. Hallmark, the leading manufacturer of greeting cards in this country since 1920, has always carried bereavement cards addressing the loss of parents, grandparents, and children, but did not start producing a sibling-specific line until the 1980s. When asked about my brother, I have repeatedly been faced with a well-intentioned person shaking his or her head sadly, saying, "That must have been terrible for your parents."

Why is the loss of a sibling such an overlooked experience? Maybe it has something to do with the pattern of infant and child-hood mortality that preceded the availability of antibiotics and modern public health measures. At one time in our not-so-distant history, surviving infancy and childhood was something of a feat. Perhaps losing a sibling was, in those years, so common an event as to have become invisible, a given, and for that reason overlooked. Or perhaps, as some researchers have speculated, siblings are more important to us now because, in the era of industrialization and birth control, we tend to have fewer. Perhaps iconic biblical stories, like that of Cain and Abel, have too narrowly drawn the emotional range of the relationship between siblings. And then there is Sigmund Freud, who thought of siblings only as rivals and elevated, above all else, the relationship of parents to children, a bias in thinking that is still pervasive in both professional and lay circles. Peruse any book in the child development section of a chain bookstore, for instance, and if you find "siblings" listed at all in the index, it will most likely be paired with the word "rivalry." Sibling relationships in childhood tend to be viewed as a parent's problem, not the unique, rich, and complex relationships that they often are, existing both within and outside the bonds parents have with their children. The nature of sibling relationships in adulthood is rarely considered at all.

At one point, in search of experts to interview on sibling loss, I signed on to Profnet, an online service that connects journalists with a nationwide assortment of media-relations specialists, the people whose job it is to help connect reporters with sources. I'd used it before, with great success, for magazine articles. It works like this: You sign on to the site, fill in a little box with your name, fill in another explaining your project and your request, and specify how you'd like the fifteen hundred public relations agencies and universities who subscribe to the service to reply (fax, phone, e-mail). Every time I'd used it before, I'd checked the phone and e-mail reply boxes. And each time, I'd gotten so many responses that sorting through my e-mail had quickly become a chore, and my phone had rung off the hook. The payoff was that I'd always found the sources I'd needed, and quickly.

This time, I said, *For a book on sibling loss, I would like to interview experts on siblings and sibling loss.* I checked only the "reply by e-mail" box. The next day, the e-mails were starting to stack up, as usual, but they weren't at all what I'd expected. Within three days,

I'd accumulated more than thirty e-mails from the media relations specialists, all of which read something like this:

I read your query on Profnet today regarding your book about sibling loss. This loss has colored my life in ways I continue to uncover as I grow older. I would be interested in being interviewed for your book.

I lost my only brother eleven years ago . . . Would be willing to talk with you.

About a year ago I lost an older brother who I was very close to. It was a suicide and was very sudden and totally unexpected. I would consider being interviewed for your book.

None of them referred me to experts. They all proposed their own stories. I would later discover that there were few academic experts on the subject of sibling loss. In fact, the people I heard from *were* the experts. Talking with them was like debriefing secret agents who'd spent years in a remote country. In all, I interviewed seventy-seven people, formally, for this book. One had not yet been born when her older brother died. One man had been seventy-one when his eighty-one-year-old sister had died. The rest were in between. The deaths had occurred as a result of a myriad of causes.

I found many of the people I interviewed from the Profnet query. Some I got from listings in grief support group newsletters, others from the website of Dr. Jerry Rothman, who specialized in sibling loss, and who had lost a sibling himself in childhood. (Rothman died suddenly March 2002." His wife, Chris Rothman, Psy.D., has succeeded him as director of the Center for Grief Recovery Institute, which he founded in 1985, and maintains the institute's website.) I put out word among friends, acquaintances, and colleagues. Colleagues knew people. Acquaintances knew people. Friends knew people. People that I interviewed knew people. And all of those people knew people.

The more I talked openly about the project, the more people surfaced with stories to tell. And they weren't just willing to be interviewed—they were eager. In a bid to allay fears, I'd put together an information packet—an article I'd written about sibling loss and my own experience with it, a consent form explaining the interview process (one to two hours, in person or over the phone, taped, anonymity an option), and a survey (for those who didn't want to be interviewed or were simply willing to fill it out). When I was contacted or contacted someone, my first step was to put the packet in the mail. But some people didn't want to wait for the packet; they wanted to be interviewed right then and there, sending me scrambling for batteries and blank tapes.

Putting out the word for volunteers, as I had, created a certain bias in the group. Most of the people I spoke to said that they had had close and happy relationships with their siblings. These were people who wanted to talk about them. I spoke to only a handful of people who'd had difficult or distant relationships with their brothers and sisters, and they were by far the most skittish when it came time to be interviewed. Some people who fit this category said they wanted to talk, and then disappeared. My sense was that it wasn't that the loss of their siblings hadn't been painful and confusing, but rather that they felt even less of a right to claim the loss as a significant event, because their relationships with their siblings had been troubled. For these people, there seemed to be an element of shame involved in their hesitation to talk.

Troubled relationships are not the ones that we expect to miss. But it's different with siblings. We learn to define ourselves, very early on, in relation to them. As adults, siblings perform this function even if they reside several states away and are almost never heard from. The way you perceive them and yourself in contrast is self-definition on a subtle scale that few of us have the time or inclination to evaluate. I suspect that those who didn't have close relationships with their siblings, in fact, may be just as stricken by their loss as those who did. That said, they're a group that has, for the most part, yet to be heard from.

There are a number of reasons the people I spoke with were so interested in being interviewed. In some cases, especially those in which the loss was recent, people simply wanted and needed to talk about their lost sibling and their grief, having found little or no outlet elsewhere. In others, the idea of participating in a book, and possibly having their brother's or sister's name appear in print—so that the sibling would still be in the world somehow—was a motivating factor. Some wanted to share their story as a way to help others. Some wanted to compare notes with me and, via my interviews, with others. Many of those with whom I spoke had never told their stories before, and never been asked to. In many cases, I had the feeling that the interview was part of a therapeutic process. One forty-nine-year-old woman, who had lost her younger brother some three years before, said so. "I feel like this was an intervention," she said, after the interview was over. Others e-mailed or wrote to say that talking about the loss had propelled them to a new stage of mourning and healing. The act of acknowledging that the death of their sibling was their story, too, was healing. Because sibling loss is so often overlooked, the act of claiming the loss, and composing a narrative of how the loss affects you, is a significant step toward moving forward.

I wasn't surprised by this, though it was interesting to see my own experience repeated. What I didn't expect was that this ongoing dialogue between myself and other bereft siblings would have a profound impact on my understanding of my own story. I thought I had done all of the hard work of grieving and understanding my brother's death before I started this book. It wasn't true. After I'd listen to someone tell his or her story, I'd sometimes end up musing about some aspect of my own that I hadn't realized or gotten to yet. It was often painful, and, equally as often, enlightening. My story, and my understanding of it, is different from when I started. I've told it, as best I can at this point in my life, in a way that follows the pattern of how I believe the loss of a sibling must be explored and integrated in order for healing to occur. By using the word "healing" I do not mean that the sense of loss of a sibling ever goes away, or that the sibling is dismissed as an important person in your life. I mean that the disabling grief is over, and we find a way to weave the lost brother or sister into our lives and go on.

I have, as a result of all of this, developed an almost reverential attitude toward the power of storytelling, especially, as in this case, when the stories belong to people from whom we don't often hear. The stories that you will read here, shared by people who wanted to help themselves and others in the telling, paint a portrait of a profound, identity-shaping loss. It's my hope that these stories will affirm the significance of the loss for those who are newly reeling from it, those still trying to put a past loss into place, or those who simply want to understand. I hope that others find solace in them, as I did.

Chapter One

FROZEN

"Life can only be understood backward, but it must be lived forward."

—SØREN KIERKEGAARD

When I talk to people who have lost a brother or a sister, I start by asking them to tell me their story—from the beginning. Most often, they start with their sibling's death or the illness that led to it. The diagnosis, the phone call in the middle of the night, the secondhand account or the breathless blow-by-blow of a horror they might have witnessed, and which they relive when they allow themselves to remember. At first, as I listened, I frequently thought, But why don't they start from the real beginning? "He was there, and then I was born" or "I was born, and then he was there, and this is who we were together."

Eventually I came to understand. Before the loss of our siblings, we think of ourselves and our siblings from the vantage point of one solid block of "I," an already baked cake. The ingredients cannot be neatly separated out after the fact, or identified when the cake is iced, sliced, and served on a plate. The ingredients become something else, something irreducible. You cannot see the flour, the eggs, the baking soda.

We begin with the story of the loss, then, because it is the shock of the impossible—the rude stripping of one ingredient from the "I." The loss is the "before and after" marker, indicating the moment at which we are forever launched—often without understanding it—into an uncertain state in which we are continuously checking our psychic pockets for something we've lost.

My story begins here: I am fourteen, sandwiched between friends in the center seat of the center row of a 747 on the way back from an exchange trip to Scotland. A mental banner, like the storm-warning alerts that run across the bottom of TV screens, keeps scrolling across the inside of my forehead—*Surprise. Surprise. Surprise*—as if something unexpected is waiting for me at home. It's persistent. Disconcerting. It nags at me, like someone tugging at my sleeve.

I try to put the annoying mental hiccup out of my mind. I busy myself with the headphones with one foam ear covering missing. I surreptitiously order red wine from the drink trolley, right under the chaperone's nose, frowning over the miniature bottle's screw-top lid, which I know means it's mediocre. I fret over the fact that my shirt, made out of a navy blue shag material, smells, as do all my clothes, because I'd been too terrified of my Edinburgh "host mother" to approach her about laundry. For the entire flight, I keep my arms close to my sides.

When we land at Kennedy Airport, still a five-hour bus ride from my Bethesda, Maryland, home, an announcement comes over the intercom. The voice calls my name. *Surprise*. It wants my attention. The voice announces that everyone is to stay seated but me. *Surprise*. It instructs me to collect my luggage and make my way to the front of the cabin. *Surprise*. I feel that I have been warned. I just don't know about what. I feel as if I'm in trouble, but I haven't stolen anything, have not, as my friend Candy and I discussed, stashed pot in my backpack. For a brief, delusional moment, I wonder if pot has mysteriously ended up in my bag anyway, as if merely thinking it has made it so. I unwedge my suitcase from under the seat in front of me, and crawl over Candy to get to the aisle. One of my teachers averts her eyes as I pass. Other faces, ones I do not know, swivel toward me.

By the time I get to the front of the cabin, the stewardesses are unbolting the door. First I feel cold air, then I smell the diesel fuel. Then I catch sight of the blue-coated airline emissary who stands on the other side. I know what the surprise is. "What's wrong with my brother?" I blurt, before he can deliver the words he has prepared. He says only that one of my brother's doctors is here to meet me.

Someone else might have guessed that my brother was the surprise long before it occurred to me. Ted had been sick for eight years. I was six, he was nine, almost ten, when he was diagnosed with a rare immune deficiency disorder. My mother's account goes something like this: He had bruises, huge purple black blotches, on his legs. She'd noticed them before. She thought it was from the football she and my father had been forcing him to play because it would be "good" for him. (My brother hated sports. His most memorable moment on the football field was the day he finally caught the ball and, to his everlasting humiliation, ran the wrong way, scoring one for the other team.) One night, as we sat at the kitchen table eating dinner, my mother glanced down at his bare legs and said, casually, "Will you look at that? He has more bruises."

My father, an oncologist, looked down. The bruises that emerge on people with blood diseases are unlike your garden-variety bruises. They are monstrous and colorful, like spilled pots of paint under the skin. My father saw them all the time, at work.

He must have known the instant he saw them leeching their way across my brother's thighs. I can't imagine what crossed his mind at that moment. Perhaps he was already considering the potential diagnoses. Whatever he thought, he suppressed it well enough that none of us suspected. He said something about bringing Ted with him to work the next day, "just to check him out," and went back to his dinner. Or pretended to. I have no idea what the rest of us did. Most likely we finished dinner, my mother cleaned up, and my brother and I ran for the front yard at the earliest opportunity, blissfully unaware that we were on the verge of the defining experience of all of our lives.

I don't remember the day he left the house. In my mind's eye, I have always seen the screen door slam, seen Donner, our schnauzer, noisily rush the door, arriving, as always, a hair too late to squeeze out; heard Ted's footsteps descending the first set of cement steps to the walkway that traversed our lawn, then the next set, down our sloping hill to the sidewalk and to my mother's maroon, Buick station wagon. I hear the sound of the car door slamming, the car ignition, the car driving away.

My only real memory of his leave-taking is vague: I am sitting in the nubbly green chair in our living room, the one that can be made into a rocking chair by slipping a peg out of its side. My parents tell me that my brother will be in the hospital for "a while." Which, in the slippery way of adults, they keep finding ways to avoid defining.

Something is wrong with his immune system, they explain. Aplastic anemia. He must stay in a sterile room. We will see him through a clear plastic curtain. I am proud to know the words, to be able to pronounce them. Aplastic. Anemia. But I have trouble with the concept. A cold can kill him. Strep throat, which I have all the time, is the equivalent of being run over by a bus. In short, the house, the school, the world, are no longer safe havens for my heretofore invincible older brother, and we are no longer safe companions. For "a while."

•   •   •

Eight and a half years passed. My brother's illness became normal
to me. Every day I went to school, my father went to work, and my
mother went to the hospital. My mother came home when I got
home. My father came home at dinnertime. And then we went
back to the hospital, which had become our family room. I only
vaguely remember the days when Ted inhabited the room next to
mine at the top of the house.

And then, the day that I return from Scotland, I am called off
the airplane and rushed through the empty, endless hallways of
Kennedy Airport, the strap of my suitcase biting into my shoulder,
the gym teacher who'd gone along on the trip as a chaperone by
my side. I am shooed through customs and presented to one of
my brother's longtime doctors. He is the one who is always quick
to smile and laugh, but his face is serious now. He explains that my
brother is sick. Sicker, rather. He's collapsed. His heart has failed.
Something about too many blood transfusions, too much iron in
his blood. This is confusing, because it is the weekly blood transfusions, the grotesque red bags slowly draining into the IV tubing,
in addition to the custardy yellow bags of plasma and the clear
bags of who knows what, that have been sustaining him all this
time. I stand there in my smelly shirt and ask the doctor if he is
going to die. He says he doesn't know. We stand briefly amid the
swirl of suitcase-toting bodies. There is nothing more to say. We
get on the shuttle to Washington, me numbly flipping through all
the magazines in the seat back, looking at the pictures. We talk
about gardens.

When we get to the hospital, my parents are there, conferring in
a huddle with another one of my brother's doctors. They look up.
I stand looking at them, they at me. I am acutely aware of my dirty
shirt again. And the bad perm a neighbor gave me before I left for
Scotland. I feel like a tourist being scrutinized by the locals. Eventually, I am allowed to go to my brother. Normally, he seems to me

as healthy as I am; he just lives behind the curtain in what we have
taken to calling The Room, gets IVs, and takes mountains of pills
daily with huge swigs of A&W root beer. Maybe he's a little pale,
but he is always himself. Smart, sarcastic, bossy, silly, full of ideas.

Now he is laid out flat, his bed pushed to rest just on the other
side of the curtain. A Plexiglas portal, like the window in an airplane, is installed in the middle of the plastic curtain, right above
two reversible plastic arms. By putting your arms in from our side,
you can safely touch something on my brother's side, or he can
put his arms in them and touch something on ours. One of my
brother's favorite ways to scare me is to grab me with them when
I'm not paying attention. The novelty of his touch never fails to
shock me. There is a doorway-sized opening to one side. On the
floor, a red strip of tape continues the curtain's line to the wall.
The words "Do Not Enter" are spelled out in red tape on the
floor. To ensure that this opening, through which my brother's
medicine and food is passed, doesn't serve as his downfall, a complex ventilation system built into the wall on his side pushes air
out at high volume, through the opening. Airborne germs can't
cross the steady gust of wind.

A shower stall is built into one wall on his side. There is no
toilet, only a desk chair. The removable seat cushion conceals a
bedpan underneath. A sink is installed under the window, at the
far end of his room. A TV sits near the ceiling on a stand that juts
from the wall. These rooms were designed for people whose
immune systems are temporarily obliterated by chemotherapy.
They were designed for a short stay, a month or two at most, by
which point their inhabitants either die or recover. They weren't
meant for the eight and a half years that my brother has stayed.

He is wearing tan corduroys and a white, gauzy button-up
shirt. But he's not wearing the clogs, the shoes he loves because
when he's wearing them he can hear himself keep time over his
electric guitar. He's not wearing the chunky rock star rings and
necklaces he loves even more, because they make him look cool.

He has IVs in both his hands and both his feet. A heart monitor blips in the corner. Nurses, gowned and masked with only their eyes showing, surround his bed. I have to concentrate hard to figure out who is who.

He opens his eyes when I say his name. I press my face into the plastic window and try to tell him about the trip, the trip I went on only for him, enduring hours of boring bus rides, field trips, the terrifying host family, to bring back the world he couldn't get to, because the idea of travel lit him up. I push against the curtain the little wooden figure, a loony, kilt-clad Scotsman with glued-on wispy gray hair, that I've brought him, and he closes his eyes, exhausted.

I am not meant to be there the night he dies. My aunt Angela, my father's sister, has come to stay, so that somebody will be in the house with me while my parents sleep in the hospital, sitting upright on two orange plastic sofas that face each other in a closet-sized room down the hall from my brother. It has been two weeks since I got back from Scotland. I don't go to school. I don't go outside. I don't see friends. I sit in my room with the lights off, watching endless reruns of *I Love Lucy, Leave It to Beaver,* and *The Dick Van Dyke Show.* I find them mesmerizing, the characters endearing, old friends. The sound of lawn mowers and crickets is a constant muffled presence outside my window. Life is like an improbable cartoon, Wile E. Coyote hovering, suspended in midair, having outrun the cliff.

When I go to the hospital, my brother seems to be improving. He talks a little. The doctors, to my immense relief, take the IVs out of his feet. In their place they put in a heart line—a big IV that goes right into the big veins that lead to his heart. More efficient, they explain. My brother insists on staying awake to watch them do it. To monitor. He is very bossy about his body. It's why he still has so many good veins left after all these years, something my mother brags about like other mothers brag about their kids' good grades. Now he's even gotten to the point where, when his heart skitters off in an erratic beat, he can use some form of homespun biofeedback he's taught himself and bring it right again, to avoid the defibrillator paddles. There is something subversive about this that I love, both because I am fourteen and well into appreciating subversion, and because it's like Wile E., defying gravity, trying to tiptoe on thin air back to safe ground.

My aunt goes home. It is Saturday, Memorial Day weekend, and my parents send me to spend the night with friends. I spend the next day by their pool. I'm wearing my mother's old bathing suit, the one that pulls up like a tube top and ties around the neck. A real girl suit, and I am proud that it fits, despite the fact that I have no chest. It's a big switch from my navy blue swim-team Speedo. When it starts to get dark we put our clothes on over our damp suits, and they take me to the hospital. We all sit on the orange sofas. Everyone tries to cover the tension in The Room by making small talk and telling funny stories, which aren't funny and grate on my nerves. My body feels like it wants to fold in on itself like a roly-poly bug.

So far there has been no question of letting me stay overnight at the hospital. But when my friends get ready to leave, I have an overwhelming desire to stay. I tell my parents I'm staying, and they let me. Around one in the morning, a code, the hospital shorthand that summons the defibrillator cart, is called over the intercom. My father, who is half drowsing, slowly sliding sideways down the slippery plastic of the sofa back, sits straight up. "This is it," he says. I think, What "it"?

Within seconds, we are standing around Ted's bed. My mother stands by him on the other side of the plastic curtain, one arm under his shoulders, propping him up. A green-gowned pietà. "Don't hold me there," he says, his voice still bossy, authoritative, but groggy now. "It's a pressure point." She adjusts her arms. My father and I stand on the other side of the curtain, with the heart monitor, a horrible, incessant, blipping reminder of the flabby ineffectualness of my brother's heart. There are no defibrillator paddles. Suddenly, I realize that he is dying, that they are letting him die. The code, this code tonight, is a signal that everyone but me has been waiting for. Only one thing is clear to me: My brother, like me, is not in on the decision. He's not going with the program. He's fighting it. The doctors keep injecting something, morphine, maybe, into his IV. Each time, he sags a little bit, but then he struggles back, heaving his eyelids open.

Time passes. I don't know how much. The machine blips. I watch it. I watch the clock. My father and I stand side by side, not touching. No one speaks. I leave, twice, and go to the ladies' room, where I don't know what to do. Everything—the sink, the floor, the tile—looks hyperreal in a way I will recognize years later when I try psychedelic drugs for the first time. But now it is just strange. I lean on the sink, look into the mirror, but I can't see my face. Only pieces. An eye. A nose. The scar my brother left on my cheek, back in the days when he was well, when fighting—real punching, kicking, and slapping—was still a major avenue of communication for us. I want to throw up, but the queasy feeling does not rise above my stomach. It sinks to my knees. My mother comes in and brings me back to The Room.

My brother's lungs are filling with fluid. I don't know if it is blood or something else. It hardly matters. He is drowning on dry land. At one point, he says, "Help me, I'm dying." The doctors just keep dosing his IV. Gradually, the line on the heart monitor grows straighter. It is not like in the movies, where a loud alarm sound comes out of the machine at the critical moment. It does what it does quietly. Almost too quietly. It seems as if it should scream a little. It is 1:55 in the morning. No one speaks. I am allowed on my brother's side of the sterile curtain for the first time ever. I touch his bare arm for the first time in almost nine years. It is limp and white as milk from lack of sun. It feels light, lifeless, foreign. My fingers don't recognize it. I want to say good-bye. I want to tell him that I love him. But I don't know how. And it is too late now, anyway. He's not here anymore. The maroon bathrobe I see hanging on his shower door, the one he liked to wear around, Hugh Hefner–like, is more alive than he is.

My parents and I leave, trace the same path out of the hospital we've walked thousands of times before. But this time we will not come back. Life as we know it, almost as far back as I can remember, is over. We don't touch. We don't speak. When we get home, we sit together only briefly. My mother, who dismissed religion the day my brother was diagnosed, says she does not want a religious funeral, that no real god would allow something like this to happen, and she takes a sedative they gave her at the hospital. We all go to our rooms. I am ashamed that I can sleep without a sedative. When I wake up in the morning, I am still wearing my mother's bathing suit under my clothes. My mother is still asleep. My father is sitting at the dining room table with my mother's address book open in front of him, making one succinct phone call after another. "Ted died last night." "Ted died." "Ted is dead."

A few days later, I find myself standing at the edge of his grave, trying to picture him, my best friend, the ringmaster of my life, lying in the gunmetal gray casket suspended by straps over a hole in the earth. I am wearing a flowered skirt my aunt made for me, one of those gauzy white shirts that is de rigueur in 1980, and a pair of my mother's sling backs, the heels of which sink into the ground when I walk. I don't own anything black. My mother has told me that girls my age aren't expected to wear it, shouldn't, in fact, wear it. But I feel wrong. As if appropriate attire is some sort of symbol of love, and I am lacking.

My brother, I know, is wearing his favorite tan corduroy Levi's with the matching vest that he liked because he could hook his thumbs in it just in front of his armpits, a gestural exclamation point usually accompanied by a piece of sailing sarcasm and a smirk, a moment when he was pleased with himself. He is also wearing a white button-down oxford-cloth shirt. I know this because it is mine. When the neighborhood ladies had conferred around my mother about what clothes were needed, they realized he didn't have one. Or it was still at the hospital. They'd stood around uncertainly, one woman nervously clutching the pile of tan corduroy.

I'd volunteered my white oxford. Though he was three and a half years older, my brother's growth had been stunted by his treatment. His growth charts as a baby had projected he would be over six feet tall as an adult, but his disease had intervened. He was no more than five-three, slightly taller than me, and thinner when he died. The grief ladies had brightened at my offer. No need to go on the strange errand of buying clothes for the dead. I was proud that my brother, whose hand-me-downs I had worn until the years I started to catch up with him, would be wearing my shirt, though I worried that he'd be chagrined at the indignity of being stuck, forevermore, in his little sister's clothing.

I picture him now in his tan corduroy suit, and I wonder about shoes. I wonder if it's true, as I've read, that your hair and nails keep growing after you die. I wonder if he has a pillow in there. I am mesmerized by the coffin, as I had been at the funeral parlor. While others had assiduously averted their eyes from it pressed discreetly in a nook against the wall, I hadn't been able to take mine off it. Now it's going to disappear, his coffin, his body, and I'm not ready. I want to look inside and see him. I want to know if he still looks like himself after the autopsy. I want to touch his face. I want to look into his eyes and see what they see.

I feel numb, incredulous. Will he be lonely? Scared? The fact that it will rain and snow on him makes me crazy. I panic at the prospect of his imminent disappearance. Forever. I make a plan. I will crawl in with him. If I can't get the casket open, I will throw myself in the hole after him. I don't care about the dirt, the bugs, breathing. I don't want him to be alone. I don't want to be left alone. I don't want to go on, brotherless. I don't know how. I might as well go on headless. He is my geography, my map. I need him.

A woman, mercifully faceless now, separates herself from the lingering crowd, takes me by the arm, and leans in close enough so that I can smell her perfume, see the lipstick on her teeth. "You'll have to be very good now," she whispers intently, sadly. "Your parents are going through a lot." Her hand is a pincer around my elbow. Her words are a jab from a sharp knife. They make me feel selfish, ashamed.

I've puzzled over the scene by Ted's grave a lot in recent years. Frankly, I'd forgotten it. But when I started to write, it was the first memory to come back. It emerged whole and with absolute clarity. I see the vivid green of the AstroTurf on the ground, the standard putty-colored folding chairs arranged in rows on top of it, see the canvas canopy stretched overhead, feel the heat of the summer sun rising on my arms. I see everything but that woman's face. I can see bits of her, smell her, but that is all.

She was trying to be kind, I suppose, trying to make some connection, searching for appropriate words. The peculiar thing was that she could not see what had been, at least for a brief moment, apparent to me—that I was going through a lot, too. Even more peculiar, in retrospect, her message was not unusual. In fact, her words and variations on them would prove to be more the norm than the exception in the days and years to come.

At fourteen, I accepted the message as gospel, as surely as if it had been explained to me by the priest who spoke at the funeral, the only religious person my mother would allow to speak because he, too, had lost a child. My brother's death wasn't a big deal to me. His life, his death, belonged to my parents. This was not how I actually felt, but my mind was obedient and it bent to the cues around it. It would take me more than a decade to begin to see the truth.

I had already, during the years of my brother's illness, learned to shunt my feelings aside. I was the lucky one, the healthy one. Whatever it was could be dealt with later, after the crisis— although the crisis, in this case, never quite ended. I had learned how to shut down, to enter an all but impenetrable interior world, a self-taught autism, where emotions were a dull tap on a distant windowpane.

And now, like an infant who learns to smile by watching others, I learned, starting at that moment by my brother's grave, to reflect the response that was expected of me. And what was expected of me, in my new life, it seemed, was normalcy. Good behavior. An appropriate somberness. Respect, but not too much grief. Not, at least, more than my parents had. I came to associate grief with self-indulgence and shame. My brother's illness, his death, what I felt about it, became a frozen lake somewhere deep inside me, one that would take me years to locate, to recognize, and ultimately, to thaw.

Chapter Two

AMBIGUOUS LOSS

"There is no agony like bearing an untold story inside
of you."

—Maya Angelou

I was fourteen when my brother died. My friends didn't bring it
up, and neither did I. Family friends, I suppose, didn't want to
intrude, or thought we would actually ask them if we thought of
something we needed. As if we knew. We didn't know what we
needed. We were lost, even to ourselves. My parents didn't talk
about Ted, or his death, alone or together. They were numb,
engulfed in their own separate miseries. I didn't talk to them,
either. I was numb, too. That summer, our schnauzer, Donner,
who'd been a gift on Ted's ninth birthday, was hit and killed by a
car. It was my mother who found him. I wondered if Ted had
summoned Donner to keep him company. We couldn't stand
Donner's absence. He was the only morsel of comfort in the
house. We got a puppy, Jackson, the next day.

Years later, when Jackson's kidneys failed and we had to put
him to sleep, our remaining dog, Rudy—a flighty character whom

Jackson had bossed around within an inch of his life—was so confused, so grief-stricken by Jackson's sudden disappearance, that he hid under my parents' bed for weeks. When he did come out, he wouldn't look anyone in the eye. He ducked his head, averted his gaze. I recognized the look. When Ted died, none of us could look one another in the eye, either. To do so was to risk seeing our own pain, reflected back. Or worse, to risk falling apart. If I let loose my grip on myself, I thought, I might never be able to pull myself together again. We hid in separate rooms of the house, my family, meeting only for dinner, at which point we strained to make conversation. I left the table as soon as possible and my parents often ended the meal by fighting.

One day, in the first months after Ted's death, my parents went out without telling me where they were going, and returned, hours later, with cardboard boxes packed full of Ted's things from The Room, as I came to think of it. They stacked them in a walk-in closet at the end of the hallway. Occasionally, when I knew they'd both be out for a while, I'd make forays into this closet, prying open box lids, peeking at what lay inside—records, a guitar stand, the suede hippie hat I'd given him for Christmas, his clogs—feeling as if he might emerge, genielike, if I opened the right container. Those boxes were a good metaphor for the place my brother came to hold in our lives. Sealed up, hidden away, unopened, except for my occasional furtive explorations. This was how it was, and how it would continue to be.

My father immersed himself in his work after Ted died. He'd always done that to some degree. But now he descended and did not come up for air. My mother, whose life had for so long revolved around my brother, then turned her formidable focus on me. I became her constant companion. Her solace for having lost one child was that she had another one in whom to lose herself. It was bad timing. At fourteen, I was just at the age when I was trying to find and assert my independence. And the years on the sidelines of my brother's illness had long since made me decide I didn't, couldn't need my parents. I resolved the dilemma by appearing, on the surface, the perpetual child my mother wanted me to be, while quietly turning to the adolescent's novocaine—alcohol and drugs—establishing a pattern of demure self-destruction that would persist for more than a decade.

Later I added an eating disorder to my repertoire of dysfunctional coping—first anorexia, then bulimia, then obsessive exercise. My school notebooks from this time are riddled with caloric calculations. I knew the calorie count of every item in the grocery store. Relationships became another common refuge, until they became demanding rather than distracting. I discovered that I was very good at shutting off emotion, abruptly. If one boyfriend got too threatening, too connected, I could exchange him for another, quite easily. It wasn't such a bad thing, in retrospect, because somehow, I always found myself in relationships in which my needs were overlooked, a state of affairs that would eventually trigger in me an inexplicable and very old rage.

I'd already learned to tune out of space and time during Ted's illness. It had been a comfortable enough way to be, the psychic version of a hammock. Slack. But this total numbness, my awareness that I could manipulate it, was a new and handy trick. No threat of unwanted feelings. I could do it at any time. Sometimes it happened involuntarily. Instant numbness. Detachment. It was like watching my life, the very life unfurling in front of me, from a front-row seat in a movie theater. I did this very well, this self-taught autism. And in the process, I blocked out almost everything that had happened in my life before I turned eighteen.

Even my memories of my brother were vague, the details gone. I was miserable, but only dimly aware of it. It felt so normal, after all those years, to be depressed, to be unhappy, to be angry. I didn't know what it felt like to be otherwise. Finally, in my midtwenties, it took the coincidence of the end of a nightmarish relationship in which I had, unfortunately for me, chosen to feel, and a bad job to break my capacity for numbness. I lost whatever control I had of it. Sometimes, I found, I was numb, and then again, sometimes even the air hurt my skin, and I could barely stand it.

When I was twenty-six, more than ten years after Ted's death, I got the name of a therapist from a friend and called and left a message. When the therapist called me back to set up the appointment and ask me what kind of issues I wanted to discuss, I said, "The usual, I guess," meaning career, relationship, and parent issues. I had no idea *why* I was falling apart. That was what I wanted her to tell me. By the time I got to the appointment, I was visibly shaking. When I sat down on the couch, the first words that came to me were an utter surprise: "I am my brother's death." And then I started to cry. Untended, the frozen lake within had grown beyond my capacity to ignore it. It was breaking into tectonic plates, heaving, threatening to crack me into a thousand pieces.

Later in that first session, my therapist explained why she thought I had started with those words: I had been shoving everything related to my brother and his death, anything that threatened to trigger memories of it, any feeling I deemed "dangerous," into a remote closet in my mind. It was so full, this closet, that the door could no longer stay shut. Things were tumbling out and hitting me in the face. The closet would not, could not, hold any more. It was time to do something about it. I had no choice. I began the process of cracking open the door, millimeter by millimeter.

It wasn't easy. Who had my brother been? I couldn't remember. Week after week, I went back. And each week, my therapist asked me questions that I couldn't answer. What had I done when I went to visit my brother? What had we talked about? What had his prognosis been? What had my parents told me about his illness? Time after time, my reply was "I don't remember." Or "I don't know." It was eerie. Each question evoked a dense, theatrical fog that rolled in and obscured my memory. For the first time,

I saw that I had shut out half my life. And my brother. He was somewhere in that fog.

The first and biggest hurdle for me was coming to understand that my brother's illness and death had happened to me, too. For years I had been told it was my parents' loss that mattered. I had to be strong for them, make it up to them. They had already lost so much. Silently, on autopilot, I bent myself to the task of the impossible, making my parents unsad. The simple truth was that, after Ted's death, they had needed me to be fine, to have been miraculously unmarked by the strange life that had ended with Ted's death. And so, I was fine.

Slowly, I began to realize that I had suffered a profound loss and that it had been every bit as shattering as my parents' loss had been. Everyone had seemed to understand their loss. But no one had understood mine. Including myself. Without that understanding, I realized, I couldn't even begin to mourn. I was carrying years' worth of intact grief inside me. It sounds obvious now, but after Ted's death, it hadn't seemed that way at all. That makes a certain sense: If every external message you receive suggests that the loss didn't really happen to you, eventually, you start to believe it.

What amazes me, when I talk to other surviving siblings, is that this theme—that the loss is not theirs to mourn—is at the core of most of their stories. There is a definite pattern: The parents of those who had been children at the time of the loss were often too ravaged by their own grief to recognize it in their surviving children. Nor, apparently, had there been others outside the family to recognize it and step in. (The exception was a handful of people who received a condolence letter addressed solely to them. I was a recipient of such a letter, too. It was written by one of my father's college buddies, who had lost a daughter. Each one of us in this small group still has the letter.)

The siblings who had been young at the time of their loss said that they had striven to be "good," which often meant not talking or crying about their lost brothers and sisters, so as not to upset their parents. They tried to make up the loss to their parents. But their parents' obvious and ongoing preoccupation with the dead sibling, which rendered them sad, distant, or downright cold, had more often than not made these siblings feel as if the wrong one— the favorite and indispensable one—had died. These families tended to be marked by a chronic and silent grief that could not be discussed, and which, in fact, became so much a part of the landscape of the family as to be unseen.

Adult siblings were often the agent of their own grief suppression. In many cases, they immediately fell into the role of caretaker for their parents and sometimes their sibling's surviving spouse and children. The loss for these people, these siblings often said, was so much bigger. And yet not. In the case of adult siblings, it often wasn't the day-to-day pattern of life that had shifted with their loss, as it had with the surviving spouse and children, but rather something deep in the foundation of their beings. Like the young siblings, most said that almost no one inside or outside their family had recognized their loss. Their loss was a burden that, for the most part, they carried alone.

For siblings young and old, all of this, inevitably, meant one thing: a delay, if not a complete suppression, of mourning. Unfortunately, as I learned, no one gets a pass on mourning. You do it or you risk getting stuck. Frozen.

Pauline Boss, a Minnesota–based psychotherapist, has coined a term to describe loss that goes unrecognized: ambiguous loss. She hasn't studied siblings. She's looked at people, like her parents, who immigrated to the United States and left behind family they would never see again. And she's looked at the spouses of people with Alzheimer's disease, who have lost the partners they once knew. And she's looked at women whose husbands were listed missing in action in Vietnam and Cambodia, who were gone, but officially, at least, not dead.

In each case, someone had been "partly" lost. Boss's Swiss relatives weren't dead; they were alive, but distant—never to be seen again. It was the same with the spouses of the Alzheimer's victims. They hadn't literally lost their spouses, who were still alive. But they'd lost the person with whom they had shared their lives, the person who had once known them so well and then barely knew them at all. The women whose husbands were missing in action didn't know what they'd lost. Their husbands might be dead, or they might return.

What all of these losses have in common is that although they are as life-altering and traumatic as a death, they are not recognized as real losses. There are no rituals to mark them—no wakes, funerals, sympathy cards, or meals made by neighbors, no social recognition whatsoever that a loss has occurred. Without that validation, the people Boss studied didn't know that they had had a loss. They were frozen in limbo, unsure how to navigate lives that no longer felt familiar.

The wives of the men who'd been listed MIA, for instance, didn't know if they were still married or if they should date or make financial decisions alone. They suffered from anxiety, depression, psychic numbness, distressing dreams, guilt, and psychosomatic illnesses. For all of them, a chronic, ambiguous grief set in and didn't go away. Boss calls this frozen grief (the same word I chose to describe my own state, long before I spoke to Boss), because of the way it sits unresolved emotionally. Without recognition of the losses, Boss observed, these people tended to get mired in their emotional pain. Frozen.

I called Boss and told her that many of the stories she'd recounted in her book, *Ambiguous Loss,* sounded like the stories I'd heard from the men and women who'd lost a brother or a sister. True, there had been a literal death, but it had been almost universally viewed as the parents' or surviving spouse's and children's loss. Few thought about what the siblings had lost, and as a result, neither did siblings. It was as if they hadn't had a loss at all. The younger the person had been at the time of the loss, the more extreme the effect. And the more extreme, the more dire the consequences. Studies on the long-term effects of losing a sibling in childhood, for instance, list interpersonal problems, difficulties in school, alcoholism and drug abuse, automobile accidents, severe nightmares, hypochondriasis, depression, and chronic guilt, to name just a few of the potential aftereffects.

Like the military wives who didn't know if they were still married, the bereft siblings I spoke with often didn't know if they were still siblings, or how many brothers and sisters they had. In fact, siblings almost universally loathed what had once been a benign social question: Do you have brothers and sisters? One woman I spoke to had stopped attending social functions because she couldn't bear having to try to answer this question. And yet, nobody, except for a small group of sibling-loss researchers, many of whom had lost siblings themselves, seemed to be able to see bereft siblings' confusion. When I related this to Boss, I could feel her nodding on the other end of the phone. "Validation," she said, "is what moves you out of the frozen place that follows a loss."

And therein lies the problem: Validation is in short supply when a sibling dies. In the broad-based group I spoke with, the ultimate equation was simple: the less validation, the more ambiguous the loss, the more frozen the grief. The younger the person was when he lost a brother or sister, the greater the ambiguity of the loss, the more frozen he tended to be. Regardless of age, the result, in the majority of cases, was this: The loss hadn't been recognized, and the siblings hadn't grieved.

Even children born after an older sibling has already died can be affected by the loss. Because it *is* a loss, although few see it as such.

The parents of these people are changed for having experienced the loss. The size, rules, and values of the family these surviving siblings grow up in are shaped by the loss, too. These siblings feel the absence of this person, but grapple with whether it is their loss to claim. They often crave information about the lost sibling, but feel they don't have the right to ask. And parents often don't think to offer information about this early tragedy. You can see their reasoning. The loss, after all, is not something their surviving children experienced firsthand. The problem is, that reasoning is wrong.

Jessica, a twenty-four-year-old artist living in Atlanta, was born a year after her older brother, Jonathan, died from a congenital liver defect. She has been circling the topic of her brother for years. She is full of questions—about her parents' experience, the size of her family, and her own identity. Her parents knew that she was interested in her brother. In fact, I'd found her through her father, who owns a store near the Connecticut town in which my parents live. One day he'd asked me what I was working on. When I told him, he said, "I don't know if this counts, but . . ."

And then he told me about Jonathan and Jessica. "I think she might have a lot to say," he said. She did. But she'd never really said any of it to him. In fact, Jessica told me she'd never had a conversation of any length about Jonathan with her parents or her younger brother. When I asked her how her father had known that the older brother she'd never met was something she thought about, she said it was probably the pictures. "I'm very big on photographs. I have about thirty or forty framed pictures all over my apartment. They're all people that are very important to me. And he's in there. So maybe that's how he knew."

Her parents had never tried to hide Jonathan's existence. His picture sits on their dresser, along with a picture of Jessica and her younger brother. But they had never offered information, either. Jessica sensed that it wasn't her place to ask, and that it might cause them pain if she did. Not asking was a way of protecting them from pain, but it was also denying herself information about her family. "He wasn't a taboo subject," she said. "But he was never really brought up unless I brought him up. We do have the same blood, but at the same time, I almost feel like my parents had a separate life before I was born. They had a separate life with him, and it's just something that was never really talked about."

Jessica said she felt her brother's presence. And even though Jonathan died as a child, she had always perceived him as older than herself. "I felt like he was watching over me, because he was an older brother. And I always wondered, 'Oh, what would it have been like?' I had some really tough times when I was a teenager, and I always wondered, If I had an older brother . . . You know, maybe he would have protected me. I would have had someone to look up to."

She was also slightly confused about her place in the family. "I've always had this strange feeling about whether or not I should be considered the middle child, even though my older brother was never really raised. Sometimes I wonder, Am I the middle child, am I supposed to have that type of behavior pattern? I have a lot of friends that are the oldest siblings, and we've all talked about what it's like to be the oldest sibling. And I know that I fit that mold. But sometimes I wonder, What am I, really?"

Jonathan's grave is not far from the house in which she grew up. She remembers as a child occasionally stopping there with her parents. "There was never really any discussion," said Jessica. "They would just stand there peacefully for a minute." When she got old enough to drive, she started going by herself. On Jonathan's twenty-first birthday, she went and put a rose on his gravestone. When we spoke, she was planning on going home for a visit. She felt a little nervous about it, but she was thinking of asking her parents to tell her more about Jonathan.

"I want to know about him. I want to know what he was like, and what they think about what happened and how it affected the way they raised us. I want to ask them every single thing that happened—what their emotions were and how it's affected their marriage," said Jessica. "I just want to know. I feel like there's something missing, that there's a part of my family that I don't understand and know about."

In her memoir, *Under a Wing,* Reeve Lindbergh, the youngest child of aviator Charles Lindbergh and the writer Anne Morrow Lindbergh, writes similarly about what it was like to grow up in the shadow of this kind of loss. In a chapter titled "The Lost Baby," she writes about the kidnapping that resulted in the death of her parents' first child, her oldest brother, Charles. Her parents, she writes, rarely spoke of him. Neither did she, or her siblings. "Our first brother's life and death was not a subject of conversation . . . as we grew up and lived our lives together in the family where he should have been the oldest son. With us, there was perhaps a feeling of constraint caused by our parents' silence . . . I think most of all there was a common understanding among the siblings during my growing-up years, that this baby, like the 1927 flight to Paris, was part of an era that had nothing to do with us."

And yet her oldest brother's life and death had had an enormous impact on her family. After their first child's death, her parents, frightened by the consequence of their fame, went to great pains to remove themselves from the public eye. When Charles died, Anne Morrow Lindbergh was already pregnant with their second child. The Lindberghs were taking no chances. They moved to a secluded house in Connecticut, surrounded by woods on both sides, backed by a lake, and separated from the road by carefully pruned shrubbery. ". . . from a boat in the cove, or from a car passing by on the road beyond our driveway," writes Lindbergh, "it would have been almost impossible to learn anything about our lives." They did this so effectively, she writes, that few people realized that there were five other Lindbergh children after Charles.

The family received letters from a number of disturbed young men who thought themselves to be the long-lost Charles. Periodically, these men showed up on their doorstep. Lindbergh describes watching, fascinated, after one such incident, as her father gently led the young man away. She often heard people refer to the kidnapping without understanding what had happened, why her name was so famous. She was aware that her name was linked with this tragedy, but she herself learned the details in the same way outsiders did—through old newsreels and mentions in media stories and on TV. "The kidnapping . . . was a moving shadow in the background of my experience . . . ," she writes, "a piece of the past that both was and was not mine."

Reeve Lindbergh was able to feel part of the loss, not only as a bystander, however, but through a tragedy in her own life. Her son, Jonny, died one night while she thought he was sleeping from a seizure brought on by infant encephalitis. She and Jonny were at her mother's home at the time. The next day, when Reeve Lindbergh and her mother made the discovery, they called an ambulance and, at her mother's insistence, sat by the crib that held Jonny. Reeve Lindbergh hadn't wanted to; she'd wanted to scream and run from the room, she writes. But her mother insisted that it was the right thing to do. Then, as they sat, her mother said, "I never saw my child's body after he died. I never sat with my son this way."

Reeve Lindbergh understood immediately. Her oldest brother had disappeared in the night, when her mother assumed he was sleeping, too. After her father had identified Charles's body, he'd had him cremated and scattered his ashes from the air himself. Her mother had never seen Charles again after she put him to bed that last night. Reeve Lindbergh felt a perverse pride, she writes, that she and her son had been able to give her mother this moment. ". . . we were sitting together, my mother and I, sitting quietly next to that crib in that house, not with one dead baby, but with two."

For the first time, she writes, she felt that the loss was hers, too. "I knew the story, had known it all my life, but on the day of my own son's death I was, for the first time, part of it. For the first time, it was absolutely real."

The most troubling stories were those of siblings who'd been quite young when they'd lost their brothers and sisters. Many had been old enough to have relationships with their sibling, but not old enough to remember him or her well or at all. They had lived, for the most part, within families that went into shock at the time of the loss and often didn't recover. Many parents receded into a chronic depression. Some came back, to a degree, and some didn't. These siblings had experienced two losses—first, their brother or sister, and then their parents, to their all-consuming grief.

In some cases, it sounded as if parents had gamely tried to cope by "getting back to normal" and pretending as if nothing had happened. Talk of the lost sibling was often discouraged, a family rule that was instituted without discussion. Everyone just knew. In one study of 159 adolescents and adults who had lost a sibling in childhood, for example, 62 percent said they had never discussed the death with anyone in their family. The most common family approach to the loss seemed to be: Erase it and the pain will go away. It doesn't work, of course. In fact, this approach tends to make the lost sibling even more of a haunting presence in a family's life.

Children, immersed within the all-consuming world of their families, often absorbed these rules and the atmosphere of subdued depression so completely that many, as adults, said that it had taken them decades—as it had in my case—to begin to acknowledge their loss and to mourn. In their stories, these people's parents sounded bereft and lost rather than ill-intentioned. Many parents who had very young children had clearly assumed that they couldn't have been profoundly affected, or not as affected as they themselves were.

This is a belief that originated with Sigmund Freud, who

didn't think children were psychologically sophisticated enough to process the meaning of death until adolescence. This message got translated as "children aren't capable of feeling grief." In the 1950s, British psychiatrist John Bowlby, the creator of the theory of mother-child attachment, challenged Freud's belief. Bowlby believed that babies as young as six months old could feel the same anguish as an adult upon separation from their mothers, and research has since demonstrated this fact. (Later studies would show that attachment relationships were not exclusive to mothers.) The truth appears to be the worst combination of Freud and Bowlby's theories: Though young children can feel loss and raw grief, they can't necessarily understand it.

Ann Farrant, a British journalist, is the author of *Sibling Bereavement,* a book in which she writes about her oldest daughter, Rosamund, who died when she was three and a half. Lucy, Rosamund's younger sister, was fourteen months old when it happened. Farrant was seven months pregnant with her third daughter at the time. "Relatives and friends did their best to comfort me, but I felt hammered into the ground by the weight of the grief," she writes. She had no idea how to explain Rosamund's sudden disappearance to Lucy. "Lucy didn't ask; how could she? At a pre-verbal stage, it is not easy for a young child to communicate the complex thoughts and fears stirred up by being in a household plunged in gloom." But this is wisdom born of hindsight. Farrant couldn't remember, she writes, if she ever tried to explain Rosamund's death to Lucy. "I rather think I said nothing and tried to appear 'normal.' But of course, I was nothing of the kind. I had changed. Her father had changed. The whole family set-up had changed."

When Lucy was fifteen, she underwent an appendectomy and was placed on an adult ward among what Farrant describes as some "unpleasant" cases during her recovery. There were complications and Lucy ended up staying longer than expected. While there, she learned of two grave events: that a favorite cousin had died, and that her grandfather had suffered a heart attack. By the time she was discharged, writes Farrant, Lucy seemed emotionally fragile.

Soon afterward, on a family vacation to Scotland, Lucy started to talk in a "baby" voice. It quickly became annoying. One day Farrant lost her temper, and Lucy burst into tears. "The crying was out of all proportion to my having snapped at her. She was weeping as if overwhelmed by some deep grief, the sort of anguished wailing I had succumbed to after Rosamund died. Instinctively and suddenly, I knew there must be a connection."

Farrant collected herself and asked her daughter to revert to the baby voice, held her, and asked her what was wrong, making the same soothing noises one might use to comfort a crying baby. "It took some time before Lucy began to speak. When she did, she had somehow moved herself back in time to the period following her sister's death. It was a remarkable and harrowing experience."

Lucy poured out a "torrent of grief and woe" about the "older sister who had cuddled and loved her, played silly games, made her laugh, been her first friend." Out, too, Farrant said, came the anxiety about what had happened, the worry that it had been her fault, the fear of losing her parents as abruptly as she'd lost Rosamund. "At last," writes Farrant, "there was a chance for Lucy to go through the process of mourning which had been denied her."

What is mourning in childhood? We're still learning. Psychologists believe at least part of the answer depends on the age of the child. Preschoolers understand absence, for instance, but have a difficult time with the idea that death is permanent. Older children, from around age six to eight, can understand permanency, but are prone to magical thinking—that something they thought, for example, might have caused the death to happen. (I can remember thinking I had made my brother ill by wishing, in a fit of anger, that something bad would happen to him.) Children from around nine to fourteen years of age start to develop a more complex understanding of death, and by late adolescence, we're thought to have an accurate understanding of permanency and the true cause and effect of what's happened.

Most people who work with mourning children will say that children need to be told what's going on, and that the information should be appropriate to the age of the child. But there's more to it than that. In her long-term study of children who'd lost a parent to cancer, Grace Hyslop Christ, Ph.D., an associate professor in the School of Social Work at Columbia University in New York City and author of *Healing Children's Grief: Surviving a Parent's Death from Cancer,* discovered that children need to renegotiate their relationship with lost parents as they reach different developmental ages in order to thoroughly process the loss. The help and support of their surviving parent in terms of providing information and being willing to talk was crucial to this process; siblings need to renegotiate their relationship with lost brothers and sisters, too. But in the case of the siblings with whom I spoke, the more common scenario was for parents to give a minimum of information to begin with, no follow-up, and to be very unwilling to talk.

John, forty-seven, was five years old when his two-year-old sister, Lisa, died. "I became aware that something was wrong in the family, and I didn't know what," he said. "The image that I remember most graphically is my sister holding her head to one side. I remember my mother yelling at her to hold her head up straighter. And I can remember wondering why my mother would be so upset with her for not holding her head up. Those were the signals that started saying to me that there was something wrong. The difficult part," he said, "is that, to this day, I don't know exactly what happened. My mother won't talk about it."

There was no preparation for what happened next. "My sister

just disappeared. I'm assuming she must have gone to the hospital, but it was never explained to us, and I don't know how much longer after that she died. We just never saw her again. We didn't go to the funeral. Pictures of Lisa were taken down. It was like this child had left right out of our life, and really didn't come back. Lisa left and was not discussed. My memory is that it was taboo to talk about." Because his sister's disappearance was so abrupt, said John, the loss was that much more difficult.

"I started having really horrible nightmares that lasted into my early teens, the kind of nightmares where terrible creatures, vicious things like gremlins, would be chasing me and I would wake up screaming. My mother increasingly withdrew from us. She became very cold. Her father was this cold, remote guy, not mean, but remote. My mother was of the same stock. And I think my sister's death just exacerbated it. Lisa was also my dad's favorite child, and his response to her death was to go for a period of twelve years working where he never took a day off. He ran a bakery that was open seven days a week. He baked all the time."

Family life after Lisa's death centered on the bakery. John's father baked in the early morning hours. His mother tended the counter when the shop opened. John and his older sister greased pans. "I can remember people coming into the bakery and saying why was I always so sad? I thought for a long time that it was because I was angry that I had to work all the time when my friends would be out playing. But I think people were picking up on a depressed child." Even more disconcerting were the times that people would come in and ask how many children were in the family. His parents' response, he said, was always "two." "I wanted to say, 'There's a third kid. She's not here right now, but there is a third kid. Two are alive, one is dead.'"

In his early twenties, during a brief span at home during college, he found the spot where his mother had hidden mementos of Lisa. "My mother finally found the courage to take all that stuff out and go through it. All of these questions came out. Even then, fifteen or sixteen years later, it was really, really hard for my mother to talk about it." He learned what Lisa had died of—a brain tumor—but not much more. "She folded up the pictures and put them away. There was this sense that she needed to keep that chapter shut. But the important thing," he said, "was the acknowledgment that Lisa existed. Up until then, she was like the child that never was."

After that, John left home and never really went back. What followed was the beginning and end of a first marriage, a few years in the military, a second marriage, and a second career as a social worker on a pediatric oncology ward, which put him directly in touch with families facing what his had faced so long ago—but this time as an adult, and in control. The choice had been unconscious, but he realized its significance later. "I look back at my life and there's this clear path of things I have done to come to grips with this major event that happened when I was five years old. One of the reasons I've been so successful at my job is because I can get in touch with pain," he said. "I can recognize pain when I'm in a room with it. I know pain. I know all the tricks about suppressing it. I know it on a very intimate level. That's been a healthy way for me to deal with it. Helping other people get in touch with their pain helps me get in touch with mine."

He joked about the fact that, because there had been no acknowledgment of Lisa's death as a child, he had grown up to be an obsessive marker of occasions. "My staff thinks I'm crazy because I insist on marking every birthday, every event." He also carried the burden of worry. Many of the people I spoke with who had lost siblings as children talked of a lost innocence—the early knowledge that life is mercurial and unpredictable, no ending guaranteed. "When I leave the house in the morning, my three-year-old says 'Be careful, Daddy.' Where do you think he gets that?" he said, shaking his head.

John didn't know if he would ever have the answers to his questions. He and his older sister, like many of the survivors of these families, were so well trained not to talk about what happened that neither has ever broached the topic with the other. "It's still one of the things I'd like to do, though. I'd like to get her memory of what happened and compare it with mine. A lot of my memories are still completely blocked." His father is dead. He hoped his mother might be more open to talking about Lisa in the future. "I would love to get the pictures of Lisa out and talk. I know where she's buried now, but I've never been to her grave. I really want to go."

Retha, fifty-two, was twelve when her younger sister died. Unlike those who'd been very young when their siblings died, she had quite a few memories of her sister and what had happened. "My sister was born with a heart defect. Back then, the doctors didn't expect her to live to be a year old, but she did survive. When she was six, she had open-heart surgery. We were very hopeful about that. But we only really had a couple of years of hope and then she started having problems again. We'd walk to school and she'd faint." Retha and her identical twin would then carry her into the school and call their mother.

"The summer that we were twelve and she was nine, our mother told us that she was going to die. That it was just a matter of time. That was really hard to grasp at that age, you know?" It was made harder by the fact that this sister and their younger brother, who was five at the time, were never told. Retha and her twin had to keep the information to themselves. "That was early summer, and she actually didn't die until almost Thanksgiving," said Retha. Her little sister spent the last two months of her life in the hospital on twenty-four-hour oxygen.

"That was very isolating for my twin and me and our little brother, because our dad was at the hospital and Mother was at the hospital, and so, we were kind of at home, trying to keep things going, and that was very difficult. My dad would spend the night with us, but he wanted to be at the hospital. Mother rarely came home. We felt pretty invisible." But the hardest part was that their parents seemed to have no idea that the siblings cared that their sister was sick, that she was going to die. They were shut out. "We really didn't get to see our sister, and so there was never really an opportunity to say good-bye."

She died one day while they were at school. Retha remembers looking up from her desk and seeing her uncle standing in the doorway to her classroom. "By the time we got home that day, the doctor had already given my mother a shot, so she was asleep. And my dad was pretty much in shock." The children were on their own. Unsure of how to handle the subject of death with them, their parents had decided to present their sister as if she were sleeping peacefully.

"So we get to the funeral home, and she's got on her little pajamas, and she's in bed, and she's dead. And my brother started screaming. He's just horrified. He screamed for hours." Their mother was still knocked out with the sedative. Their father, she said, wasn't good at soothing. "So my sister and I took turns rocking this screaming, horrified child, trying to get him to sleep. My brother doesn't even remember that she was part of the family now. He has no memories."

For the children, no real mourning took place. "Our minister had been to the hospital a lot there at the end, and most of their friends went to that church, so you know, they did the meals. They were wonderful. I can remember my mother's friends ironing whatever it is we were gonna wear for the service. And that was nice. But they were there for Mother and Daddy. I don't think they knew that we needed anything other than soda to drink and something sweet to eat. I see it as just a total lack of awareness about what we might be feeling, or what it might be like for us."

Just before Christmas, their parents decided to go through her sister's toys and clothes and give them to an orphanage. "They went into her room, and I can remember the door literally closing in our faces." Retha and her siblings stood there, she said, wanting to be let in, not wanting to be left out. "I know that it was because they were grieving that they didn't see that. But they never really did seem to understand that we had a need to grieve, you know?" From that point on, her mother became what she described as fragile. "She never really came back after that," said Retha. Communication about their younger sister stopped altogether.

"What happened was that when we mentioned her name, and when we would ask questions or talk about her, our mother would start to cry. And then of course, my dad would be very protective. The cues we got were, 'You don't talk about it because it will upset Mom.' And so it got to the point, and still is this way, that we never, ever mention her name. It was like, if we didn't talk about it, we would protect my mother. But then we also didn't talk about it when we were alone. She just never comes up. It's like, we wiped her off the face of the earth, the way we dealt with her death."

Looking back, she said, there have definitely been ripple effects in her life. She has never visited her sister's grave. In fact, she has gone out of her way to avoid it, and she does not attend funerals if she can help it. "There are some flowers that people always send to funerals, gladiolas, that make me sick to my stomach if I smell them. I honestly think I'm going to hurl every time I smell or see them. It's just a horrible reminder." She feels that she and her twin both chose first husbands who would not consider their needs, a continuation of their childhood experience as the healthy siblings.

Her divorce from her first husband, Retha said, propelled her into therapy, where she finally began to explore the long-ago loss of her sister. Like John, she had never really discussed her sister's loss with her surviving siblings. In fact, she told me she recently took a chance and brought the subject up with her twin. The conversation didn't last more than five minutes. Although Retha describes herself as a stronger, more empathic person because of her experience and is now happily remarried, it is clear that she is still sad about the missed opportunities to mourn her sister. "I wish we had been able to say good-bye. And I wish we'd been able to talk about her. I would hope that, if it were me, and I lost a child, that I would be able to keep that child as a part of me and keep the child alive in my heart, and in my day-to-day life. We really lost this sister in every way. Not just physically, but we lost her."

Pleasant White, Ph.D., a Missouri–based psychotherapist who specializes in working with adults who lost siblings as children, lost her only sibling, a thirteen-year-old sister, to cancer when she was fifteen. Twenty-five years later, when her son turned the same age her sister had been, the grief she'd suppressed hit her full force. She had such a hard time finding a therapist who took the reemergence of her feelings seriously, she said, that she decided to become a therapist herself. "One person told me I wouldn't still be grieving if I wasn't getting attention from it." She is still plagued by feelings of guilt over her sister's death. She'd known her sister wasn't feeling well when they'd gone away on a family vacation, but her sister had begged her not to tell their parents for fear that they'd cancel the trip. Soon afterward, her sister's symptoms grew worse, and advanced cancer was diagnosed.

White's description of her typical patient was an apt profile of me and most of the surviving siblings who'd been children when they lost their brother or sister. "A huge percentage of them come into therapy depressed and they don't think it has anything to do with the loss of their sibling," she said. "It usually doesn't hit until around mid-life. And there's usually a trigger, like their children reaching the same age the sibling had been, or another loss, like a divorce." I asked her why the loss tends to pop up like that, so many years later. "Repression only works if you have the energy for it," she explained. "When there's a lot going on in your current life and you have to redirect your energy to respond to it, the repression sometimes lifts quite suddenly."

White had moved several times, just before her son turned

thirteen, and that upheaval had drained her. In my case, it had
been a recent breakup and a horrifying job that tipped me over the
edge. Message boards on the handful of sibling-loss sites on the
Internet are sprinkled with hesitant e-mails from people in just
this state. They want to know if anyone has ever heard of anything
like this. They want to know if they're crazy.

White describes the psychic space where the loss resides,
unexplored, until repression lifts as "shielded space," a term
created by bereavement expert Therese Rando, Ph.D. (My therapist's "closet" analogy describes the same phenomenon.) "When
certain events are too traumatic to deal with, you take that event
and hide it inside you and shield the space," explained White. "You
grow everywhere else except that space. No one else can get in
there, except someone who has been through it. It's why I've been
so successful in working with other bereaved siblings," she
explains, echoing John. "They let me in."

As adults, siblings don't necessarily live near, talk to, or see one
another often because of geography or busy lives consumed by
tending to families and careers. In other cases, however, siblings
have, for one reason or another, become alienated. In these cases,
said Ken Doka, Ph.D., a professor of gerontology at the College of
New Rochelle in New York who specializes in issues of loss, siblings might feel even more strongly that they don't have the right
to mourn. "They'll say, how can I grieve for my brother when I
haven't spoken to him for ten years?" And the list of "rightful"
mourners ahead of the bereft siblings is often long. While parents
are often seen as the truly bereft in the case of childhood sibling
loss, in adult sibling loss, this category extends to include the
spouse and children the sibling has left behind. It is, once again, a
situation rife with ambiguity, one that leaves adult siblings wondering if they have a right to the loss.

It isn't unusual for them to decide that they don't, which has predictable consequences. Lynn, forty-eight, is the second of three children. Her younger brother, Mike, who was forty-six, died a year and a half ago from a sudden heart attack, the same way their father had died. Though her mother and older sister were still alive at the time of his death, the task of providing emotional support to most everyone—her mother, her brother's wife, his four children—fell to Lynn. She and Mike had been close companions as children. They'd played together, had "adventures." Throughout college and their early twenties, they'd kept in touch and visited one another in the various cities they'd lived in. "We were good friends," said Lynn. But then Mike got married and had four daughters, and the needs of his family, financial and otherwise, had taken precedence over their relationship.

For Lynn, Mike's immersion in his family had felt like a loss. She'd felt somewhat supplanted. "With four daughters, he already had so much *female* energy in his life," she said. "We never really had a chance to have much of a relationship after that. We didn't have a tight relationship as adults. I wish we did. At times, I had hoped that we would be able to be close again. His death destroyed that future, you know? It took possibilities away. It will never happen. I'll never have that chance. I feel like I am less joyful, that my heart is heavier, because of that." It is common for adult siblings to talk of a double loss—the loss of their sibling, and the loss of the possibility for reconnection.

What Lynn and Mike had had were twice-a-year visits in which they'd laugh together like little kids, and the shared worry of an elderly mother who lived with Mike and his family. Lynn had just moved to New York City to start a teaching job when she came home to an answering machine full of frantic phone calls from her sister-in-law and her mother, informing her of Mike's death. By that evening, she was on a plane to Iowa, where Mike, his family, and her mother lived. She cried for the entire two-and-a-half-hour flight. "That was the last time that I allowed myself to feel it," she said.

When she got to Mike's home, it was to a family in a severe state of crisis. Though her mother had been living with Mike and his family for some time, it had not been a happy arrangement. Mike, said Lynn, had been a "typical male" and ignored the trouble, hoping it would go away. It hadn't, and with his death the pretense was gone. Mike's wife and children, in their distress, were blaming his mother for his death, claiming that the stress of her presence had triggered his heart attack. Lynn's mother, for her part, was undone both by her son's death and by the antagonism she now felt cast her way.

"So I flew down into the middle of this wild situation, and I had to be the adult, because everyone was in such a state of crisis. I had to move my mother out of the house and get her reoriented to a new living situation, and I had to deal with her grief over losing not only Mike, her son, but losing what she thought of as her family, too." And then there were Mike's wife and the girls, the youngest of whom was just six. Lynn had to put her loss—in the interview she didn't claim Mike's death as "hers," she referred to it as "it"—aside. "It was just that, the impact on their daily lives is just so great, it's like, their loss is so much greater."

When she spoke of her early relationship with Mike, how they'd shared in exploring the world, she began to cry. Though their relationship had receded over the years, that intimate early connection with him and with her father had represented happy memories of the family she grew up in. Her father and her brother, both now dead of heart attacks, had been her foundation. She was starting to realize that, whatever their relationship had been as adults, Mike, on a deep and hidden level, had been her remaining anchor, the last person from her early life who had rooted her in the world.

There's a tendency to speak of "worse" losses and "easier" losses. The truth is there are only different losses. This was just beginning to occur to Lynn, and it was leading her toward giving herself permission to mourn. Her grief, she said, was starting to bubble up on her unexpectedly, and she found it unnerving. She said she realized she needed help. She was considering taking care of herself, going to a therapist. "It's all very confusing," she said. "Maybe in the safety of a therapist's office I can . . . deal with it a little bit. I have this feeling that I need to get in some sort of safe place in order to sort things out."

Those who lost a sibling as an adult differed from those who experienced the loss as a child in that, although they were often denied the opportunity to grieve, they could more readily question the response to their loss and create innovative ways to cope on their own. Amber, thirty-five, was someone who found her own way to mourn. She was just nineteen when her seventeen-year-old brother, James, and their cousin were killed in a car accident. "They were driving across a bridge. It was raining, my cousin was driving, and their car hydroplaned as they were on a bridge and hit an abutment and blew up." Two men tried to pry the boys out, but were forced to step back because of the flames.

Amber was the first, but not the last, young adult I encountered who'd been called upon for such grim adult tasks as identifying bodies, making end-of-life and organ-donation decisions, and planning funerals. It was as if the parents felt they could collapse if there were surviving siblings to take care of these things. Amber was, in a way, happy to do this for her brother. But the fallout for her, and for others like her, was severe.

"I had to view the body, because my parents couldn't. And as the oldest, I volunteered. He was burned on ninety-five or ninety-eight percent of his body. He wasn't recognizable. Except for his foot. That's how I identified him, his right foot. His toes were intact. He didn't wear shoes a lot, so I knew his feet really well. At first I thought, it's not him. He's been kidnapped; it's the wrong person, all these crazy things. But once I saw his foot, I knew."

She experienced symptoms of post-traumatic stress disorder

afterward. "I got into crisis," she said. "I felt very suicidal, because I thought if I killed myself I'd be with him. I'd rather be with him than in this pain. Over time it subsided, but I definitely had a lot of suicidal thoughts. A lot of dreams. A lot of nightmares, too. A lot about fire."

In the aftermath of his death, she found herself searching for comfort, without much luck. "I felt like there were a lot of outlets for my parents, but I felt like there was nothing for me. People would interrupt my grief to say, 'Boy, that must be really hard for your parents.' I really felt like saying, 'You know, it was, but it's really hard for me, too.'"

Her mother, a family therapist, encouraged her to get into therapy. "I did therapy on my own with a Freudian analyst, and that did *not* work for me, because I was in crisis and he really wanted to explore from birth on. I needed to start at the crisis." She quit after three sessions. Ultimately, she found her own solution: Outward Bound, a rigorous wilderness program, in the Colorado mountains.

"James had gone on it the year before and he had been there on his birthday, and I was going to be there on his birthday a year later, in the same place. I did it because I thought it would be therapeutic. And it was. I was able to grieve openly for a month and a half, and people thought it was just because I was on this grim program and it was really hard. I could just grieve for him and be in the wilderness." The loss is not, by any means, over for her, she said. "It's amazing, you would think fifteen years is such a long time to still be feeling it," she said. "But it's like, time doesn't really matter."

In her book, *Ambiguous Loss,* Pauline Boss writes that the family you see is not always the one in the minds of its members. Without some kind of adjustment to the new reality of a lost sibling, the greater the confusion and dismay of the family. Witness John's family, for example, in which Lisa had been silently erased. The goal, according to Boss, is to work toward melding the physical and psychological reality. But in sibling-loss stories, particularly in those in which the surviving siblings are young, what you often see is families too paralyzed by the shock of the impossible—parents outliving children, siblings outliving siblings—to function.

Occasionally you see a family that manages to grapple with this more successfully. In Amber's family, for example, they were allowed to talk about her brother, which she attributed to the fact that her mother is a therapist. "It's not taboo. It's okay," she said. And they have devised a number of rituals to mark that they still consider James a member of their family, even though he's no longer with them. On his birthday, a red rose sits in a bud vase in the foyer of the family home. At Thanksgiving and Christmas, they set a place for him. "My husband thought it was funny. He'd come over for Thanksgiving, and there'd be a place set for James at the table, and his picture sitting there."

Kathleen was forty-eight when her sister, Janie, forty-four, died. Their father had died just two weeks earlier. He'd been sick for quite a while, and Kathleen, who lives in the same town as her parents, helped take care of him during his illness. When he died, her younger brother, the middle child in the family, flew in from Oregon for the funeral. Janie, the baby of the family, flew in from Colorado. Two weeks from the day of their father's death, Kathleen put Janie on a plane back to Denver.

Her husband and three sons, then sixteen, eighteen, and twenty, picked her up at the airport. Once home, she changed clothes, poured herself a glass of wine, and sat down to tell her sons and her husband about the funeral. "She took one sip of wine, stood up, grabbed her head, and said, 'My God, this is the worst migraine I've ever had,' and dropped to the floor," said Kathleen. It was a cerebral aneurysm. "I talked to a friend of hers, who was a nurse, and she saw the CAT scan. She said my sister must have died instantaneously, because her entire cranium was filled with blood." The paramedics asked if Janie was an organ donor even before they pulled away from the house.

"I was with my mom when we got the call about my sister. And I immediately had to take care of her," said Kathleen. Her own children were also thoroughly undone. "My sister was my kids' favorite aunt, and they loved her dearly." Her son's migraine headaches, which he'd suffered for years, got dramatically worse. Her daughter, already struggling with anorexia, dropped ten pounds. Her brother-in-law, with whom she'd never really gotten along, was overwhelmed by single parenthood and began to call her regularly, asking her what to do. And her nephew came to spend the summer. "I'm the surrogate wife," said Kathleen. "And I'm the surrogate mother of his kids."

No one really understood her loss, she said. Empathizing with her mother, for instance, was harder for her because her mother didn't seem to realize that she, too, had had a loss. "She is just so wrapped up in her grief," Kathleen said. "Sometimes she'll say things like, 'God forbid this ever happens to you. She was *my* daughter.' A couple of times I've made light of it. She'll make some comment and I'll say, 'Okay, you win, you're grieving more than I am.' It's like, I can't get in there. It's very hard. My mother is an articulate, intelligent woman. I know that she knows I grieve. But does she realize that my grief is as big a deal as hers? No, I don't think so."

Kathleen had become aware that she felt drained, and unable to take care of herself and her own feelings. She decided she needed to do something about it. "It's only within the last month or so that I've thought, 'I've done enough.' In essence, I told everybody that they have to be on their own for a little while. I really have to take care of me. And that's the advice I would give to someone else. Given the tenor of society around you, people try to be nice, but it's like it's not a big deal to lose a brother or sister. So my advice is to know that you're going to be basically alone, and you need to take care of yourself and whatever it is you feel."

When I asked her what that meant, she said she was still figuring it out. She'd learned to request a hug if she needed one, or that somebody sit and talk with her about her loss. "I sit out in my garden and do nothing. And if things don't get done around the house, I don't worry. I've pretty much closed down my kitchen. I don't do dinners every night. I read about grief. If someone says to me, 'How are you?' I tell them. I don't assume they don't want to hear. I figure, 'You asked, I'll tell you.' I talk to my friends. And I try not to put me and my sister on the back burner."

Some of the more visible examples of adult-sibling caretaking can be seen in the newspaper, or on the five o'clock news—anytime there's a story about an untimely death. Most often, it's an adult sibling who is appointed the family spokesperson. Is it because the family perceives him to be in better shape, because his loss is "less"? Is it because the newspeople assume this is the case and approach him?

In a *New York Times* article dated March 17, 2002, for instance, the reporter offers an update on the case of Kristine Kupka, a pregnant, twenty-eight-year-old student at Baruch College in New York City. According to Kupka's family, one of her professors, with whom she allegedly had a relationship and who was the father of her baby, had been trying to convince her to have an abortion she didn't want. She was last seen shopping with him on October 24, 1998. Then she vanished. Though the man has been listed as a suspect in her disappearance, there hasn't been enough evidence to prove anything.

Kathy Kupka, Kristine's older sister, has done many television and magazine interviews in the years since Kristine's disappearance and even put up a billboard featuring her sister's picture and the details of her disappearance in New York City. She says hello to her sister every day when she passes it. But she sidesteps talking about her own loss. "It's ruined my mom's life," she said in the article. "She just cries every day."

One of the few bereft siblings I've spoken to who said he felt his loss was recognized was a seventy-seven-year-old man named Leon, who'd lost his older sister, Irene, to cancer some five years earlier. I'd wondered if there came an age where sibling loss seemed like a more normal part of life. If so, it had not come for Leon. His mother and father had lived well into their nineties. "When Irene died at eighty-one," he said, "we thought she died young."

Irene had helped raise him. She used to joke that she was also raising Leon's wife, Marilyn. Marilyn had referred to Irene—affectionately—as her second mother-in-law. They'd always been close. They'd vacationed together and eaten at one another's houses regularly. But they'd become a particularly tight threesome after the death of Irene's husband. When Leon spoke of how much Irene was missed, he said "we," not "I."

They've keept in touch with Irene's son and daughter, who don't live in the area anymore. They're close to them, he said, but not like they were with Irene. His voice became teary when he spoke of her. "It's almost five years, and, of course, we still talk of her. I've got a picture of her in my head." Leon had a hard time articulating what the loss of Irene meant to him. "I just miss everything, there's a void." He'd start sentences, trail off, and then say, "You see? You see?" I did. What he was saying was, how do you describe the way someone fit into your life, if they have always been a part of it?

Leon didn't feel his loss had been overlooked. Part of the reason had to be that Leon and Marilyn had experienced Irene in the same way—as a wise, older sister who'd always been there for both of them. That was just the way the relationship was. They had shared and validated each other's loss of Irene. They still go to places and comment on whether Irene would have liked it. Leon told me that they said a prayer and cried at the hospital after Irene died. In the background, I could hear Marilyn say, "I'm still crying."

My challenge was the opposite of Leon's. He was trying to articulate a lifetime of memories with his sister, all of which floated within reach. I was trying to find less than half a lifetime's, all of which I'd taken great pains to hide. I spent a good number of years in therapy rummaging around in that back closet, just trying to catch a glimpse of my relationship with my brother. Gradually, bits of my life with him began to flutter out. When this happened, I was both thrilled and sad. They illustrated with painful clarity just what I had had, and what I had lost.

Scene 1: The Christmas that he is nine and I am five, in a fit of spite or a need for someone to share and admire his savvy, my brother lets me in on the whole Santa Claus ruse. He wakes me up Christmas Eve and takes me to sit at the top of the stairs. From there, we can peek through the railing and see our parents wrapping presents, eating the cookies and carrots I've naively left out for Santa and the reindeer. "Don't tell," he says, nodding his head toward them. I'm not disappointed. I am, in fact, aglow in his confidence, awed by his savoir faire, the way he *knows* things. How had he kept cool while I'd worried over selecting just the right sugar cookies? In the morning, I follow his cue, feign surprise, check to see if the cookies have been eaten. My parents smile, all innocence. From now on, the tables will be turned. We will indulge *them* with insincere references to Santa Claus. Lesson: Knowledge is power.

Scene 2: Soon afterward, my brother takes me sledding up at the elementary school we attend, which has the only hills in the

area that don't lead straight to the street. It's considered by parents
to be safe. We are on our way home late, my brother trudging
through the snow, pulling the sled behind him. No one else is
around. It is ice-cold and quiet, in that late-afternoon, gray, snowy
way. We get to the top of the black path, which leads from the back
of the school down the hill to the sidewalk and street below. It
goes without saying that this is a no-sled area. It is icy. Steep. It is
unlikely you'd be able to stop at the bottom. You'd be bound to
end up in the street. My brother stops, turns, asks me if I want to
sled down it.

We contemplate it, silently, for perhaps a second before climb-
ing on, him in front, steering, me in back, clinging. The path is icy
and bumpy. We slide down it unevenly. The wind is cold, racing
by my ears, my eyes tearing, but I am aware, in a removed way,
that it is still quiet all around us. As we near the bottom, my
brother pulls back on the rope attached to the steering levers, tries
to brake. It doesn't work. We hit the mogul of ice that has hard-
ened on the sidewalk and fly, landing midway in the street. No
cars. It is beyond exhilarating. We climb the hill to our house and
go inside, shaking our boots off. My mother asks, How was it?
"Fine," we say. Lessons: Rules can be broken. Risks are worth taking. Don't ask, don't tell.

Scene 3: That summer, we go to San Francisco. My father is on
sabbatical, working at Stanford. We live in someone else's house,
which has a jungle for a backyard. Hummingbirds flutter around
the trees, and chameleons skitter on the patio. We find their skele-
tons and pick them up by their bony tails. We eat lots of Ghirardelli
chocolate bars with raisins. I break four of the absent family's plates
tripping over the dog's water bowl. My brother teaches himself to
crochet with a pencil for a hook, teaches me, and then, because we
don't know how to make second rows, we make long strands of
crochet loops with multicolored yarn. Toward the end of the trip,
my brother comes down with something. We drive partway back
home, with Donner, our schnauzer, in his crate in the back of the

station wagon, my father, mother, and I in the front seat, my brother lying down in the backseat, sick with fever.

We get home from California. My brother gets better, and life goes back to normal. I start first grade at Ashburton Elementary, and my brother starts fifth. He walks me to school in the morning, delivers me to my classroom, picks me up in the afternoon. At home, he watches me draw and evaluates whether the pictures are good or not. When he approves, I am pleased, my sense of possibility stretching inches beyond the visible boundaries of my body. I want to read. I want to catch up with him. By the time Miss Adrian breaks out Dick and Jane, I am champing at the bit. My brother is already writing stories and plays, reading thick books. I am insane with jealousy. I read Dick and Jane as fast as I can, eschewing recess. I want to read. I want to write. Like my brother.

And then, one day in September, I wake up and he is gone. Lessons: Life is unpredictable. Trust no one.

Chapter Three

DISENFRANCHISED GRIEF

"O lost, and by the wind grieved ghost, come back
again."

—THOMAS WOLFE

There's a term for what I experienced standing by the side of my
brother's grave, and for the similar experiences related by other
siblings: disenfranchised grief. Ken Doka coined the phrase in 1983
to describe the experience of divorced spouses mourning the death
of their former partners. These people often weren't allowed the
right to grieve because their relationship with the deceased didn't
make them "legitimate" mourners. Before long, Doka realized that
the term was applicable to the grief of other people, as well.

Those who've undergone miscarriages or abortions, for example, may find themselves short on sympathy. The grief of children
can be disenfranchised because they tend to mourn differently
from adults and their grief is not always recognized. The grief of
the mentally retarded and those with mental illness is also often
overlooked, the assumption being that they're too disconnected to
register death, or incapable of understanding it.

And then there are people whose relationship to the deceased doesn't fit the strict profile of the nuclear family—gay partners, ex-spouses, lovers, grandparents, and friends, to name a few—who may also find their grief overlooked. It's a surprise that siblings should find themselves sitting under this particular umbrella. They are, after all, part of the nuclear family. And yet, the most universal feature of the sibling-loss stories I heard was some version of my story, of standing at the side of my brother's grave, being exhorted to take care of the real mourners.

"The focal point is always on other relationships," said Doka. "If it was a young person, it will be the parents. If the person was older, it will be on his or her spouse and children. The sibling relationship, wherever it is in the life cycle, is just very easy to neglect."

But why?

To understand, we need to start with Sigmund Freud. Freud was born in 1856, the first child of Jacob and Amalia Freud. By the time he was ten years old, he had seven younger siblings. He lost one, too. Julius, his younger brother by less than a year, died from an intestinal infection when he was just six months old. Freud biographer Louis Breger, M.D., speculates that this loss had much to do with the man, and the scientist, that Freud became. So did the fact that his mother delivered Anna, the next of Freud's siblings, within a year of Julius's death, and that she would produce four more siblings—three girls and a boy—in quick succession.

When Julius died, the grief of his parents likely made them emotionally unavailable to Freud. And soon there were new siblings clamoring for attention. Freud sought his parents' attention by cultivating their pride in his intellectual precocity. But he never regained even a fragment of the attention he'd enjoyed before Julius's birth and death.

Later in his career, when he created the theories he offered as templates for the human psyche, Freud immortalized his own sibling relationships by dismissing all siblings as rivals who would gladly be rid of one another if they could. He never revised his opinion. Though siblings and sibling loss turned up in the stories of many of his most famous cases, he routinely chose to ignore their potential significance.

Only in two personal letters to his friend Willhelm Fleiss, written during an intensive period of self-analysis, would Freud ever let down his guard on the subject of siblings. In the letters, Freud muses over the significance of Julius's death. He writes of an enduring sense of guilt over it, something he attributes to the fact that he must have wished to conquer his new rival. And he speculates that the death had left him with "a germ of self reproach" and a lifelong need for a "hated enemy." His relationship with Julius, he wrote, had contributed to "what is neurotic, but also what is intense, in all my friendships."

Only Freud can speak to the guilt he felt. But his propensity for "hated enemies" is well-known. Most of his enemies were young protégés whom Freud initially mentored and eventually snubbed, usually when they tried to emerge as psychiatrists in their own right. Freud, the consummate older brother, could tolerate only followers, not leaders. And he hated competition.

One of the exiled was a young Viennese physician named Alfred Adler, relevant to our tale primarily because he was first to propose that birth order confers on us certain personality traits. Adler, too, based his theory on personal experience. He was the second of seven children. As a child, he suffered from rickets so severely that he didn't learn to walk until he was four years old. One of his most vivid memories was of sitting bundled up on a bench, an invalid, envying the ease with which his older brother moved and played. He spent the rest of his childhood trying to surpass him. Adler infused his particular experience into his observations on siblings. When he went to assign the traits of first-, second-, and third-born children, for instance, he listed ambition, competitiveness, and a profound desire to better their chief rival, their older sibling, among the common traits belonging to the second-born.

The relationships that Freud and Adler each had with their siblings, essentially based on the notion of rivalry and rooted in the experience of growing up in very large families (the norm, in their era), would become the accepted paradigm for all sibling relationships in the decades to come. In fact, until the early 1980s, almost every academic article on the subject of siblings took up the topic of rivalry or birth order. That the sibling relationship might meet other needs, or evoke any emotion other than competition, rarely came up. In 1970, when psychologists Brian Sutton-Smith and B. G. Rosenberg came out with *The Sibling,* a landmark book (in terms of the weight it gave to the relationship—a whole book!), the word "love" appears in the index only in relation to the word "mother."

After Freud's death, research on child development and the critical importance of the mother-child bond to children's psychological and emotional well-being began to emerge and, in the early fifties, blossomed into a major area of new research. It still carried Freud's imprint—mother, father, and child were still the trio of featured players in the scenario. But while Freud's theories revolved around the idea that a child's relationship with his or her parents was based on forbidden sexual fantasies, the new theory proposed another explanation for what bound parents and children together: love. In the early days of this research, the emphasis was on the mother's role. Eventually, these scientists would get to wondering how fathers fit in. It wouldn't be until the 1980s before anyone thought to ask that question of siblings.

The Sibling Bond was the first major book to make the case that the sibling relationship is important and often composed of deep, complex, and intimate bonds that play an instrumental role in the development of identity. The first edition of the book came out in 1982, two years after my brother's funeral. In its first chapter, authors Michael D. Kahn and Stephen P. Bank, Ph.D., both

Connecticut–based psychotherapists, write about how baffled they'd felt when confronted with patients who needed or wanted to talk about their siblings. And they explain why that had come to be:

"We had been taught that siblings are, at best, minor actors on the stage of human development, that their influence is supposed to be fleeting, and that it is the parents who principally determine one's identity. We had also been taught that, after one leaves home, the main influences upon an adult's life and sense of self are spouse, children and job . . ."

The notion that siblings could only be rivals, proposed so many years earlier by Freud and Adler, had become accepted psychological truth. This, at least in part, explains the blind spot. It was not, as I had assumed, that no one had thought to ask: "What about siblings?" It was that anyone who might have asked that question had been taught that we already knew the answer. As a result, it was possible, until quite recently, for psychologists like Bank and Kahn to listen to their patients talk about their siblings without the foggiest clue what to make of the information. When patients discussed their brothers and sisters, Bank and Kahn confessed, "We felt as if we were in a foreign country without a map."

They were among the few who investigated the chasm between what they'd been taught and their real-life experience with patients. They had, as most pioneers do, written the book they'd needed to read. I was grateful to discover it, some years after my brother's death. It helped explain the woman at my brother's graveside, and all the others who'd reiterated her message, in one way or another, in the years that followed. If generations of psychotherapists (who pride themselves on their insight into the human psyche) hadn't understood the relationship, or the loss, who could?

When sibling research did begin to emerge in the 1980s, much of it had the name of developmental psychologist Judy Dunn, Ph.D., attached to it. Dunn, the undisputed matriarch of this field, became curious about siblings when she found herself the mother of three children under age two. "I was seeing all of these things happen right in front of me," she explained when we spoke. Though she herself was doing research on the parent-child bond at the time, it quickly became apparent to her that siblings were an integral part of the developmental story, too. She promptly went to look up the clinical literature on siblings. "And there was nothing there," she said. "It was such an interesting gap. I knew from my own family experience what a big deal this was. How anyone with more than one child could think that the parent-child relationship is the be-all and end-all is beyond me.

"In 1985, I went to a conference that was a huge, biennial congregation of developmental psychologists. Among the thousands of academic papers being presented, there were two on siblings, one of which was mine. I remember it clearly. I gave my talk, and then afterward, this person sitting in the front row jumped up and said, 'I'm the other one!'" When we spoke, Dunn had, in fact, just returned from the annual meeting of the same conference of developmental psychologists. The topic was still so poorly represented, she said, that a small cluster of sibling researchers had held a meeting to discuss it. Why was there still comparatively little research on siblings?

Siblings, as it turns out, are both easy and difficult to study. They are easy if you want to do a short-term project and interview them—Dunn said young brothers and sisters are quite candid about the things they like and don't like about one another. "They let it all out in front of you. They don't try to hide anything. Interview a four-year-old about her relationship with her siblings and she'll be more articulate about it than would anyone in any other relationship." There are a number of yearlong studies on topics like the emotional attachment between siblings. These kinds of projects are just the thing for a graduate student who is looking to undertake a relatively short-term project, says Dunn. But what the field lacks, she says, is the difficult, more long-term research on the course of the sibling relationship across the life span.

Dr. L. Alan Sroufe, a professor of child development at the University of Minnesota's Institute of Child Development, said that's because the relationship doesn't bend well to the strictures of systematic science. You can round up a bunch of pregnant women due to deliver at the same time and watch the parallel development of their children. But you'd be out of luck, he said, if you wanted to follow this research with an orderly study on the dynamic between these children and later siblings—unless you could persuade all those mothers to have a second child at exactly the same time. "To follow that group into adulthood would cost millions of dollars and take an entire career." (Unsaid: To devote one's career to studying a relationship that the psychological community has shown little sign of valuing is risky.)

Peer research—meaning the impact on one another of friends and children the same age—has actually been a much more fruitful area of research. "You'd think that siblings would be studied more. But it's a trick," said Sroufe. "Peer research is really easy to do." If you want to do a study of siblings in which you have only eight-year-old and five-year-old pairs, it would take time and money to build your sample. You'd have to search long and hard for pairs that exactly fit your specifications. "But if you want to study peers in those age groups, you could just go to a couple of elementary schools and you'd have your sample within two weeks."

There's also a whiff of academic territorialism in this saga, as evidenced, most recently, in the 1998 publication of Judith Rich Harris's *The Nurture Assumption: Why Children Turn Out the Way They Do*. In the book, Harris proposes an idea that the majority of developmental psychologists consider heresy—that it is peers, not parents, who have more influence on making us who we are. "She was really posing a challenge to all the people who were studying the parent-child relationship. And they pilloried her for it," said

Dunn. Harris proved that even interesting ideas can be unpopular if they challenge the status quo. Were someone to make a similar claim on behalf of the importance of sibling relationships, they might find themselves equally unpopular. It's the kind of situation destined to repel rather than lure new researchers. In fact, after I contacted people who had done sibling research earlier in their careers, about the time *The Sibling Bond* came out, most took great pains to distance themselves from the topic.

Ultimately, no one really has a simple answer for why sibling research is still so scant, relative to research on other topics. "It's a real puzzle," said Dunn. "It's part of a curious gap between what people will say is important in their real lives, in which context most would say the sibling relationship is important, and what they study as an academic topic. It's absolutely mad that there is such neglect."

Fortunately, a small core of sibling scientists has been doggedly working away at the questions that interest them. Dunn and her husband, behavioral geneticist Robert Plomin, for instance, have been pioneers in sorting out what makes siblings in the same family so different. They attribute this phenomenon to the fact that, beyond the obvious things siblings share in common—parents, a home, some genes, perhaps a room, and some physical characteristics—they each have an intimate circle of nonshared life. Among the nonshared elements are friends, different school experiences, their ages, different treatment by their parents, and often even different experiences growing up in the same family. Taken together, say Dunn and Plomin, the components of non-shared life can result in very different personalities and traits, even among those who share a significant amount of the same DNA.

Other researchers are plumbing such topics as how the quality of sibling relationships is related to the quality of marital relation-ships; the purpose of sibling conflict (the new, politically correct term for rivalry); the way that siblings deliberately adopt different roles in the family in order to limit competition for parental attention; and, in a renaissance of birth order research, the way birth order and the gender of our siblings shape us into who we are. Scientists are also coming to believe that siblings are one primary avenue through which we become aware that others have feelings and thoughts different from our own. You can see this in action, according to Dunn, in the way that even very young siblings have a knack for knowing just how to please or, alternatively, infuriate one another. Only a handful of researchers study adult sibling relationships. And other sibling arenas are all but untouched—step- and half-sibling relationships, for example, and sibling relationships in situations other than white, two-parent, middle-class homes.

When I asked Dunn what she finds particularly compelling about the sibling relationship, she said that it was its contradictions. "The relationship can be dramatically different between different siblings. You might find that while one pair is closely attached to one another, there is another in which there's really no close emotional tie. And they know each other so well," she continued. "It's a very familiar relationship. Their interests are often alike. What excites them or scares them tends to be alike, and they are the people with whom what happens in the family is experienced similarly. And yet," she said, "it can be so ambivalent, such a mixture of hostility and companionship and affection and rivalries. We tend to think of intimacy as an unequivocally good thing," she said. "But in the sibling relationship, intimacy can involve a lot of unpleasantness, too. One of the interesting things about it is that it challenges a lot of our assumptions about relationships."

A handful of researchers began looking into sibling loss at just about the same time Dunn started looking into the sibling relationship, putting them in the unfortunate position of having to try to both understand the relationship and the impact of its loss simultaneously. And this, as the saying goes, is where the rubber meets the road. Because much of the negative experience of those who have lost siblings has to do with the fact that the relationship has never been recognized as an important part of people's lives.

"Those things change very slowly, " said Sander Abend, M.D., a New York City–based psychiatrist who wrote one of the early case studies on adolescent sibling loss, and then mostly watched the slow development of the field from the sidelines. "Even in a world more interested in communal relationships, and relationships in general. I just don't think it's caught up yet."

Helen Rosen, Ph.D., a New Jersey–based psychotherapist who lost a sister growing up, wrote the first book to appear on sibling loss, *Unspoken Grief.* Rosen's book focuses on people who lost siblings as children. In it, she concludes that children suffer greatly because their loss is unseen, that self-blame of the kind Pleasant White described is very common and intense, and that it gets repressed for years and creates horrible guilt for the surviving siblings. "Our social process just doesn't encourage people, especially siblings, to talk and express loss, and that's what keeps it going," said Rosen.

Joanna Fanos, Ph.D., began looking into sibling loss in the early eighties, too. And like Rosen, the subject was personal. Her older sister, Judy, died of cystic fibrosis when Joanna was fifteen and Judy was twenty. Her conclusions were very much like Rosen's: though some siblings had received enough support to get through, they were the exception. The norm tended to be that the loss often wasn't acknowledged by others, families were unable to see their surviving children's grief, and the grief became a chronic condition that undermined survivors' lives for decades.

Betty Davies, R.N., Ph.D., came by her interest in sibling loss a generation removed. Her grandmother lost two brothers growing up. Her mother also lost two siblings: an older sister in childhood, and later, an older brother during World War II. Davies's book *Shadows in the Sun: The Experiences of Sibling Bereavement in Childhood,* explores the childhood loss of a sibling to cancer. In it, she concludes, "Siblings do not get over the loss of their brother or sister. Rather, to varying degrees, they learn to live with it." How well depends very much on how the loss is treated. "These siblings follow paths that they don't necessarily need to follow," said Davies. "They're alone. They think they're the only ones in the world who feel the way they feel."

Yet, "It's a million times better than it was," said Fanos. "More and more people are doing work. But it still isn't generally well recognized, in the medical community or beyond. There has been an increased emphasis on family-centered care in medical centers, for example. But what people mean when they say that is the parents. I'm one of the few who keeps saying that 'family' also means the siblings."

Fanos recently received the go-ahead to begin creating a sibling center at the California Pacific Medical Center in San Francisco, where she is a research psychologist. "Any time a child is diagnosed with an illness, the sibling will be referred to the sibling center for four sessions of therapy. It's a total preventive model," she explained, noting that the usual model for sibling loss is retrospective—a bereft sibling struggles alone for decades and then, in a state of crisis, has to dive to untold depths to bring up and understand the past trauma.

Most of the siblings I spoke with said that few of those around them—parents, friends, coworkers, bosses—had recognized that the relationships they'd had with their siblings had been significant to them, that their death was a profound loss. "I had a performance review about four weeks later," said Jeanann, who was twenty-four when her younger brother, Sam, died at age eighteen of a congenital heart defect. Five years later, it still stung. "I was reamed. [My boss] said, 'You're not the person I hired.' I thought, 'No *shit*. I will never be the person you hired. I will *never* be the same again.' She wanted me back, she wanted me happy, she wanted me perky, you know? And I didn't even want to tie my shoes in the morning. She didn't get it at all."

It's one of a number of reasons that bereft siblings tend to loathe the question: Do you have any brothers and sisters? This question, which I took to calling "*the* question" in the course of my interviews, sits at the juncture of private and public lives. Answering honestly can expose the loss to myriad unpredictable responses, many of which are dismissive. And it's in the context of "*the* question" that you often see the ambiguous sense of the loss emerge. Are they still siblings? How many do they have? Almost every sibling said, "It depends," when I asked them how they answer. What it depends upon is generally their gut response to the person asking.

It's problematic, not only for the social experience of the loss, but for the implications for how that grief is then processed—or not. "The very nature of disenfranchised grief creates additional problems for grief, while removing or minimizing sources of support," writes Ken Doka, in his most recent book, *Disenfranchised Grief.* Disenfranchised grief can end up in what (in the language of loss) is known as "complicated mourning"—grief that, unexpressed and unexplored, takes on an unhealthy form, becomes the model for all future losses, and/or goes on and on, unresolved, undermining your life.

That was my story.

Chapter Four

CLAIMING THE STORY

"All sorrows can be borne if they can be put in a
story."

—ISAK DINESEN

While I was busy interviewing other people who'd lost brothers and
sisters, hearing their stories and beginning to understand what they
meant, I was also trying to write my own, and feeling enormously
frustrated. Whenever I tried to write about Ted's illness and death
from my point of view, I ended up writing his or my parents' story
instead. Words flew out of me, until I typed the word "I," at which
point I grew confused and uncertain. I was unable to tell my story.
I felt as if I didn't have a story. Ultimately, this writing block proved
to be revelatory. Though I had, with the help of years of therapy,
been confidently saying *this happened to me, too,* on some level, I
didn't believe it. At some level, I was still the fourteen-year-old
standing by the side of my brother's grave, shamed into silence.

Ironically, given that I was the one writing the book, it was
hearing other siblings' stories of loss that helped me to understand
that I had a story, and gave me the confidence to tell it. Somehow,

listening to others awakened the "I" in me. Haltingly, I began to write. My first attempts were inarticulate, guttural. The sentences had the slurry quality of a stroke victim learning to talk again. Gradually, I found my voice. I began to be able to start a sentence with the word "I" and complete it. I remembered things—scenes, conversations, people—that I didn't know I'd forgotten. And I remembered my brother in ways that I had forgotten, too—his voice, his silliness, his intensity, his anger, the look he'd give me before proceeding to bait our mother into her trademark sigh. And I saw all of this anew, from the vantage point of an adult, rather than the child I had been.

I found this process of narration, of telling with a point of view, healing beyond all expectation. It wasn't simply the catharsis of releasing long-suppressed emotion, although that did happen. It was the act of storytelling itself. I wasn't the only one to have this experience. As time passed, I began to get calls, e-mails, and letters from some of the siblings I'd interviewed, all of whom indicated that telling their stories had been a significant event. None claimed to be healed. We all knew there was no "getting over it," to borrow the phrase most often misapplied to loss. But they had come to a different place with their losses, embarked upon some sort of journey. Somehow, the process of narration had helped them move forward.

From my experience and that of the others I was hearing from, I drew a few conclusions. In acknowledging our losses, we had given ourselves permission to speak that had often been denied us by others, permission that we, on our own and in response to others' cues, had often denied ourselves. We had found our voices. And in telling our stories, we had made sense of them and claimed them as our own. It was the difference between saying, "Yes, it happened to me," and knowing it as certainly as you know anything. One was lip service, the other was profound.

Other bereft siblings before me have discovered the power of narration, most visibly, in recent years, in the form of memoir. In

My Brother, for instance, Jamaica Kincaid struggles to resolve her ambivalent feelings toward her younger brother, Devon, after he's died of AIDS. "Someone I did not know I loved had died," she writes, "someone I did not want to love had died, and that dying had a closed-door quality to it, a falling-off-the-horizon quality to it." She makes it clear that she is writing, telling her story, for the express purpose of making sense of it and claiming it—recognizing specifically how his loss impacted her. "When I heard of my brother's illness and his dying," she writes, "I knew, instinctively, that to understand it, or to make an attempt at understanding his dying, and not to die with him, I would write about it."

In *Phoenix: A Brother's Life,* J. D. Dolan wrestles with the death of his older brother John, from whom he'd been alienated for years. In that strange reversal not uncommon to siblings, J.D. had turned out to be the successful one, while the brother he'd looked up to had struggled in his adulthood. They'd never found a way to reconnect before John suffered serious burns over 90 percent of his body in an accident. Much of the story takes place in Dolan's head, as he goes back and forth from his hotel to the hospital, and paces from the hospital lobby to John's room, trying to find a way to speak to his brother, who is barely conscious. Margaret Diehl's *The Boy on the Green Bicycle* is a memoir written from the perspective of the nine-year-old child Diehl was when her brother Jimmy was killed riding the bicycle he'd gotten for his fourteenth birthday. The writing of these books was a necessity, an act of self-salvation.

Sibling loss was there in literature long before memoir became such a popular form of writing. It was just more hidden. It's quietly slipped into Charlotte Brontë's *Jane Eyre,* for example, in the form of the noble heroine Helen Burns, who dies of tuberculosis contracted at the harsh boarding school in which she and the main character reside. Helen is based upon Charlotte's oldest sister, Maria, who died in just such circumstances in just such a school.

The death of Beth in Louisa May Alcott's *Little Women* is a thinly fictionalized account of the death of Alcott's own sister,

Lizzie. Henry David Thoreau wrote his first book, *A Week on the Concord and Merrimack Rivers,* as a memorial to his older brother, John, with whom he was extremely close. John died, a few years after this boating trip, of lockjaw contracted from a rusty razor. The book, which celebrates the natural order of birth and death in nature, is Thoreau's attempt to come to terms with his loss.

One fundamental theme in all sibling-loss stories is disruption: It isn't supposed to happen this way. What we expect of sibling relationships is varying degrees of competition, love, loyalty, friendship, ambivalence, conflict, and support that waxes and wanes throughout our lives, and is available if and when we want it. When that story line is cut off abruptly, the world and all our assumptions about it get thrown in the air. It's a violation. You could say that the natural response to this kind of chaos, after the initial shock, would be to regroup, to begin to incorporate this unthinkable occurrence. What does it change? What does it mean? How does it recast the past? How do we reorganize the narratives of our lives in such a way as to accommodate and make sense of this death, this disruption? Do things look different, now that this has happened? Are we different?

They are necessary questions to ask after any loss. They can be difficult to answer. And they're impossible to answer if you haven't owned the loss in the first place. And this is where so many of us get frozen, stuck in ambiguity. Storytelling is a remedy for ambiguity. To tell a coherent story, you have to pose yourself as the narrator, tell with a point of view, sift through a lifetime's worth of memories, events, assumptions, and anecdotes. The woman who told me after our interview that she felt as if it had been an intervention was right. What she didn't know was that it had been one for me, as well.

•   •   •

The first step needed in order to tell the story is knowing it and understanding it. Pauline Boss had told me that if you can't make sense of a loss, you can't move on. Boss didn't mean "sense" in the larger scheme of the meaning of this loss in your life. (That's something we get to later.) She meant it in the most literal sense— what happened? This is a problem for some siblings. There are circumstances in which the details or logic of what happened can't be or aren't known—murders, suicide, remote accidents. And those who were children when their siblings died often get few details about the death. Witness John's story, for example. How do you tell your story if all you know is that your sister disappeared one day?

"Closure" is a word I don't like, because it's often used to imply that you can neatly seal off a loss and go on. You can go on, you can even go on healthily, but losses are always losses. With that caveat, I do think "closure" works if we use it strictly to describe the place we get to in knowing the literal story of what happened and making sense of it.

Laura's story embodies the predicament of young siblings. When she contacted me by e-mail, her message was rife with that particular brand of ambiguity so common to surviving siblings. It began "I don't know if it counts, but . . ." and then she went on to write that she'd been just one and a half when her four-year-old sister, Debbie, had chased a ball into the street in front of their house. "From what little my mom has ever told me," she wrote, "there was a woman driving down the street who'd just gone to the grocery store. She had a car full of kids who were distracting her. She didn't see Debbie, and she hit her." Though Laura had feelings of both love and grief for Debbie, she had no memories of her or the accident that had taken her life.

By the time I called Laura, a day or so later, she was anxious and already doubting the wisdom of having sent me the e-mail. She didn't know anything. She didn't remember. There was nothing to tell. No one in the family talked about Debbie's death. She didn't know what else she could tell me. And then she uttered a phrase that I hear in every interview with someone who was young at the time of their loss, and which has come to me to symbolize their plight: "To this day, I don't know what happened."

She doesn't know when it happened. She doesn't know who was home. She doesn't know the sequence of events that followed. She does know that after Debbie's death, her parents did what a lot of us try to do—outrun the memories. They picked up and moved to another state. No pictures of Debbie were kept on display in their new home. Neither she nor the accident was ever talked about. "I don't remember being told not to talk about her. I just knew, without being told, that *we're not talking about that,*" said Laura. "Before I learned to talk, I learned what *not* to talk about."

The irony, of course, is that trying to outrun loss usually has the reverse of the intended effect. Debbie's ghost haunted the family. Their lives were shaped by their attempts to ignore her absence and avoid their grief. "Her death was like the elephant in the living room that everybody stepped around," said Laura. "It was there, all the time." Laura was in the same difficult situation Ann Farrant's daughter, Lucy, had been in. She had had a relationship with her older sister. That experience was somewhere inside her, but she hadn't had the language to express it, or the developmental skills to store the memory. And her parents had assumed that she'd been unscathed by the loss.

It wasn't true, of course. As a child of eighteen months, Laura must have wondered what happened to her older sister, where she'd gone. And then there were all the other ways that Debbie's death affected her. In her book, Grace Hyslop Christ talks about a "cascade" model of loss, meaning that losses are not just single events, but rather events that trigger and/or are worsened by following ones. In Laura's case, for instance, her mother suffered from depression, the onset of which Laura suspects coincided with Debbie's death. It's a well-known fact that maternal depression thwarts the development of the mother-child bond. And the

quality of that bond—secure or insecure, anxious or unanxious—
becomes a child's internal gauge for experiencing the world. What
happens to all those surviving siblings—particularly those, like
Laura, who were at particularly sensitive developmental ages—
who report that their parents distanced themselves from their surviving children and never came back? What effect did that have on
those children's emotional hardwiring?

Laura said her mother's depression gets worse every year
about the time of the accident. Laura, too, suffers from chronic
depression. Her relationship with her mother has always been
difficult. "She was sort of numbed by her own pain. There was
this layer of something around her that was impenetrable." She
told a story about a series of pictures of herself at age three—the
first family pictures after a nearly two-year gap following Debbie's
death.

"I'm on roller skates. And I fall down. I've skinned my knee,
and I'm crying. My face is all squinched up." The pictures
bothered her for a long time. Finally, she went and talked to a
therapist about them. "She said, 'So, your mother was taking your
picture.' And I said, 'Yeah. *Yeah.*' There I am, hurt and crying, and
she's taking my picture. Not dropping the camera and picking me
up. Not holding me and comforting me. Taking my picture. That's
a good illustration of the sort of disconnection I grew up with."

Laura's father took the opposite approach to the loss—stoicism.
"He didn't understand depression. He couldn't crumble, and my
mother couldn't let herself feel it. They spent the rest of their life
together soldiering on." She tried to lure her parents' attention
toward her, to make it up to them. She became a tomboy, her
father's buddy, and an A student. "I felt like I had to get their attention away from missing her, because it seemed like they were
always missing her. But it never worked. I always felt like a second-
best substitute."

Later, she said, she took the opposite approach to get their
attention. "I got arrested a few times. I'm lucky I don't have a

record. But I still kept up my A average. The judge was really confused." When I asked her what had happened to make her take this approach, she said, "I wanted credit for being me."

As she grew older, she became aware of her own sense of loss. For the longest time, she'd been cognizant of the hole Debbie's death had left in her parents' lives. Increasingly, she was becoming aware of the void Debbie had left in her own. But she knew next to nothing about her. It made it hard to define what hurt and whom, in fact, she was mourning. The sense of loss, she told me, had only grown over time, as had her need to know more about her sister and the accident. She managed to pry bits of information from her mother over the years, but the sum total of those fragments sketched little more than a stick-figure image of Debbie. "Usually, after the first question or two, it's like, 'I don't want to talk about that anymore.'"

She also wanted badly to know what happened on the day of the accident. She was worried that she had somehow distracted her mother at the moment of the accident, keeping her from calling Debbie away from the street. "If I had just been a good little girl," she said, speaking as if her guilty fear were fact, "maybe it wouldn't have happened." She was grimly resigned that she probably never will know more: "There's nobody left to tell me anything. My grandparents are gone. My father is gone. The only person left is my mother, and she's not going to talk about it."

She has a few pictures of Debbie, one of which is extremely important to her. It is of the two of them together, shortly before Debbie's death. "She's this pretty blonde girl, wearing a dress with bows, smiling. And I'm sitting in her lap, and she looks just thrilled to have me there," she said. "I've imprinted it on my brain. I hold it as, not quite a memory of her, because I don't remember her, but as the image I have of her." She does feel as if Debbie looks out for her.

Once in a while, she said, she'll look up at the sky and acknowledge Debbie's presence. "I don't talk to her out loud, but

I think of her. I'll look up and talk to her in my head. I tell her I can't wait to meet her." She hopes she will get to see her again when she dies. "I believe we get that," she said. "I hope it's true." Meanwhile, Debbie's amorphous outline, and what might have been, continues to be a strong presence in her life.

Over the course of our conversation, her voice became lower and tearful, then trancelike and heavy. Toward the end, it almost dropped to a whisper. Her voice was literally fading on the other end of the line. "If I could have anything I wanted, I would have Debbie here, sitting in this room, the two of us talking, and not having to share her," she said faintly. "I feel almost like, through you, I'm sending a message to her. I feel my parents were the barrier to my knowing anything about her. Maybe if I had known something about her, I wouldn't have been so lonely growing up. There's a part of me that's angry about not knowing about her. She was kept from me, you know? I feel like I love her, but I don't know her."

This was how my interview with Laura ended. What was she, or John, or any of these siblings who possessed only a handful of facts, to do? How were they to make sense of what had happened to them and find a way to move forward? Sometime after we'd spoken, I e-mailed Laura and asked if we could speak again. I wanted to update her story to see where she'd come to with it all. She said she was in a very different place—and she had solved the problem I'd worried about.

In the time since I'd spoken to her, Laura's mother had moved out to the West Coast, into a retirement community near Laura, against Laura's advice. Her mother was somehow expecting a miraculous "Kodak moment" transformation of their relationship, said Laura, and was waiting for the relationship to become close. It hadn't. Her mother had moved back home again, angry with her for not being a better daughter. They'd since become estranged, which Laura wasn't thrilled about. "It's sad, but it's the way things are."

Our first interview had made her resolve to try to get more information from her mother about Debbie. "I remember distinctly sitting down with her in her retirement-community apartment and saying, 'I really want to know.' She gave me the same answer she always had, but I pushed more this time. I said, 'I know you don't want to talk about this, but it has been forty years. I know it's painful, but I need to know this.' And she refused to talk about it. And I pushed a little more and she got angry. I wasn't being a good daughter." It was at that point she realized that the puzzle of Debbie was one she would need to solve herself.

"What I do is think of her and imagine how she would be now. And unfortunately I have to fill in some of the gaps. When I was younger, I filled in the gaps with feeling I was to blame." She's filled in some of the blanks via her relationship with her sister-in-law, who is the same age Debbie would have been, had she lived, and of whom Laura is extremely fond. "I often feel that she is like Debbie would have been, or how I imagine or wish Debbie would be."

Now that she has focused more on her feelings and her needs, rather than trying to assuage her mother's, her feelings of guilt have ceased to be the focal point of her connection to Debbie. As a result, Debbie is more present for her. "Lately I have really found that she's become a companion. I think about her a lot. I think about the fact that I would have a big sister. And I imagine sometimes that she is watching out for me. There have been so many things in my life that could have been really terrible that have not been so bad because I often imagine that she is taking care of me. So, I've filled in the gaps with imagination more than anything else."

She refers again to the picture she described in our first conversation. "There's that wonderful picture I have of her holding me in her lap. And she's smiling and she looks like I'm her own little doll. So I like to think of that. I imagine her now, three years older than me, in her late forties. I like to imagine scenarios where we would go out for lunch together and share our lives and talk about stuff. And sometimes I do. I talk to her. It's funny, though, because in my imagination, she's not a little girl. She's the adult she would be if she were still alive."

Some of the people I talked to saw their older or younger brothers and sisters frozen in time at the age they were when they died, but still thought of them as their older or younger siblings. This had been the case with me, and with Laura, in her first interview. Some imagined their lost siblings had aged right along with them.

I knew this was a marker for something, but I wasn't entirely sure what. I'm still not. I do know that we look on siblings as signposts, of a sort, who help locate us in space and time, and in our own families. We know how old we are in reference to them. We know what goals we want to achieve by certain ages, if our siblings have set the standard. Our siblings prod us into moving forward and achieving milestones we might not otherwise consciously reach for.

What happens to this aspect of our life—locating ourselves, being prodded, and prodding—when a sibling dies? Do we get stuck in time? It seemed to me as if those of us who envisioned our siblings as children, frozen in time, were the most likely to be frozen in time ourselves. This idea evokes Pleasant White's comment on "shielded space"—"You grow everywhere else except that space." Is it possible that the loss of a sibling leaves our sense of our own age and place in time frozen? Or is the loss of a parent to his or her grief the trauma? Or both? For years, Laura had envisioned her sister as a child. When I asked Laura about the change, from seeing Debbie as a little girl to an adult sister, she said it was a change that had taken place in the past year.

Her mother's failure to give her the information she needed, followed by her abrupt departure, seemed to be the catalyst. "My mother's leaving made me feel guilty. It sent me right back into therapy and an emotional crisis. It helped me separate from trying to please her all my life. And that let me become a grown-up. And that's why Debbie's probably grown up with me now," she said. "And that's what finally left me free to acknowledge my sister, to acknowledge that it was okay for me to miss her. We have to allow ourselves to claim things and know that we have a right to do that."

Many other bereft siblings have found ways to come to understand what happened to their brothers and sisters. Amber, whose brother, James, was killed in a car accident, went to the scene of the accident. She found some residual debris from it, including a button from James's Levi's. She also read the accident report and the autopsy notes. Other siblings who have lost brothers and sisters to accidents have gone to the site and tracked down eyewitnesses. One magazine article I read described the saga of a woman who had solved the mystery of her twin's murder and disappearance by dressing and acting like her sister, in effort to gain access to people who had information. John, the social worker on the pediatric oncology ward, had unconsciously and then consciously chosen to work with families in which he saw the same kind of tragedy that had unfolded in his own family.

They were all trying to make sense of deaths that were senseless, in one way or another—a random accident, an undiscriminating disease, a senseless murder. I asked Pauline Boss about that, and she surprised me with this answer: "Sometimes, the only sense you can make of something is that it doesn't make sense. But even that meaning, that it doesn't make sense, is enough to help you go on."

I was one of those whose story began in childhood. My parents were silent on the topic of my brother. Talking about him was too risky. It might bring on the pain. It might cause us to break down and cry—in front of one another. My family believed in stoicism, that crying was self-pity—and who were we to pity ourselves, given what Ted had endured? It just wasn't done. "Pull up your socks!" my mother used to say. Looking back, I can see that, for lack of any outlet, I shut down, suppressing anything that might make me feel—love, hate, anger.

I learned that in order to move on with my life, to allow myself to feel again, I had to excavate the grief I'd buried. But this was a problem. I couldn't grieve without knowing what had happened, and my information, in many ways, hadn't been updated since I was six years old. I still explained my brother's illness in the same words my parents had used to explain it to me thirty years ago, the day they'd told me that my brother would have to live in the hospital for a while.

My break came one day, amid the debris of the Thanksgiving table, well into the period during which I was working on this book. My father told me that he had all of my brother's medical records on microfiche. He said he would give them to me. "There might be something interesting in them," he said. "Maybe some nurses' notes." This offering did not come unprompted. I had just been telling one of the guests at our table about my concerns about the vagaries of memory, how hard it was to write from the perspective of a child. I wanted to write about the emotional experience of losing Ted. But I was disconcerted by the fuzzy areas, and my inability to connect a memory with actual fact. I still didn't really know what had happened.

My father's offer, I knew, was as close as he could come to giving me the details he couldn't talk about. It had been my father who had told me, when I was a freshman in college, to just forget about all "that stuff" and move forward in my life. It was done, over. It was a rule he seemed to live by. After my brother died, he'd directed all his energy to his work running the cancer center. When he was not at the center, he kept on working, reading piles of medical journals in his home office, which had once been my brother's bedroom. He threw himself into other all-absorbing hobbies—biking and opera. It seemed to me that opera, with its unreal melodrama, was the only context in which he felt safe to feel. I'd heard him say my brother's name only a handful of times in the more than two decades since his death. Once, years earlier, I called him and asked him a question about my brother's death—I couldn't remember if one doctor in particular had been there when Ted died. "I can't talk about this," he said, and hung up on me.

Now, this direct address of the topic of my brother, much less the offer of his medical records, was a startlingly straightforward gesture. It caught me off-balance. I thought that, perhaps, the presence of another couple, my father's friends, might have made it easier for him to make such a daring move. It was because of them that the topic had come up—they had asked how the book was going. My parents rarely questioned me about the book, and when they did, it was only in the most general terms. They didn't really want answers. Maybe my father knew that this couple's presence would prevent any delving into places he couldn't go. Maybe, in his social mode, he'd felt emboldened, emotionally disconnected enough, to make the offer.

I hadn't quite formulated an answer when my mother jumped in, furious. She hated the idea that the notes of nurses should be considered a valid perspective on my brother and his life. What did they know? She was trying to keep a layer of social veneer over her rage, and having a hard time of it. She got up from the table, and angrily gathered plates, with her lips pressed together and a sour face.

The truth was that my mother had loved some of the nurses, and so had my brother. Many of them had gone out of their way to tend to him and make a personal connection. Others—control freaks who had done things like take all the toys out of his room because he hadn't gone to bed on time—had been less kind. (Taking things out of The Room was a big deal—it meant that every item would have to be resterilized, which could take days.) But my mother wasn't making distinctions. She was mad, it seemed, at all the nurses.

My father and I remained at the table. He reiterated—sotto voce—that the notes might be helpful, while my mother could be heard clattering plates in the kitchen. By the time she came back with the next course, we'd changed the subject. But by then I understood. My brother and his illness had been my mother's whole world. His death had left a black hole in her life. While she didn't talk about him, she couldn't stand the idea that somebody else's words might be considered authoritative. He was hers, not theirs. This was her story. It was only then that I realized that I was not only breaking a taboo by speaking about Ted in the book, but also, somehow, treading on her turf by calling the loss "mine." It spoke to the solitary way we'd all treated Ted's death.

It took me months to go to the apartment my parents kept in New York and get the box of notes. It was interesting that my father had kept it there all these years, not in the family home, but rather in his oasis in the city he loves, where he goes to think and write. "It's on the bottom shelf of my dresser," he told me when I called him to ask where to look. "I've never read them," he added. I found it right away, a three-by-six cardboard file box, unremarkable except for an orange paper seal plastered on the flip-top lid reading: SPECIAL: DEPARTMENT OF HEALTH, EDUCATION, AND WELFARE.

My father had broken the seal. Perhaps he had started to read the notes and thought better of it. Why he'd asked for them in the first place was a mystery. Maybe it had been his researcher's instinct for collecting information. Maybe he'd wanted some physical relic, some proof of my brother's battle. In any case, it had to have been his paternal instinct that had prevented him from reading them. After all, what was the point? He knew the whole story, had known it, probably, the instant he'd looked down at my brother's legs at the dinner table that long-ago night.

For me, it was different. I'd seen with a child's eyes. Though I'd witnessed and experienced everything, a lot of what had happened was kept from me, with the notion that I was being protected or that I wouldn't notice or understand—or under the assumption that I, like an adult, could cope with it on my own. I didn't know if the box would hold answers for me, the kind of answers that mattered. But just holding it had a strange effect on me. I sat and held it in my lap and cried. I had the distinct sense that if I flipped the lid open, Ted would emerge in a puff of smoke. (How old would he be? The age he was then, or the age he would be now?) I wanted to rest my head on the box, press my cheek against the cardboard. I'm not sure if I wanted to comfort him or myself.

Finally, I wrapped the box in a plastic bag and carried it under my arm as I set out, on foot, for my office, twenty blocks away. I felt as if I had just been to a funeral and was responsible for carrying the ashes to the mausoleum. On the way, I stopped at a stationery store to pick up something, and the security guard insisted that I check the bag. I was quietly and irrationally horrified, as if I were handing over my brother's ashes. How irresponsible. But I did it. The bag was there, ten minutes later, when I anxiously presented my ticket. I met a friend for coffee near my office, and the box sat like a third person between us, making us both nervous. He finally insisted on displacing other things from my satchel and placing the box inside, so there'd be no chance that I'd drop it and spill all the microfiche cards on the ground. I didn't like the idea that my brother and my lunch were occupying the same space, but I acceded, thinking it would be just my luck to drop him amid the foot-stomping chaos of midtown Manhattan.

It took me a week to make the next move, to go the midtown library and find the microfiche room. I settled at a microfiche reader, and inserted the first card. I didn't know what I expected. Daily notes, starting from the beginning of Ted's care, I suppose. But the first card contained the typed transcripts from my brother's autopsy. Before I could look away I was reading, with growing horror, the weight and color of his eyeballs, the length and color of his kidneys. The noted lack of marrow tissue in his bones. The lamentable condition of his heart, enlarged and flabby, damaged by years' worth of iron buildup from the blood transfusions that, ironically, also helped keep him alive. One of his lungs is full of fluid. His trachea is, too. Or was. This body was long gone.

In the reflection of the machine's glass, I saw the circles under my eyes grow deeper, saw the lines in my face appear in darker relief, my eyes grow glassy. Around me, I heard the faint buzz of the characters who people a Manhattan library, reading old microfiche. They didn't notice me; they were too engrossed in their own projects—genealogies, history papers, conspiracy theories. It felt surreal to be reading this strange memoir of my early life amid strangers who couldn't care less, who didn't even notice that the world had tilted under my feet. I breathed heavily. I pondered the advisability of doing this. The necessity of it. And read on.

I learned things I hadn't known—that they'd autopsied our parakeet, Danny, who had died a day after my brother went into the hospital, to see if there was a connection; that they'd tested the model glue my brother was in the habit of using to construct airplanes because one of the ingredients was thought to be a possible trigger for aplastic anemia; that my brother had taken antibiotics not long before his diagnosis (a rare trigger for his disease, according to some of the medical literature); that some pesticide spray had been used on the trees in the backyard shortly before he got sick; and that a box of oranges someone—probably my grandparents—had sent us from Florida had been so coated in pesticide spray as to make the oranges inedible, though my brother, alas, had eaten one before they were thrown away. Ultimately, they had no idea what had caused my brother's illness.

I learned that he was first diagnosed on September 6, 1972, a little less than a month shy of his tenth birthday, the week after the scene at the dinner table. My parents had tried to have him treated outside the hospital after the diagnosis, but within a week he'd come down with a fever and they'd rushed him to the hospital late one night and had him admitted. This explained a big hole in my story, one that had puzzled me for years. I didn't remember my brother leaving because I was in bed, asleep, when he'd been whisked away. That scene in the nubbly chair did, in fact, take place after he was gone. Overnight, my brother had been snatched from my physical life.

I couldn't read all of my brother's files that day. There were too many—eight years' worth. Just copying some of the sheets had cost me forty dollars, and produced a barely portable pile, and I'd only gotten from September through March of the first year. There were other reasons I didn't go further. I couldn't take it. I found myself suppressing hysteria and sadness and anxiety, a sensation that felt disconcertingly familiar, reminiscent of childhood. Reading the cold, hard facts after having lived amid soft, gray ones for so long, the transition from no knowledge to arguably too much was devastating. As an adult, I could understand the emotional truth the clinical notes hinted at. The situation had been even sadder, more stressful, more desperate, and, in the record of my brother's daily struggle, more moving than I had remembered. I was bringing myself up-to-date on fast-forward. But I couldn't do it in one sitting. I would need many days and many visits to the library, punctuated by periods when I would simply put the file box, my brother, away in a drawer.

But opening that box had set something in motion. After all these years, I still didn't understand my brother's disease. I had accepted the definition my parents had given me the morning after he was gone, and never challenged it, never upgraded it to fit my adult ability to understand. I did some research.

Aplastic anemia is an orphan disease, meaning it's rare enough that it hasn't inspired too much excitement in the field of scientific or pharmaceutical research. Only five to ten out of every million

Americans are diagnosed with it each year. About the same number that are hit by lightning.

Encased in the center of our bones is a soft core of tissue central to our survival. Bone marrow is the factory where key blood cells—red cells, which carry oxygen to the body's cells and remove carbon dioxide; white cells, which fight disease; and platelets, which are integral to the clotting process—are produced. These cells circulate through the bloodstream in numbers measured in hundreds of thousands.

In the case of aplastic anemia, the body is suddenly and brutally deprived of all three varieties of cells. The onset is often insidious, increasing in intensity as the old cells die off and new ones fail to replace them in sufficient quantities. There is bruising. Fatigue. Dizziness. Pallor. Shortness of breath upon exertion. Maybe a rash or bleeding gums. All ignorable symptoms if you subscribe to the wait-and-it-will-pass approach to minor maladies. Meanwhile, blood cell counts are plummeting. Often by the time people are diagnosed, they're in or near a danger zone in which a simple infection can turn into a life-threatening problem.

The first person to take note of the disease was a famous German pathologist by the name of Dr. Paul Ehrlich. In 1888, he did an autopsy on a pregnant woman (in some instances, pregnancy can trigger the disease) and found that she had almost no functional bone marrow. But it wasn't until 1904 that the disease was actually given a name: "Anemia" is the umbrella term for a deficiency of blood cells. "Aplastic" is the term that makes it specific. It means, according to my father's old medical school dictionary, "having no tendency to develop into new tissue." The name was based on the idea that the marrow simply lost its ability to make new cells.

Why it happens is a puzzle. Among the suspected causes are exposure to radiation, like that released in the 1986 Chernobyl nuclear plant accident. After the accident, many people in the surrounding areas developed the disease. But catastrophic events aren't necessary. Other possible causes include exposure to environmental chemicals, pesticides, fertilizers, glues, and any chemical that, like the glue my brother used to assemble his models, contains benzene; to certain viruses such as hepatitis; to some over-the-counter and prescription medications; to street drugs; and to a cornucopia of other chemicals. And despite this laundry list, more than 50 percent of cases are deemed idiopathic—the scientific term for a shrug. Cause unknown.

It strikes people of all ages and ethnicities and both genders, though it tends to be more common in Asia, Russia, Vietnam, Mexico, Africa, India, South America, and other developing nations, where there may be increased exposure to chemicals, than the United States. It can be mild, more chronic than life-threatening, or acute. Those with milder cases sometimes recover on their own, or are treatable over the long term with supportive care such as transfusions of blood and platelets. Advances in technology over the last decade have made transfused cells last longer, which has the added advantage of reducing the likelihood of side effects associated with too-frequent transfusions.

In 1972, when my brother was diagnosed, the only true hope of a cure was a bone marrow transplant, in which a dose of healthy marrow is removed from a donor and transplanted to the patient. The idea was that the donor marrow would take root and begin producing blood cells in its new environment. But bone marrow transplants were a new concept back then. Given the novelty of the procedure, you needed a donor whose bone marrow was as close to an identical match as possible—an identical twin or sibling—in which case there was about a fifty-fifty chance that it would work. Statistically, there is only a one-in-four chance siblings will match.

There was a slim chance that one of my parents would be a match, but I was the best candidate. I have memories of being dragged down hallways to face an array of needles, fighting panic as the techs held my arm down and drew blood. They didn't have to take any marrow from me to see if I was a match, they said.

They could tell by my blood. I was lucky. In an attempt to take control of the situation, I told my parents I wasn't going to go see my brother in the hospital anymore if there was going to be more needles. Okay, they said. No more needles. The next day, when we went in, I got a finger stick. They said that didn't count as a needle. It was the same kind of rationalization my brother and I used when trying to cheat at board games. But it shocked me to see it in adults.

In the hospital, some people wore white buttons with the words "I'm an HLA match!" printed on them in red. This meant, my mother explained, that their marrow matched someone else's, that they were bone marrow donors. I wouldn't be wearing the button. My bone marrow didn't match. I don't remember being told, only knowing it. I was acutely aware of my failure, as if I had cruelly refused to share a toy that I wasn't playing with. My body had failed my brother. I had failed my brother. What's more, the season of needles (which had probably lasted only a matter of weeks) had been so terrifying that I was, in part, relieved, which made me feel even guiltier. And this was on top of the conviction that I had caused my brother's illness by wishing, in a fit of rage over some tyranny of his, that something bad would happen to him.

The only reasonable thing to be done, then, was to isolate him in the laminar airflow room, give him transfusions, and hope for the best in the days and weeks, maybe even months or years, to come. Maybe there would be a miraculous, spontaneous turnaround. Maybe a new development, a new insight, a new treatment. Man had landed on the moon. All things seemed possible. Of course, this is the adult me talking, reconstructing. I didn't know all this at age six. Back then, all I knew was that my brother could get sick and that he was no longer living in our split-level suburban house in the bedroom next to mine at the top of the stairs.

It was a sacred space, his room, into which I had to be invited, except when called upon by my mother to wake him up. It was there that I had learned to play. We made fortresses, castles, and ranches with wooden blocks, using the legs of his desk chair as a corral. We made up stories involving my Best-of-the-West figures and his G.I. Joes. It was there that he'd showed me how to split the seams of plastic sandwich bags in order to make parachutes for his army men, which we hurled out the window, watching as they made slow, graceful arcs to our mother's flowerbeds. We ran from invisible enemies hiding in closets. We piled all his chairs on his bed to approximate the bridge on *Star Trek,* his favorite TV show, and therefore my favorite, too. He was Captain Kirk. Always. I was usually a minor character, like Chekov. Spock seemed a bit of a stretch, even to me.

We would no longer be sharing the bathroom with pink and black tiles. He would no longer be walking me to school in the morning and picking me up in the afternoon. We could no longer fight, at least in a physical way. All I knew was that I was getting stuck with endless needles which made me frightened to visit him. I knew that he would be in the hospital for a while because my bone marrow didn't match. At age six, I must have absorbed the unspoken tension and anxiety around me, but I had no conscious idea that there was need of hope, of a miracle, in fact. I learned the true desperation of his—of our—circumstances only as an adult.

In the sad days that I go to the midtown library to read my brother's medical files, I learn that my brother didn't like taking his medication, that he was a creative kid who withstood the pressure of confinement with remarkable strength, but that he'd struggled with its limitations. They tried, again and again, to jump-start his marrow's production of white and red blood cells with various medications, only to have them rise briefly and fall again. From the age of almost ten, he was expected to take an enormous quantity of medication several times a day—which he fought, according to the nurses' notes—shower frequently, and use body sprays, to keep germs at bay. I read that he fought everything at first, and got himself a reputation as a bit of a disciplinary problem.

From the one diary my brother ever kept, which covers only a few weeks in the spring of his first year in the hospital (it might have started earlier, but a chunk of pages had been ripped out, probably by Ted himself), when he was just ten, I know how onerous these routines were for him. He refers to The Room as a prison. He writes, in his outsized block print, that his toys have been removed from The Room in order to force him to comply with all of the medical procedures. "The Room," he wrote, "is beginning to feel more and more like a prison . . . I do hope," he added, "that I will be able to leave soon. I am beginning to feel like the lost prisoner of Alcatraz. Hopefully I will get my Big Josh sterilized and passed in soon. I am sure that will help to harness my temper and calm my nerves." Later in the same entry he wrote, "I am tired because I did not sleep well on account of the IV I had which finally came out at 2:00 in the morning." The entries end abruptly after one about how Ted had apparently insulted his doctor (the same doctor who would meet me at the airport eight years later). The doctor responded by taking away his toys again. "I am an American," he wrote. "I have the right to say anything I feel without being punished."

According to his medical records, the "protocol" of germ-ridding rituals associated with his disease was eventually altered. There were no more body sprays. Showers didn't have to be taken every night. And he'd gradually given in on most of the medication. He was periodically depressed and withdrawn, especially around holidays, his birthday, and the anniversary of the day he'd entered The Room. He'd fought depression by cultivating his interests—music, reading, writing, war games with miniature soldiers. This I remembered. He took on new interests and devoured them. Some he discarded, some he stayed attached to, like his music. He worried about losing the will to fight, and fantasized about what he would do if and when he got out, but he avoided attaching a date to the fantasy.

Among his things I found a pencil draft of a thank-you letter he'd written to a wealthy lady who'd given him money to buy musical instruments. In it, he laid out his contingency plan should he not get out by the time he finished high school. (He had two tutors who came to his room every day.) "This is my last year in high school," he wrote, "and since I am still here, and don't plan to go to college until I am out of the hospital, I have been planning to take some correspondence courses. I'm interested in science and history, so I thought I'd pick up some extra credits so I'd be that much more prepared for college. There is also a computer electronics course I am interested in. This would also give me a skill with which I could maybe get a job and earn some money myself. This would probably be something I could do from in here. . . ."

In the records, I see that he had blood transfusions several times a week, and that my father was worried from the first about the potential impact of the blood transfusions on his heart. Later notes said that Ted still hoped he would get out, but that he knew it might not happen. On May 14, 1980, at approximately 6 P.M., when I was, in all likelihood, seated on a Scottish tour bus taking ill-advised pictures through the glare of the window, my brother was eating dinner when he fainted, woke up, vomited, and called for a nurse. When they hooked him up to a heart monitor, they saw that his heart was beating irregularly. Subsequent readings showed his heart to be failing. In the notes is a record of all the ways, all the drugs that they tried to keep his heart working— digoxin, quinidine, Dilantin, pronestyl, lasix, nipride, potassium, norpace, calcium, verapamil.

All of them failed.

It is clear from the clinical notes that the administration of those last drugs, one after another, had been a formality. No one expected them to work. The last entry said that Ted died on May 27, 1980, at 1:55 A.M. This I knew. I'd been there.

One day when I went to the library to read Ted's files, I decided I'd had enough. I wasn't even halfway through, but I felt like I was finished. I rested my forehead on the glass of the microfiche machine. I was thinking about what my brother had gone through. The daily gravity of his situation. The constant poking and prodding. What he had lost. What had been taken from him by some small accident in his life. Had it been his penchant for model airplanes? Playing within inhalation's reach of pesticide-sprayed trees? A pill? The eating of a single orange?

And as I was thinking that, strangely, suddenly, time shifted, and I was an adult, and Ted was a little boy who'd suffered a lot, and not my big brother. And I was looking back on something that had happened twenty years ago. At that moment it was not hysteria I felt, or even the familiar depression. What I felt was an encroaching, all-consuming sadness. Grief.

Grief for the fact that Ted, my brother, lost his battle against a nasty disease in prisoner-of-war conditions. Grief for the way his struggle had been cheapened, first in a shitty made-for-TV movie. The writers of the movie, *The Boy in the Plastic Bubble,* had combined the story of a boy in Texas known in the press as "Baby David," who'd been born with a genetic immune-deficiency disease, and my brother's. In the movie the boy was named Tad. Astronauts came to see him, as they had Ted. Tad had a girlfriend, as had my brother (the niece of a patient who was being treated for cancer on the same ward).

We saw the movie in *TV Guide.* No one had consulted with us before making it. We wouldn't have talked. My parents' best guess was that someone at the hospital with access—a nurse, a doctor, a patient?—had talked, and that the producers had merged the two boys' stories to avoid lawsuits. When I'd asked my brother if he was going to watch it, he said, "I have to live it, why should I watch it?" My parents said they would boycott it, too. Nobody asked me. I watched it on the TV in my bedroom with the sound turned down low. What confused me was the ending: One morning, Tad simply walks out of his bubble room. The last shot is of him walking down the beach in the morning light, looking wondrously at the world around him.

Was there a chance that Ted really could have walked out and been okay? Or was a little bit of "real" life, the life we all knew, better than the uncharted territory of life in a bubble? Was John Travolta, who played Tad, choosing death? It confused and angered me. The movie had made out that his life was all tragedy and suffering, that the life he lived inside his room was nothing, a mere approximation of the real thing, that leaving the bubble room for a few days or weeks was better than a whole life inside. This wasn't true. My brother had made a choice, and instead of curling up and dying, he'd become an artist, a musician, an intuitive, empathic, intellectually curious, reaching human being. A seeker. The movie had gotten that all wrong.

A boy's boy, the type who's life pleasure was solely to run and play, would have shriveled up and died, emotionally, if not physically, within weeks in The Room. My brother's inner life, his eccentricities, served him well. He wrote and edited a small newsletter that he circulated, full of hospital gossip, which he culled from the nurses and lab technicians who entered his room on errands. On Halloween, he dressed up for the younger kids in the hospital and, wearing gloves, dispensed treats from a bowl just on the other side of the entrance to his room. He taught himself magic. As he reached adolescence, he started staying up all night and listened to the radio stations and eventually began calling in, befriending the disc jockeys who, before long, were frequent visitors and friends. He got a CB radio, and chatted with people who drove the highways around Washington, D.C., keeping maps on hand to guide those who were lost. In fact, he gained a certain level of fame this way—he once made the cover of *CB Magazine*.

My brother wanted to have a New Year's Eve party. But most everyone was out of town on the holidays, so he decided he'd schedule his party in the summer. My mother made Swedish meatballs; my Italian grandmother in Connecticut made twisted pizza, an enormous Stromboli-like concoction shaped like a horseshoe. The food was sterilized on the outside and passed in to him. And into his room—the accordion door that connected The Room with the nonsterile half of another room next door was open to allow for traffic flow—strolled doctors, musicians, disc jockeys, writers, family friends. Invitations were coveted. My brother would stand in his doorway, dressed in his Johnny Cash outfit—black jeans, black shirt—arms crossed, mouth in a slightly more expressive version of Mona Lisa's smile, rocking back and forth on his heels. This meant he was pleased.

The family lore—the party line, which could not be discussed, which I had been swallowing whole all these years, despite the lingering emotional pain that had haunted me—was that Ted was intrinsically noble. He was a gifted person who possessed the unnatural gifts and talents it took to live in that tiny room day in, day out for eight years without going insane. This wasn't true, either. The notes and my brother's brief diary had told the true story. He'd struggled, daily. He'd worked for equanimity, for peace of mind. In celebrating his triumph, in celebrating him as a superhero, an otherworldly being, we had erased the tracks of his struggle. I had been barely conscious of the struggle, at least on an intellectual level. Perhaps in erasing the tracks of my brother's struggle, my family had tried to erase the tracks of our own. Perhaps his death felt less like defeat to us if we pretended that it was he, not the disease, that had been the conqueror. Perhaps that version had seemed more fair. But the truth was that his suffering and transcendence were intertwined.

For now, I am the only one who chooses to go back and look at what happened. What he went through. What we went through. What we all lost. I lost my brother, and because of my family's inability to find a way to cope and to attempt to heal, I lost the grief. I stuffed it into that back closet, under the mistaken impression that this was what I was supposed to do, that this was being strong like my brother. And because of that I lost my brother even in the way I might have kept him. I lost the lesson of my brother's life. We'd turned away from struggle. Pretended it wasn't there, as if you could simply go to the funeral, grieve for a month, and then turn it off, and go on. We had all climbed into a bubble of our own devising. Reading the records, I witnessed it again—the world falling off its axis, the pain, the fear, the guilt, the grief. I realized that what I had read wasn't just the day-to-day record of my brother's struggle; it was mine, as well. But my brother's story, that struggle, had stopped in 1980. Mine had continued.

And then again, it hadn't. I had been stuck. Frozen. It was only by digging through the details of Ted's medical files and years of therapy in which I'd pieced together shards of memory as elusive as shattered glass that I'd been able to start piecing the bits together in the form of a story—my story. That was how I began, finally, to move on.

Chapter Five

RE-FORMING AN IDENTITY

When I spoke with Judy Dunn, she lamented the fact that far too much time was still being spent making generalizations about the importance or unimportance of sibling relationships. "This is the wrong question," she said. "What's important is what kind of relationship you have with that sibling." Most of my energy had been consumed by coping with the question of whether my loss was important, too. Having finally gotten beyond that by claiming the story, Dunn's statement became the next hurdle. What had my relationship with my brother been? How had he affected who I was?

For my entire life, I'd been a sister. For more than half of it, I'd been the sister of Washington's bubble boy. My life, my personality had been molded, in one way or another, around those two facts. Without Ted, I didn't know who I was anymore, in my family or as an individual. Later, when I tried to label and quantify what I'd lost when Ted died, I found myself sketching stick figures with limbs missing. It was an accurate analogy. Ted's death had left me feeling like an emotional and psychological amputee. I had adapted to his absence, I had functioned well enough. But it had been a struggle. I'd often felt as if I was compensating for something I was missing—as if I was perpetually in the process of maintaining, losing, or reclaiming my balance. A cripple without a crutch, flailing her hands in the air.

And I still felt phantom pain at the site of my lost limb. Except that the site of the cleaving—him from me, me from him—was not a neatly severed wound, obvious for all to see. It was internal. Amorphous. Dispersed within me. I couldn't point to the injury because the injury *was* me. It's another reason that many of us who have lost siblings start our stories with their deaths: It's our clearest view of the wound. In my case, the ambiguous nature of the loss, the it-didn't-happen-to-me syndrome, only exacerbated my confusion. I knew I was expected to "get over it" and get on with my life, unhindered. Be strong for my parents. Make it up to them, somehow. All of which was the equivalent of telling someone who's just lost his leg to run a road race, which is to say to move outside the realm of the possible.

I was totally unprepared, in too much pain and too confused to see straight, much less run straight. I had spent so many years as the sidekick, Robin to my brother's Batman. And I had spent too many as the healthy one, a quiet observer to Ted's center-stage performance, to be able to step into the limelight and put on an equivalent show for my parents. I didn't know how. His death gave rise to a certain genre of dreams that still haunts me: I have just walked onstage. The audience waits. Suddenly, I realize, I do not know my lines, I cannot play the guitar. I am a failure, a flop. I burn with inadequacy.

Many people I interviewed described similar sensations. In fact, some even used the analogy of amputation and phantom pain to describe the unsettling nature of the loss. One of them was Kathleen, who lost her younger sister Janie. "You know of the phantom limb of amputees?" she asked. "She's my phantom sister, ripped from me by death, but ever present."

She went on to explain, "After my sister died, I have a clear memory of looking in the mirror and mourning the loss of *me*. I so depended on her to mirror me, to reflect back who I was, that when she left, I was truly at a loss. I honestly did not know who I was any longer." "Mirroring" is a term developmental psychologists use to describe what happens when babies gaze into the faces of those around them. Laugh and they laugh. Frown and they frown. But as Kathleen continued to talk, she described a more complex version of mirroring, one that was more about affirmation than imitation.

"When my sister was alive, she called me for help and for support and for information. I was the one that gave advice. She was always telling me how much she loved me, and how important I was in her life. And I sat and acknowledged that, you know? Okay, I'm the oldest, I'm the wisest. She really validated me. She constantly did that. My mother, God bless her, loves to talk about what a horrible kid I was, and how much I put her through when I was a teenager. My sister, she would be honest with me, she would tell me my faults, but she did it in her way. She reflected me back, but with my hair in place. I was always much nicer in her reflection."

Kathleen's remarks reminded me of something Helen Rosen had said. She had been a budding concert pianist when her older sister, Karen, was killed in a car accident. After Karen died, Rosen had explained, her music fell apart. "I hung on for a couple more years, but I couldn't play after she died, and I couldn't perform anymore. It was too painful. I would cry. There are still pieces of that, that I don't understand. Somehow, my sister was tied to my ability to be creative and expressive."

In fact, signs of mingling sibling identities came out in many of my interviews. As I read over the transcripts, I constantly stumbled upon phrases like "He was my confidence." "He was the one who knew I was funny." "She was the one who understood me and my career." "She was my conscience." "He was my introduction to the world." "He was the problem one." "She was nicer." "I was the hard-ass, she was the softy." "He was the social one. After he died, I didn't know how to make friends." "She was the scholar, I was the athlete." All of which made me wonder, how does one identity become dependent on, or even embedded in, another?

Susan picks me up at the train station in a commuter town about an hour outside New York City. She is forty-three. She has long strawberry-blonde hair, fair skin, and seems to be on the reserved side, like me. As we walked toward her car, we struggled to find conversational equilibrium. What we knew about each other so far, that we'd each lost our older and only brother, didn't offer much in the way of light conversation. I was struck by the fact that, while I am almost always utterly unacquainted with the people I interview, the one bit of life history we share in common sparks a strange and immediate intimacy that is not unlike meeting a relative for the first time.

As we entered her house, she motioned for me to follow her to a large family room where she kept family pictures in frames. "This is my brother about two years before he died," she said, pointing to a picture of a thin, tired-looking man with her coloring. His name was David, and he was forty when he died, nine years earlier. "He died of AIDS, so he'd been losing weight and he's not looking so good there." She took another off a shelf and handed it to me. "That's me and my brother and sister," she said, pointing to a black-and-white family portrait in which the three of them are elementary-school age and the epitome of 1960s respectability.

Her brother, who was her elder by seven years, is wearing a suit and a white shirt, and his hair is clipped close to his head. Susan and her sister, Janet, who is older by five years, are each wearing immaculate dresses with crinoline skirts and white gloves, their hair neatly coiffed. They all beam for the camera.

"My father was a small-town school superintendent in Okla-
homa," she said, still gazing at the photo. "And my mother was his
wife," she said wryly, looking up to make sure I caught her meaning. The perfect portrait of the three perfect siblings was an illu-
sion of family bliss and normalcy that her mother aspired to, said
Susan, but that never really existed. "She always wanted to fit in."

The truth behind the portrait is clearly not so neat. But Susan
wasn't ready to talk about that yet. She took one more picture off
the wall and handed it to me. It was one of her brother and sister
as adults, before David was showing signs of his illness. They are
grinning and wearing straw hats and Hawaiian shirts. "They both
moved to San Francisco," said Susan, who was wearing a green
tweed skirt, an off-white blouse, and plain black pumps. "They
were both counterculture. Hippies," she said, as if reading my
mind. "I was the conventional one."

Ask any mother what her children are like, and she'll probably
exclaim over their differences. Ask any sibling what their brothers
and sisters are like, and they're likely to do the same. How can it
be that people who share so much can wind up so different? In
1976, psychologist Frances Fuchs Schachter proposed an answer
in an academic paper called "Sibling Deidentification." In it, she
suggested that siblings parcel out traits (with deference given to
innate strengths and weaknesses) in order to limit competition for
their parents' attention, especially when they are of the same gender and/or close in age. Hence the family jock and the family
scholar. It's an interesting notion—a sense of self, the maintenance of which is dependent on the presence of at least one other
person, all set against the unique backdrop of a single family.

Others have proposed explanations for this kind of behavior.
In 1996, for example, Frank Sulloway suggested a Darwinian angle
on deidentification in *Born to Rebel,* his book linking birth order to
the capacity for creative thinking. "Siblings become different for
the same reasons that species do . . . ," he writes, "to minimize
competition for scarce resources." Darwin first described this phe-

nomenon in the finches of the Galápagos Islands, who solved the problem of competing for food by splitting off into groups, each with a beak adapted for a specific, and very different, source of food. In the ecosystem of family, argues Sulloway, the necessary resource, from the children's point of view, is their parents. "Personality," explains Sulloway, "is the repertoire of strategies that each individual develops in an effort to survive childhood."

This social comparison theory also supports the idea that deidentification is about survival: It posits that how we feel about ourselves is, to a large extent, determined by the people around us. There are two basic rules by which we behave: If someone close to us has a success in a realm we, too, are invested in, we feel bad about ourselves. If someone close to us has a success in an arena in which we're not invested, we not only celebrate it, we like to bask in the reflected glory. Social comparison may also have its evolutionary roots in group survival. Historically, groups of people—such as families—may have stood a better chance of survival if they'd divvied up the labor, thereby simplifying life and allowing each member of the unit to shine in one arena.

And, as previously mentioned, there's the theory proposed by Judy Dunn and her husband, behavioral geneticist Robert Plomin. They have suggested a more subtle explanation for the often stark differences between siblings: the many aspects of life—friends, gender, age, type of parental treatment, and a host of genes, to name a few—that siblings don't share in common. What's more, it's possible for siblings to have radically different interpretations of the relationship they have with one another.

In their book, *Separate Lives,* Dunn and Plomin illustrate this last point with a fragment of an interview with ten-year-old Nancy, who waxes poetic on the subject of her younger brother, Carl, six. "I think I'd be lonely without Carl. I play with him a lot and he thinks up ideas and it's very exciting . . . He's very kind . . . Don't really know what I'd do without a brother." Carl, in a separate conversation, isn't nearly as flattering. "She's pretty disgusting and we don't talk to each other much. I don't really know much about her." When the interviewer asks what he actually likes about his sister, his response is "Nothing."

Sibling researchers, as scientists with an investment in certain points of view, might argue for the primacy of one of these arguments over another. For those of us who simply want different lenses with which to view our relationships with our brothers and sisters, each of these theories has a lot to offer. In fact, I thought I saw elements of all of them in the transcripts of the stories I'd collected. The overarching theme that linked them together was a paradox, which seems aptly complicated, given the relationship in question: Siblings are connected by their differences.

Susan was born into a family that already had two children. She had always sensed that David was different. But when she was little, it had been hard for her to define in what way. For a long time, she thought that maybe it was just that her whole family was eccentric. They were all "bookish," she said. "I make us sound like we were this Tennessee Williams family. But we had good times, too. We all liked talking and reading and words." One of the favorite family games had been Dictionary. Each player picked words from the dictionary and invented definitions. Then they'd choose to read either the real or made-up one aloud. The other players had to guess which definitions were real. It was a game at which David particularly excelled. "Once, he got this word 'globergerina,'" she said, starting to laugh at the memory. "His definition was 'a female globerger, or one who sorts figs in a haphazard manner.'" She laughed again. "And he would just say it, very deadpan."

When she was about seven and he was fourteen, she became aware that David was different in a way that wasn't connected to family eccentricity. "He was going to public rest rooms and cruising," she said. "At the time I had no idea what was going on." All that she knew was that he was getting arrested. A lot. And that her parents were extremely upset. But they never spoke about what he had been arrested for. "There was a terrible sense óf something very, very wrong in the household," said Susan. But no one would talk about it. The exact nature of David's difference wouldn't be revealed to her for several more years. And even then, it was an accident.

One day, Susan overheard her mother say something that made everything clear. Her mother was upset, which was why she couldn't stifle the words before they erupted. "She said, 'Now everyone in town will know that David is a *homosexual.*' All of a sudden a door opened and I said, 'Ahhhhhhhhhhh. *That's* it.'" Her mother's dream of the perfect family had been crumbling for years. When I asked her how long David had known he was gay, Susan said, "From birth." His task had been to learn to understand and accept himself in the context of his mother's dream of the perfect family. Susan's had been to do the same thing in a family that, by the time she arrived, was already partly defined by David's struggle. She was like an actress being thrown into the second act of a play without a script.

Susan's story illustrates how two different siblings can have different experiences in the same family. David was the different one, the one who was the source of family turmoil. Susan was a bystander to that angst, rather than its source. Her task had been to read what was going on around her and find another role to play. It was a long, ambivalent struggle, she said. She felt bad for her parents and tried to be the "good child" that David was not. But at the same time, she felt a certain alliance with and loyalty to her brother. "He was, in a lot of ways, a good, regular, older brother. He took me driving around all the time. He was in drama in school, and he had lines to memorize, so I would read him his cues while we were driving, and he'd drive me past the house of the boy I liked."

As she reached adolescence, her allegiance toward David grew stronger. "I started hanging out with my brother and sister and their friends when I was about thirteen. David turned me on to pot," she said. "I became sexually active at an early age. I thought the way he conducted his love life was the way I was supposed to do mine, because he was cool." It was at this stage, she said, that David became the arbiter of her artistic taste. "He started taking me to movies that I wouldn't have seen, like *2001* and *M★A★S★H,* and all the Robert Altman movies from the late sixties and early seventies."

She naturally gravitated more to David's point of view of the world, rather than her older sister's. "My sister was a real earth mother kind of hippie. She's a very literal, earnest person, in that late-sixties way. And she doesn't get camp, really. And for whatever reason, she was able to establish herself without being buffeted around by what was going on in the family. Even now, she's sort of New Agey and does tai chi and takes all kinds of nutritional supplements. And I think, it's just nonsense," she said, sounding irritated even by the idea. "I meshed more with him and his outlook."

Susan talked of contradictions within the relationship, too. She felt sorry for David, because of her parents' disapproval, and was afraid of him. "He was so smart and could be so cutting. He could really put you in your place." She envied him, too. She wanted to be like him, and yet she didn't want to be him, because there was so much trouble and strife in his life. "He had wit and a sharp tongue and sense of style, and good visual taste. They were all qualities that I admired and yet were a real conflict, a real paradox, because those were also the things that caused my parents, and my mother in particular, such anguish."

Eventually, as she wrestled her way through adolescence, Susan found herself leaning toward being the perfect child, to make up for the continual anguish David was causing her parents. She deliberately became, in many ways, his opposite. "I felt great pressure to be perfect because he was so flawed. He was overweight, and that was one of the external things my mother focused on. They had him on diet pills. So when I was about fifteen, I developed anorexia."

It was a perverse way of getting noticed, trying to please, and being different from David, all at once. But it didn't work. "I stopped because no one was noticing. I tried to be everything that he wasn't, to do my parents proud, because they were ashamed of him," she explained. "And I resented it, and him. And yet at the same time, I admired him greatly, intensely. His wit. And his panache. And his ability to rise above the situation. He created all this chaos and still went ahead and was what he was."

Eventually, they all grew up and left home. David and Janet both moved to San Francisco, each to pursue his or her own individual notion of the hippie life. Janet became a social worker and continued to be an earth mother. David also became a social worker, and reveled in the sexual freedom of San Francisco in the 1970s. Susan still had her role to fulfill, too, and she kept at it. "I went to college and I taught for a couple of years. And then I went back to graduate school for a couple of years. I met myself a medical student, and I started getting my ducks lined up."

By the time the eighties rolled around, she was married to her doctor, living in New York City, and working as an editor at a health magazine. Things between her and her brother and sister remained the same. "They were living the free life and I was still fulfilling the obligation," she said. "My brother would come out and visit me and my husband, and he would go out to the St. Marks baths all night." Though she adored him, she also still resented the role she felt he forced her to play, and he, with a sibling's unerring eye for a sore spot, mocked her. "He ridiculed me. He would talk about how narrow-minded and conventional I was," she said.

It was in the context of her work that she first started hearing about the frightening new disease then associated with gay men. "The first time I read about AIDS, I knew that he was going to have it. In a way, because his gayness was treated like a disease, growing up, I somehow knew he would die of it. It was like a train coming," she said. "It was almost unreal." For a time, she lapsed into denial. "The more I was in denial, the more I tried to have the perfect life to counter it." That was how she'd always anticipated and responded to David's upsets. But the laws of the universe work differently from the laws that govern families.

A few years passed. Susan had a baby, a daughter, and she and her husband moved to the suburbs of New York, to the town where she still lives. And then, one morning in 1987, while David was visiting, he delivered the news over breakfast. "We were eating bagels at this really awful mall, and he said, 'I think I need to get my affairs in order.' I still can't go in that mall. The sight of it makes me queasy." Four months later, her mother was diagnosed with lung cancer. She died a year later. David survived for three more years.

As her mother and brother, the two forces who had so shaped her identity, neared the end of their lives, Susan found her identity slipping away. Her father, meanwhile, seemed finally to be finding peace, even admiration, concerning his son and his lifestyle. And it unsettled Susan. "It pissed me off. I thought, Why not me? I'm the one who's done everything right here." If David was acceptable, being conventional was for naught. "No matter what I did, it didn't make a difference." Being good hadn't made up for David, and it hadn't saved him. And with David nearing the end of his life and shedding his "bad" child identity in the family, it left her feeling at a loss for her own.

As we talked, Susan wrestled visibly with conflicting emotions—her love and admiration for her brother, the fact that she missed him, her anger over the role she found herself in, the shame over some of his behavior, the confusion over who she really was now that he was dead. David's death had robbed her of the identity she'd created for herself, first within her family and then within the outside world. She didn't know who she was anymore. In some way, he had taken her with him. Three years after her brother died, her father died, and then, a few months later, her marriage fell apart, and the disassembly of her life was complete. "It's funny," she said, "the facade just crumbled. It was like I really lost all my moorings."

Now, nine years after her brother's death, she lives in the suburbs, near her ex-husband, so that their daughter has an easy com-
mute between the two of them. She is still struggling with who she
is. She sees another dimension to her loss now, too. David, though
he had mocked her conservative ways, had been her connection to
what she considered her artistic, eccentric side. That piece of her
had always been alive when David was. Now, it isn't. Downstairs,
in her bedroom, she keeps the Wizard of Oz books and the paper
doll collection her brother left her. "I like to think of myself as having a camp sensibility because of hanging out with my brother and
his friends," she said, when she showed them to me. "But I feel like
I lost that identity. Now, I'm just a suburban divorcée."

She is toying with change, though. "Just recently, I threw it off.
My aunt, my mother's sister, was very ill and needed someone to
come right away. I couldn't because I had just started this new job.
And I called my sister and I said, 'You've got to go.' And she didn't,
so now my aunt has survived and she's really mad at both of us
and she's cut us out of her will. But I'm not going to play the role
anymore. Of course," she said, referring to the anger and the will,
"there are consequences."

In some families, it seemed as if each sibling had taken on a role,
and that when one sibling died, the others took on different pieces
of the roles they left behind. It appeared to be an automatic
response, often unspoken, that comes from the needs of both the
parents and the surviving siblings, as a way of maintaining the
integrity and identity of the family.

You could write an entire book on the Kennedy family and this
subject. Their saga is well-known, starting with the presidential
aspirations the family patriarch, Joseph Kennedy, had for his eldest
son, Joe Junior, before World War II intervened. On the evening of
August 12, 1944, Joe Junior, then a twenty-nine-year-old navy
pilot, volunteered to fly an airplane loaded with explosives over

the English Channel. At a certain point, he was supposed to bail out, leaving the plane under radio control en route to its target—a cache of German missiles that had been located in Normandy. But shortly after takeoff, radio control heard a gasp from Kennedy's cockpit, followed by an explosion. His body was never recovered.

John F. Kennedy, Jr., like his older brother, was educated at Choate and Harvard. But while he and Joe Junior had been rivals—Joe Senior was known to encourage his children to compete for his affections—John had had no intention of competing with Joe in the political realm. He was going to be a teacher or a writer. But two years after Joe's death, JFK ran for a seat in the eleventh congressional district of Massachusetts and won. He served three terms in the House of Representatives and then, in 1952, was elected to the Senate. In 1960, at the age of forty-three, he became the thirty-fifth president of the United States. Who knows what path his younger brother, Bobby, might have taken, had JFK not been assassinated three years later?

"The great fault-line in the life of Robert Kennedy was the assassination of his brother," writes Thomas Powers, in a review of *Robert Kennedy: His Life,* by Evan Thomas, in *The New York Review of Books.* "The person he had been—right arm, door-opener, detail-man, enforcer, adviser, devoted and loyal brother—died in Dallas and was eventually replaced by a different sort of person." The new Bobby was searching for a new meaning, and determined to live life without fear, and impassioned by the plight of the "oppressed and impoverished," writes Powers.

Soon after JFK's death, Bobby, who'd been attorney general under John, resigned his post and won a seat in the Senate. Five years later, he announced that he was running for president. Unfortunately, we know how this story ends. After Bobby's death, the only remaining Kennedy son was Ted. He was the youngest of the nine siblings, and had been only twelve when Joe Junior was killed. He hadn't been groomed for the role of president either. His attempts at approaching the presidency ended in failure.

Today, he appears to have made some peace with his legacy, living the family ideal of political service from his seat in the Senate.

Not all siblings have to take on such lofty aspirations. Amber, who was just nineteen when her seventeen-year-old brother, James, was killed in a car accident, has two other sisters, both younger than James. James was smart and athletic, the pride of the family. There was no question that he was going to be the one to go to their father's Ivy League alma mater. "I was like, great, the pressure is off me. I'll go through school and get C's," said Amber, now thirty-five. "But when he died, I was like, you've got to do it now, you have to get serious about school and you have to change your life and turn it around because he's gone."

At the time that James died, Amber was in school studying fashion. When we spoke, she'd just finished a master's degree in social work in New York City and was beginning a Ph.D. program. "Every one of us has filled the void," she said. "Mine was academics. My youngest sister was very athletic and she got even more athletic. And then my other sister had a lot of kids. She's got three kids, and she named her son after my brother." (Naming children after lost siblings is common. Interestingly, a number of people said that their children didn't particularly like the fact that they'd been named for their lost uncles and aunts. Their complaint: Too much baggage had come with the name.)

This phenomenon is so common to sibling-loss stories, in fact, that I sometimes stumble upon it in the most innocuous places. Once, sifting through magazines in a doctor's office, I came across a *Cosmopolitan* profile of the model Cindy Crawford. Her brother, Jeff, had died of leukemia when he was three and she was nine, according to the article. "When my brother died," the author quoted her as saying, "we all took on traditional 'boy' roles to fill the void. My sister was an athlete and I had to be the best student, so my father could play ball with her and talk physics with me. My success means I'm like the son my dad didn't get to have. He loves the fact I am who I am and I don't have to change my name, even though I'm married." (I found it was common for women who had lost a sibling to keep their last names, especially if an only boy had died.)

Val Kilmer, the actor, fulfilled the dream of his younger brother, who drowned when they were teenagers. The famous Japanese director Akira Kurosawa became a director because it was what his older brother, who committed suicide, had wanted to do. After the death of Ronnie Van Zant and several other band members in a plane crash, the rock band Lynyrd Skynyrd disbanded, only to be resurrected, a few years later, by Ronnie's younger brother, Johnny, who looks and sounds like him, as the lead singer and guitarist.

Sibling-loss literature tends to refer to this phenomenon as "living for two." But I find that phrase vague. Some people interpret it to mean that they live their lives thoroughly and consciously, because their dead siblings cannot. Others take it to mean fulfilling dreams left behind by dead brothers and sisters. One of the things I don't like about the phrase, aside from the fact that it's not specific enough, is that it establishes the phenomenon as a thing solely between the siblings—the two in question. But it seems clear to me that this happens, at least in part, within the context of identity in the family. In the Kennedy family, for example, the fact that someone had to be president was very much a family aspiration put in motion by Joe Senior.

When I think of this phenomenon, I think of the pieces we use as markers on a game board. We mark the sibling's onetime presence in the world—a living monument to the fact that the person once existed. Keeping him or her present, in this way, means the sibling stays in our lives to some degree. Siblings are reference points, and we often gauge where we are in life with comparison to them. By "living for two," we keep them as reference points—a marker of what once was. When a sibling dies, we become different. But it doesn't show right away. It's the phantom limb sensation—a sense of both absence and presence. We find ways, like naming children after them, of marking the alteration.

• • •

Of course, the identity crisis that can come with the loss of a sibling doesn't always lead to growth. A number of people spoke of the sense of having held themselves back, deliberately not succeeding, because they felt guilty surpassing their brothers or sisters. They felt guilt at being the one, quite randomly, not to be sick, not to be the victim of a random accident or violence. That was mentioned as a reason for both achieving and not achieving. I struggled with this. I felt bad growing older than my brother, and worse, surpassing him. Besides, I had relied on him to lead the way. I was often at a loss as to how to move forward. I made moves forward in my life in fits and starts.

Because I had not mourned my brother, there was also only a wall where he'd been. I was no longer relating to a person, I was relating to death, loss, and grief. That's what I think I was getting at when I walked into my therapist's office that first time and said, "I am my brother's death." And because I was an adolescent when he died, trying to understand who I was independent of my family, the grief for my brother became a major reference point for me in forming my adult identity. My touchstone, in this regard, was not my brother, but his death. There is not a lot of give-and-take, prodding and competition, that can happen in a dynamic like that. In my case the situation had also been worsened by the fact that, having lost one child, my parents were not anxious to lose another, even to the process of growing up. I submerged a lot of my separating. I hid it from them, or I didn't do it, because it caused them not only pain, but fear and anger.

Research suggests that this is the quandary of many adolescents who lose a sibling. In her book, *Sibling Loss,* which is based on interviews with seventy-five adults who lost siblings to cystic fibrosis in childhood, Joanna Fanos talks about the phenomenon of "refocusing." She found that parents, whose attention had once been diverted by their sick child, often suddenly refocused all their anxiety on their adolescent children, who were often desperately trying to form identities separate from their families. It tended to fill adolescent siblings with conflict, anger, and resentment. "Separating from parents," she writes, "was accomplished with increased difficulty, sometimes due to the sibling's own premature sense of responsibility for parents and sometimes due to parental inability to allow their adolescent children to grow up."

Other research by Fanos on adolescent sibling loss suggests that adolescents are at high risk for long-term anxiety, depression, and guilt. She also found that an enormous proportion of these survivors were hypochondriacs, and had health complaints that seemed to have their roots in troubled emotions. They had a difficult time sleeping, and they feared intimacy with others. Nancy Hogan, Ph.D., a nurse who specializes in sibling loss in adolescence, said adolescents maintain ongoing attachments to their lost siblings. Some may even fantasize about following them. Pleasant White says that adolescence marks an uncomfortable juncture— an adolescent can understand and feel a loss fully, and yet does not have the adult capacity to get the support he or she needs.

In November 2001, a car carrying two teenage boys plowed into a giant spruce tree in East Haddam, Connecticut. The driver survived. Fifteen-year-old Daniel Dombrowski was killed. Five months later, Daniel's brother, thirteen-year-old Michael, and his friend, fifteen-year-old Jeffrey Barton, chose to follow Daniel. With Michael in the passenger seat, Jeffrey drove the Dombrowski family's Ford Bronco straight into the same giant spruce. It was a deliberate death, a double suicide, a fact that was known because the two boys had called friends from their cell phones to say good-bye en route to the tree. Most people thought that Jeffrey, who was vaguely described by some as "troubled," had gone along as an act of friendship toward Michael.

Nobody really seemed to understand what had motivated Michael, or what he must have been going through in the months between his brother's death and his own suicide. The press dubbed the tree "the Suicide Tree." The town pulled it down, worried that it was a draw for other suicidal teens. The school superintendent, Steven Durham, was quoted as saying, "Why East Haddam?" A friend of the boss's was quoted as saying, "I don't know why they felt like they had to do this." And the police spokesperson assigned to the crash said, "It's always an unfortunate event when youths have permanent solutions to temporary problems."

I don't know what was going on inside Jeff, and I can't be sure what was going on inside Michael. But that policeman had missed a key point that may have driven Michael over the brink. The "problem" Michael was facing was not temporary. Nor was it easily solved. It was one that, had he chosen to live, he would probably have had to work on all his life. Imagine a complicated story like Susan's, for example, and how difficult it might have been for her to negotiate who she was in her family if David had died when she was an adolescent. As surviving siblings are prone to say, "You don't get over it, you learn to live with it." The learning curve seems to be particularly steep in adolescence.

Part of the process of reconstituting yourself after the loss of a sibling is to become conscious of what role you played in your sibling's life, and he or she in yours. With that knowledge—a process of locating the wound in a period of time less traumatic than the time of his or her death—it is possible to renegotiate who you are. One example of this is Jeanann, whose brother Sam died unexpectedly. Jeanann is from a blended family with six children. The three oldest children are from her mother's first marriage. The three younger children, of which she is the oldest, are from her mother's marriage to her father.

"I thought he was mine," she told me, laughing. "I was six years and five days old when he was born, and I thought he was my birthday present. With my little sister, I was only two and a half. And that was fine. But I was so ready for this baby. I was in first grade and I had learned to read already. I had learned about the bicentennial that year, and if he was a girl I wanted to name him Betsy Ross." She was adamant on that point, but her parents were just as adamant that it wasn't going to happen. Fortunately, it didn't become an issue.

"I was the only child taken to the hospital to pick him up. That was probably a coincidence, because I was also probably the best-behaved child. But I got to go, and I got to turn the key off in the ignition of my dad's truck, and we picked him up. And I babied him, and I carried him around. I held him captive in his little seat and tested my new reading skills. I would turn the picture pages toward him, just like my teacher did at school. He was *mine*. I mean, there was no doubt about it. I look back at pictures and I am just all over him. And it was just always that way. Of course, we had moments, you know, years where we weren't what I would call friends," she said. "But once I went off to college we became confidantes again."

After college, she moved back to her hometown to be nearby for Sam's senior year in high school, and for the birth of her little sister's first child. "I spent a lot of the last year and a half or so of his life with him. And we had a great time. It felt like, not only was he my little brother, but it was that he had become my dear friend. I took time off work to go to his football games, and I got to know his friends. I felt like it was part of my sisterly duty. I felt like, I'm the one he's closest with, I want to be here for this. I feel like we lived that last year and a half perfectly together."

Sam dropped dead one Friday night during his senior year of high school. "It turns out he had a congenital heart defect. His heart was never formed right in the first place," explained Jeanann. She thinks that he knew something was wrong, and it horrifies her that he went through that alone. She was devastated by his death, but stayed on autopilot as the big sister, because Sam's friends were looking to her for cues as to what to do. "I went back to work after three or four days, because if I didn't, they wouldn't have gone back to school. I was the Pied Piper. They were definitely looking to me for behavioral cues. I thought, Oh God, now I have twenty little brothers," she said.

She went to their high school graduation, though she knew it would open up scar tissue. "I wanted to go, and I needed to be there for his friends." And she saw them all off for college in the fall. This was the time of sleepwalking, when shock, which she calls a "wondrous drug that should be bottled," was getting her through. But after that, the shock wore off and she had to confront the losses that Sam's death had brought.

"I lost my touchstone," she said. "I lost the person who understood my family just as I did. I lost the mirror that was our face. Out of six kids, we were the only two who looked alike. That made me really feel like I'd lost a part of me. I lost someone who would be most like me, who would have gone to college and gone on to professional life. I lost someone who would have helped me care for my parents. I lost a dear friend.

"And I lost having someone to baby. That was the hardest thing, when he was first gone," she said. "I thought, I've been his big sister my whole life, even waiting for him to be born. That was my job. I was the big sister. And I took that over with his friends for a while, to try to fill the void, and they needed a big sister then. But it was hard to be out of a job. I thought, I'm not done yet! I'm not done yet! How am I ever going to get that back? How am I ever going to fill that hole inside of me?"

She took on some of Sam's role. She moved back in with her parents, because she felt bad that they had been so abruptly empty-nested. "I feel like I do some of his family work," she said. "You know, trying to be all that for my parents. I'm the one to wake up with my parents on Christmas morning. And my sister is probably done having kids, and the older kids are done, so I'm the one who's left. I'm sort of the last fulfiller of grandchildren, and I'm thinking that's my thing, too. I have all the cleanup." She laughed. "I'm the last one to get married. I feel like I'm the finisher for him, carrying on for him."

When I spoke with Jeanann, her life was beginning to change. She and Mike, her fiancé, were planning their wedding, and she was preparing to move out of her parents' house. She was thinking about moving on in her life, too, and assuming new roles. She had always been the one to take care of everyone else, she said. "I'm the caretaker. I'm the one who made good grades, and was a good girl, and did everything right."

By joining Mike's family she would become, along with Mike, one of the family's youngest members, and that felt like something she was ready to welcome. "I think I'm looking forward to being a baby sister," she said. "My thought is, You know? I've done my job and I've done it well, but it may be okay now to let somebody else sort of take care of me, or learn things from other people, because I've always been the person who's had to do that. And I might not have been willing to give up my old role if I still had Sam."

Some six months after I spoke with her, Jeanann and Mike got married. A year later, I received a card in the mail announcing the birth of her son, Sam.

One of my brother's favorite ways to tease me used to be to rock back and forth on his heels (a behavior that usually heralded some form of torture pleasing to him) and singsong: "My life was perfect for three and a half years." Then he'd smirk, cross his arms, and rock some more. He was referring to the period of time he'd spent as an only child. He knew this drove me insane, partly because, to some degree, it was probably true. I was the younger sibling. There are three and a half years of Ted's life before me that I can't account for. All that I have from this time with which to reconstruct him are pictures and the few stories my parents find it not too painful to tell. I know he was born on October 2, 1962, in the Washington, D.C., hospital where my father was doing his medical residency.

My mother said she should have known about his personality

from the get-go. During labor, he jammed himself into a breech position, further complicating matters by positioning himself with one leg up and one down, all of which was confirmed in a series of disconcerting X-rays. "Contrary," my mother was fond of saying. "Stubborn. Hardheaded." She had to have a C-section, the incision for which, back in 1962, was huge and vertical, unlike the relatively dimunitive incision used today.

Our parents named him Vincent Theodore, after my father and grandfather. They called him Teddy, and when he got old enough to make his preferences known, Ted. I know nothing of his infant years. In his baby picture, which hangs in the proper order, above mine, in my parents' bedroom, he is all but hairless and slightly cross-eyed, lying on his stomach, head tilted to one side, smiling a quirky, gummy smile. This baby is a stranger to me. I can barely see my brother in him. He looks way too sweet, for one thing. Only the shape and hint of humor in his eyes suggest to me the person I came to know. He is not yet the person who would come to dominate and guide my life with the authoritative nonchalance of a traffic cop. He is not yet the person who knows he is the most capable child in the family. He is the first child, the heir apparent, the center of his own and his parents' universe, his own point of reference. New. He is not yet an older brother.

In later pictures he is a chunky toddler, legs divided into sausage-like segments barely contained in their skin, fat escaping little white anklets. In one picture, he sits halfway out of the passenger side of the car clad in a little boy suit—miniman gray flannel jacket, button-up white shirt, short pants, anklets, and dress shoes. He is scowling up at the camera, ticked off, perhaps, to be documented in such ridiculous garb.

Another photo catches him, bathing suit barely visible amid his belly folds, eating an ice cream cone, a melted slick of ice cream exploring the ripples of his stomach, feet stuffed into tiny Keds. In yet another, he is sitting at the Thanksgiving table. All eyes are trained on him as he lifts an enormous turkey leg to his mouth, a Pilgrim hat balanced precariously on his head.

I was born on April 16, 1966. My mother chose my first name simply because she liked it. My middle name, Anne, was after the grandmother who'd raised her. My other grandmother, upon hearing that I was due, climbed into her Persian lamb coat and her '57 Buick, stuck a Chiclets, which she never chewed, in the corner of her mouth, and drove the two hours from Yonkers to New Haven, Connecticut, where we were living—or rather, where I was soon to join the others—while my father completed yet another leg of his medical training. I was a complicated birth, too. Another C-section. My mother now had two hardheaded children on her hands.

My brother, who had newly acquired this big brother title, was, by all accounts, displeased by my arrival. He blew a whistle over my bassinet while I was sleeping, provoking a panic-infused few days during which my parents thought I was deaf because I didn't even flicker an eyelid. I was just a sound sleeper, as the pediatrician demonstrated by holding me upside down by my ankles while I slept on. When I learned to crawl and then walk, Ted took to plowing over me, so that I learned to scream and flatten myself on the ground whenever he approached. He put his hand over my mouth when I cried. He didn't like me to touch his things.

I know all of these things not because I remember, but because these are the few things I have been told. These are the blank years, during which I surely felt and saw and thought, but did not absorb conscious memory. It has occurred to me to wonder what really happened, unfiltered through the eyes of others. It has occurred to me to wonder where or how that early sense of him, of us, got stored—when I began to look up to him, when I accepted him as the leader, when I began to see him as a different kind of authority figure from my parents, and when and how I began to trust him above all others.

. . .

It's a strange thing, the amnesia that cloaks early childhood. Most people's first memories take place after age three. Before we have language, we're unable to identify, label, or store the events of our lives in such a way as to be able to recover them at will, or even have them jogged loose by some triggering event. What happens to our sense of our early lives, during which we are, undoubtedly, forming our opinions of the world and deciding how to respond to it and interpret it? What happens to those unmoored events and encounters that have floated off into the ether of our psyches? Who do we learn from and what do we learn? Our early experiences are the foundation of our experiences of the world.

We remember some events of childhood, the bigger events, that are most often witnessed by others and that tend to become the stuff of family stories, like my brother blowing the whistle over my bassinet. That is a story that neither my brother nor I remembered, though we'd both heard it so many times we felt as though we did. But it's the day-to-day moments and the things you yourself can't remember that constitute the true basis of the relationship.

It's a process of hardwiring, learning the world with someone by your side as witness, peer, protector, antagonist, or all of the above. It is what makes you know, at a later date, when your mind is sufficiently developed to wonder about such things, that these people are intimately, sometimes even uncomfortably, connected to you, without being able to articulate in any convincing manner, to yourself or to others, exactly how or why. At some point in time (a time that most of us won't remember) siblings become interstitial: lodged between your cells. They are the invisible glue that holds your interior architecture together.

There were probably thousands of ways I'd been shaped by my brother that I had not been conscious of. I recognize this most obviously in the way I have a hard time turning down a dare, because I was always trying to prove myself to him, and never lost the habit

of saying "sure," no matter how stupid the dare was or how little I
wanted to do it. I recognize it in the way I like to trade wisecracks
and banter with friends, a way of communication typical of siblings,
but not those who've grown up as only children. I recognize it in
the way it has always been easy for me to have boys and men as
friends. And I recognize it in the way I will often defer leadership to
others. I wasn't groomed for it, and I don't want the job.

But I don't have the memory of the mundane day-to-day
moments in which I became this way. Not being able to find them
frustrates me as I attempt to describe a relationship I don't
remember forming, that I only have a vague sense of living within,
because it was always there. The only remotely objective evidence
of the relationship that I possess is pictures. One of my favorites is
a Sears's portrait of myself with my brother. I am perhaps three,
sitting on a bench, wearing a smocked pastel blue dress with
sleeves that gather high up on my arms. I am smiling gleefully. My
brother is sitting in back of me, knees flanking mine, smiling also,
but less gleefully. There is something else in his expression. Calm.
Competence. A certain level of tension, perhaps.

The story behind the picture as told by my mother (here I am
again, relying on somebody else) is this: My mother wanted a picture of me by myself. I refused to cooperate, screamed, was well
on my way to a tantrum, when my brother climbed up on the
bench with me, at which point I instantly broke into the smile
captured in the picture. My mother used to relay this story with a
bit of exasperated amusement, as if the frustration of dealing with
me and being shown up by a six-year-old is still fresh in her mind.
My brother, whenever he heard this story, was smug. He'd cross
his arms. Smirk. In the tally of who got what from whom, I think
I can take credit for the evolution of his superior smirk—it was
usually about or aimed at me.

But in looking at the picture now, I can see why he developed
that smirk. In the picture, his life may not be totally perfect anymore. He may have more responsibility than the average first

grader cares for. And more frustration and annoyance from dealing with his younger sibling. But with regard to me, he is compe-
tent where adults are not. He has insight and expertise, a subtle
authority. He could be wearing a gun and a sheriff's badge. It is
clear that we have an understanding. What it is based on, beyond
rank, is anyone's guess. But, from both our expressions, it is quite
evident that, in this picture, he is a big brother.

Our early years were quite different, as were our later ones,
maybe because my brother and I lived in such extremely different
environments. I found Dunn and Plomin's work on nonshared
environment helpful when I was thinking about this. But I saw the
unshared environments in less literal ways, as well. My brother's
illness had an enormous impact on the shape of my life. It was
something that I, obviously, experienced differently from him. His
illness became his burden, while my health became mine. He was
the center of the show, needing, while I sat backstage providing
invisible support—the prop lady. He thrived on attention. I worked
to require as little as possible, and felt ashamed when I failed.

But as my brother struggled with his surroundings and grew, I
receded. My existence was based on his, and I increasingly defined
myself by his achievement, his importance, his struggle. It wasn't
just that that's how it naturally evolved; it was how it needed to be.
There was no energy left, no family, when we weren't in The
Room. And when we were in The Room, my brother was the
focal point. When I was away from him, I didn't know who I was,
or I feared the worst—that I was nobody. Looking back, I see the
signs of the stress I was under. I had a favorite pair of pants,
maroon crushed corduroy. I have a mental vision of my maroon
legs stalking the playground at recess with visions of various alter-
cations and exchanges playing in my head. I was a bully looking
for a chip to push off someone's shoulder, but the only person I
bullied was myself. That's where I aimed my anger and confusion.

One memory: I am about ten, standing just outside an empty
stall in the girls' bathroom of my elementary school, slamming the

door on my fingers. I want to break them, but, much to my annoyance, the awkwardness of my one-handed grip on the door and some sort of self-protective flinch mechanism keeps me from slamming it hard enough. It hurts, but not enough. "Will you do it?" I ask one of my classmates, who is standing by the sinks, transfixed and horrified. She shakes her head from side to side, a soundless no, and leaves. I tried to break my fingers often—in the doorjamb of my bedroom, in my wooden laundry hamper—but I never succeeded. My body, it seemed, was embarrassingly sturdy.

Looking back now, I see my own peculiar logic: In my experience, a life unchallenged by trauma, by tragedy, by something to overcome, was meaningless. It made you invisible. It was the struggle, the pain, that gave it purpose. I was the healthy one, the lucky one, as I was often reminded, the one who appeared to sail through the world without challenge. Mine was a meaningless and ordinary existence, not worth noting. The travails of my life were small. My mother's favorite phrase for quieting me was, "Save your tears for something important." But nothing that happened in the daily course of my life ever came near to what had happened to my brother. Ergo, there was never a time when I was entitled to cry, to feel bad. Breaking my own fingers was a way to gain entry into a world that mattered. It was also an attempt to make my inner pain, an amorphous, edgeless ache, something real and identifiable that I was allowed to have. A cracked bone you could see on an X-ray.

Sometimes I was more direct in my attempts to communicate what I now realize was depression. Only I couldn't name it. I remember, when I was ten or eleven, standing in front of my pediatrician, a kindly, quiet man with a long horsey face and iron-gray curls cut close to his head, who had been my doctor since I was a baby. I stood, shivering in my underwear, as he pressed the pronged TB test into my forearm, aimed the light in my ear in the way that always made me feel something was going to crawl into my head, gagged me with the dreaded tongue depressor. He asked me how

I was. "I'm always tired," I told him. "I'm tired *all* the time." I saw him flick his eyes across his desk at my mother, who was sitting, watching in a chair. He had an amused twinkle in his eye, and I knew, from his glance, that I was a joke. Or about to be one. "Well," he said, looking back at me. "Do you go to bed on time?"

Times when I was sick were frightening, because they often made my mother angry. If I said I was sick enough not to go to school, she threatened to take me to the doctor to expose my fakery. It must have been the extra stress, the contrast between what my brother was going through and what I was complaining about that so irked her. Maybe it was frightening that I, too, was vulnerable. And then there were times that I wasn't sick, or not in the way I said I was. These were times I was what I would now call depressed or anxious.

Once, as a teenager, I truly did feel sick. I called her from school and went home. She yelled and threatened to take me to the doctor. My illness escalated; later it would be diagnosed as mononucleosis. But before that, what I remember is my mother in terror, racing me to the home of one of my brother's doctors. He looked at my swelling throat, gave me steroids, and told her to take me home. She should bring me to the emergency room for a tracheotomy if I appeared to be having any more trouble breathing, he said. That night, I remember sleeping fitfully, waking up and seeing my mother, rigid in a chair next to my bed, watching me breathe.

Because my brother and I couldn't touch, fight, or play, we reconstructed our relationship as a verbal approximation of what it had been. Once, we had fought, pushed, shoved, helped each other, played, been allies. I had been his sidekick and his nemesis, he my leader and my nemesis. Then, at an age when siblings didn't have to work on their relationships, we had to work on ours. We talked, sometimes. We found interests that we shared—books, plastic

models, music, ideas. We honed our fights into verbal ballets, trad-
ing insults in a game of one-upmanship to see who would be left
speechless in the end, a practice that amused us and disturbed anyone who was watching. But this was all in the few moments when
we were alone. Usually, there was someone there. Our private sibling relationship had become public. We learned to communicate
without words, too, with subtle eye rolls and mouth shapes, ways
to transmit commentary on the egregiousness of our parents'
behavior.

Sometimes, on Saturdays, my mother dropped me off alone at
the front of the hospital, and just he and I spent the day together.
It was the only time we were ever alone. Sometimes we watched
movies on TV, or talked. Sometimes he showed me how to play
something on the guitar. He was already good. I was taking
lessons, wanting to be just good enough without surpassing him.
Sometimes he had an agenda in mind. We'd design a spaceship,
draw out plans. He recited bits of plays and poems that he'd
memorized, acting out parts, especially those involving swords,
for my entertainment. On really good days, the hospital recreation
department wheeled up a projector and aimed it at the back of the
door to his room, and we'd watch Mel Brooks movies. Sometimes
he wanted no part of me, no part of the fact that I, a child and his
younger sister, no less, was increasingly one of his peer contacts
with the outside world. On these days, I made myself quiet and I
read, or roamed the hospital on my own.

Whatever normal competition my brother and I might have
experienced, had he not been sick, was contorted. I learned to be
a noncompetitor in all ways. When I got his teacher for fourth
grade, in school, it was a misery for me. She had loved my brother,
adored him, thought he was brilliant and creative. He'd had a
"wonderful" year, my mother always said. When I got her for
fourth grade, I shrunk into myself, partly because I was afraid of
competing with my brother, who was, by then, in The Room. The
teacher saw me as a faint shadow of him. I could read it in her face.

That was the year I stopped doing my homework, and nobody, not even I, knew why.

When I enter a classroom or auditorium, I still look for a seat in the back. Performers who recruit people from the audience are my nightmare. I can't stand being photographed or videotaped. My most horrifying day-to-day adult experiences usually have something to do with introducing myself to a group, or worse, speaking in front of one. At these times, I feel the way you might feel if a cluster of onlookers tromped into your bathroom one morning and whisked back the shower curtain while you were in the shower. Which is to say, exposed and vulnerable.

I, the one my mother once described as "the social one," became an observer after my brother got sick. I was not seen and not heard. It's one reason, as my memory of those early years started to come back, that I remembered so many details. The wet Magic Marker smell of Betadine. The rough texture of floor tile. The sound of the air rushing from the fans in The Room. The Houdini poster that hung on a wall just to the nonsterile side. All my energy had been consumed in observation. That was my coping mechanism. It still is. I am still the watcher, which might be why I still panic when all eyes turn to me. It not only violates my sense of my role in the world, it strips me of my most practiced mode of coping with it. And it goes a long way in explaining why I was so horrified when my parents turned their attention to me, as star of the family show after my brother died. I could not be what they wanted. It was too late for me to become, again, the "social one." It also made it inevitable that I would seek a behind-the-scenes career dependent upon the observation of detail. My writing goes out into the world, not me.

Because I knew that my brother's illness seemed weird to other people, I also became the consummate outsider. No one else lived a life like I did. I was always acting like other people, other kids in my grade, with the conscious knowledge that I was acting. I studied smiles and laughs, phrases and body language. I assessed these pieces of people the same way beauty contest judges assess contenders for the crown. My goal, early on, wasn't to stand out but to blend in. I could act like them and get by. At first, I felt bad about this, as if my life had denied me entrance to normality. Later, differentness became something I embraced, normalcy something I scorned. I still do. Suburbia, that bastion of normalcy, the land of my childhood, is now alien to me. I prefer places like New York City, where differentness is all around. It makes me feel normal.

My brother is now long gone. I am older, I work. I have significant relationships outside the family I started in. There are different expectations of me now. But I still carry his imprint. Every sensory signal sent to my brain zips through nerve fibers, through my conscious and unconscious mind via circuitry soldered while Ted was still alive. I couldn't change that now if I wanted to.

Chapter Six

CARRYING

"I love that old phone with a passion. It was the only real property Seymour and I ever had in Bessie's entire kibbutz. It's also essential to my inner harmony to see Seymour's listing in the goddam phone book every year. I like to browse through the G's with confidence."

—Buddy Glass, explaining why he doesn't want his old phone disconnected four years after his brother Seymour's death.
FRANNY AND ZOOEY, BY J. D. SALINGER

Buddy is the second oldest of the seven Glass children in *Franny and Zooey.* Seymour, a brilliant eccentric who'd taken it upon himself to educate his younger siblings on the finer points of Eastern philosophy and religion, is the eldest. Seymour appears in the novel offstage, but he is an enigmatic and dominating presence, despite the fact that he's been dead for years when the novel begins. I love the lines above because they illustrate, with typical Salingeresque humor, a common practice among surviving sib-

lings: the tendency to find a way to "carry" our lost siblings forward into our present-day lives.

How people try to do so may vary, but why we do it is more
straightforward. We try to carry our siblings forward because they
are part of our identities, and our half of the relationship doesn't
end with their deaths. We need them as reference points to
remember who we are. We do it because loyalty and fairness are
two aspects of life we learn within the sibling relationship. They
continue to inform it well after we've become adults, whether our
siblings are alive or dead. We do it because it can feel too disori-
enting and disloyal to move forward and leave our siblings behind.
We carry them forward in order not to leave part of ourselves
frozen, unaged, in time. We carry them forward because siblings
were meant to be parallel travelers, in life's longest relationship.
We carry them forward because in order for us to go forward with
our own lives, whole, unhampered by guilt at having been the
ones chosen to survive, we often need them to come, too.

And so we find a way.

I first learned about Meredith through an article in a magazine.
She was twenty-nine, and for the past three years, she'd been running marathons in memory of her brother, Jon. When Meredith
was fourteen and Jon was sixteen, he died of neuroblastoma, a
common childhood cancer that begins in the nervous system but
is most often diagnosed after it's spread throughout the body. For
each marathon she ran, she gathered $3,000 in contributions and
donated them to help fund cancer research. In the picture in the
magazine, she is standing on an indoor track, water bottle in hand,
wearing a light blue T-shirt with the words "For Jon" printed on
it in black. There is also a smaller inset picture of the two at the
beach as children, with Jon giving her a piggyback ride.

I called her, thinking I would interview her specifically about
the marathon running and the notion of "carrying." We met in a

coffee shop across from her office in midtown Manhattan. Like most people I spoke with, she had rarely been asked to tell her story before or to talk about Jon. And so, amid the bustle of the coffee shop, we started from the beginning: Jon's diagnosis and death, their fiercely loyal and protective relationship, her devastation after his death, and her attempts to go on without him. "I've lived more of my life without him than with him now," she said, a fact that saddened and bewildered her. Before long she had tears running down her face, and I was reaching for extra cassette tapes and trying not to cry myself.

"When my parents brought me home from the hospital, they handed me to Jon and said, 'This is your baby and it's your job to take care of her now,'" she said. And that's exactly what he did. When she took naps, he dragged a chair outside her door and sat there for hours, guarding her. He wouldn't even allow adults who came by to enter. When he heard her wake up, he went in and got in the crib with her. "My mother was always afraid he would sit on me, or something. But he never did."

When she started school, she was annoyed to find that she was in a different grade and different classroom from Jon and his friends. "My parents were called in for a conference because I wouldn't have anything to do with the other kids in my class. I never smiled at them. I never talked to them. At recess, I just wanted to go play kickball with the third graders. I couldn't be bothered with the first graders." And she had her own Mafia. If someone dared to be aggressive toward her on the playground, Jon and his friends were on them in a heartbeat.

Time passed, and things continued much the same way. When she went to freshman orientation before starting high school, she was in the group assigned to Jon, who'd volunteered to be a student guide. To her, it was a happy coincidence. For Jon, it was the culmination of a summer's worth of lobbying. She discovered that he'd pestered the woman coordinating orientation all summer long in order to ensure that she was in his group. "For the first fourteen years of my life, my brother was everything to me," she said. "He was not even two years older than me. He was my best friend. He was my mentor. He pushed me. He had a knack for getting me to do things."

He also taught her how to handle their parents. "One night when I was little I asked my mother if we could go to Carvel's. I said, 'I really want ice cream. Can we go?' My mother said she didn't feel like getting in the car and it was too much bother and blah blah blah," said Meredith. "So I walked out of the room, and Jon had been listening to the conversation from the living room. He turned to me and he said, 'Watch this.' He just walked in and he put his arm around my mom and he said, 'Come on, you know, let's just . . .' and he lays the whole thing out. Next thing I know, she's grabbing her keys and we're in the car," she said, laughing. "He had a way. He could make you want to jump off the Brooklyn Bridge without thinking twice."

Jon was diagnosed with cancer at Memorial Sloan-Kettering Cancer Center in New York City, three days before his sixteenth birthday. "It happened so suddenly. He was diagnosed in November of eighty-five, and he died in June of eighty-six. He was diagnosed with terminal cancer, it was already stage four. It was a type of cancer that he'd apparently had since birth. It's really a pediatric cancer that had been dormant," Meredith explained. "When he got to Sloan-Kettering, he was the oldest case they'd ever seen, and they had absolutely no treatments for it. Everything they did was pretty much experimental. Looking back, I can see there was no way he was ever going to survive. But back then, it wasn't until the week before Jon died that I realized he was going to die. I never believed it was going to happen."

Meredith's story is rife with signs of ambiguous loss. Her family went into shock after Jon's death and, like many families in this situation, had a hard time re-creating the family in a way that adapted to it. Before, he and Meredith had always eaten dinner together upstairs in front of their TV set, while their parents ate together downstairs. After his death, the family didn't think to change the routine. Meredith found herself eating upstairs alone. "When I went to college and I got to go to dinner with friends, my friends would say, 'Why aren't you eating?'" Everyone else would be finished, while all of her food would still be sitting on her plate. "I was so excited to have people to talk to," she explained. "I didn't know how to talk and eat at the same time anymore."

Her grandparents told her Jon's death was worse for her parents than for her. None of her friends talked about Jon or his death. "For freshmen in high school to try to come to grips with death and be there for you, well, they really just weren't," she said. Her school guidance counselor, a woman she'd adored, chastised her one day for crying. "She said, 'You're being selfish. You're crying for yourself, not for Jon.' Mentally, I thought, Fuck you," said Meredith. "But I also thought, I'm a kid, and this woman, who is much older and a guidance counselor, must know better, must know something." She resigned herself to the fact that she was on her own. "I had to do it all by myself." That was the year she developed a gray streak in her long dark hair. "It just never went away," she said.

She grew up, went to college, and landed a good job in a highly competitive city. But there remains a fundamental sense that something is missing in her life. Jon. She feels his absence, and she wonders a lot about what her life would have been like if he had lived. She believes it would have been a lot different if he had been here to guide and lead her. Jon is still an important person in her life, though she knows that people might think that's strange.

She told me a story about an eerie moment of synchronicity, when she turned on the TV set and, in a sitcom she'd never seen before, saw her brother's full name—the name of a character in that episode—painted on a wall in one scene. Stunned, she called her parents. They weren't home, so she called her grandparents. "My grandmother basically told me there was something wrong with me," she said. "I've only seen that show twice, and both times, it was the same episode."

She told another story about meeting for dinner with one of Jon's friends when he came through town. As they were talking, she mentioned that she still thought about Jon every day. He was shocked. "He said, '*Really*, you still think about him every *day*?'" Though she's no longer fourteen, and she's better able to interpret that kind of response as someone else's problem rather than her own, these reactions make it hard for her to feel normal sometimes, and make her leery about discussing her feelings about Jon or his importance in her life.

In college, four years after Jon's death, she found a grief support group. She went only a few times. Most people were there for recent losses, and they found her presence strange. "People want you to be over it, done with it." The problem is that Jon was instrumental in shaping her into who she has become, and his death, his absence, has shaped her, too. To be "over" Jon is to be "over" herself, which contradicts the impetus to go forward with her life.

"For the first fourteen years of my life, his life was my greatest influence, and for the past fifteen years, his death has been my greatest influence," she said. "I'll never get over it. He is the core of me. His loss is the core of me. The day I get *over* it is the day I'm dead. But as long as I'm alive, I'll never be *over* it." In fact, that was the universal opinion of people I interviewed: You don't get over the loss of a sibling. So the questions Meredith, and all of us bereft siblings, face are: If moving forward with your life is not about "getting over it," what is it about? And how is it done?

Different people have found different answers, and many have tried several routes before finding the right way to carry their siblings forward. I don't know how many things Meredith tried before she discovered marathon running, but it was clear that it was the right solution for her. Jon had been a natural athlete, and running had been one of his passions. He'd often dragged Meredith out to run with him. She hadn't shared his enthusiasm, nor did she possess his natural ability or speed. But he'd always pushed her, encouraged her, helped her to improve, which was the role he played in the rest of her life, as well.

After he died, running was something she let go. Then, some years back, a friend she'd known since she was two called to tell her she'd just run a marathon, and that thinking about Jon and what he'd endured had gotten her through both the marathon and all the long training runs. "I cried," said Meredith. "It just made me so happy." When the same friend called again and told her she was moving to New York, Meredith decided it would be nice to be able to run with her, "because Jon had been important to her, and to be close to him."

A self-acknowledged couch potato, she started by taking a running class, in which she began at the beginning—walking one minute, running the next. It was slow going, at first. Her goal was three miles. "The first class, someone told me I should run a marathon, and I thought, Yeah, right. I can't even run three miles." Then she happened upon a pamphlet about Fred's Team, a group of marathon runners who each pledge to raise $3,000 for cancer research in honor of Fred Lebow, who founded the New York City Marathon, and who died of prostate cancer in 1994.

It was the right confluence of factors—an activity she and Jon had once shared, a way to do something meaningful in his honor, and a way to keep his name alive. And the funds went to aid cancer research at Sloan-Kettering, where Jon had been treated. She persevered with her training and eventually was able to start running with her friend and, in time, graduate to marathons.

She wears the shirt that says "For Jon" on it so that people on the sidelines can cheer her on by yelling, "Do it for Jon," which keeps her focused and helps get her through. Inevitably, she cries during every race. During the New York City Marathon, Fred's Team runs past Memorial Sloan-Kettering Cancer Center. Patients stand outside and wave. There is, she said, no better reminder of why she is doing this.

Through the marathons she can think about Jon, and she can

travel, which makes her happy because Jon loved to travel. And she can raise money to fight neuroblastoma, "so no other little sister has to go through what I went through," she said. Ever the little sister seeking approval, she also gets a kick out of thinking about what Jon's reaction would be.

"I graduated from high school, I graduated from college, I got a job. I've done things that I should be proud of, but this is the one thing that would blow him away. If Jon were standing here and I told him I just ran the New York City Marathon, he would fall to the ground," she said, smiling. "I think he would think it's really cool."

She's also driven by the knowledge that anything can happen anytime, and that she wants to experience things—for her and for Jon. She was leaving for Mount Everest shortly after we spoke. She was also planning to run a marathon in Antarctica. She was taking boxing lessons. And she was considering other marathons to run.

What she aspires to now is as daunting a struggle as training to run a marathon—finding happiness in a world that has already failed her once. She is still puzzling over how she is going to attain that, what it involves. Taking on physical challenges in the past several years seems to be the outward sign of that inner struggle. Running has given her a way to keep Jon with her as she moves into the terrain of her own future, one that she looks to more willingly now. She has invented a new relationship with him, one that acknowledges that he is dead, gone from her life but present, too.

Running has helped Meredith to redefine life after loss, outside the limited confines of "getting over it." It has taken her half her life to come to this, because she's had to figure it out all by herself. "I was just talking to somebody recently who read some of the articles about my running, and he said he was so impressed and so proud. It took me a long time to get to this point. Jon died when I was fourteen. At that point in time, just dealing with it was enough. It took me a long time to find a place where I feel like he's still involved in my life."

When I spoke with her, she had seven marathon medals sitting on her bureau. She hears them clanking every time she opens and shuts the drawers. "Looking at them, I think, Who knows what the future will bring?"

Stephen Chanock is a doctor with whom I share an unusual connection. I met him the last week of May 1980, the same week that Ted and Stephen's older brother, Foster, died. Ted and Foster shared a doctor in common, and it was in conversation with this doctor, standing in a hospital corridor, that Chanock and I first crossed paths. He'd just graduated from college and was spending the year in France studying music with his fiancée when he got word that Foster, the elder by five years, had been diagnosed with cancer.

Foster had surgery to remove the tumor immediately, and by the time Chanock returned to the States, he'd already lost his hair to chemotherapy. Chanock spent the next year traveling between Boston, where he was starting medical school, and the National Institutes of Health, where Foster was being treated. (Chanock is also the child of an NIH scientist, so returning to NIH was also coming home.) When it became clear that Foster wasn't going to make it, Chanock arranged to take his final exams at home, so that he could be with his brother when he died.

Inspired by the missionary zeal of the doctor who'd treated our brothers, Chanock made the decision to train to become a pediatric oncologist. He said he wanted to bring that same purpose and passion to his practice of medicine. Making that decision, he said, was transformative. Foster had been a star at whatever he'd done. There had been pressure on Chanock, too, from his parents and himself, to do well. The choice to become a pediatric oncologist meant years more of training, at a time when his parents were hungry to witness their son's achievement. But it was the right decision, said Chanock. When he made it, all the pressure melted away.

When I first interviewed him, he was working at NIH for the same doctor who'd treated Foster and Ted. His office was within five hundred feet of the intensive care unit where Foster died. Chanock said that although he believed he would have brought commitment to his chosen field had Foster not died, it had been his death that had impassioned him. "The minute I'm not one hundred percent committed to work late, early, or on weekends to do whatever I can to get kids better or help them when they die, is the day I walk out of here," he told me.

Since that early interview his office has been moved to another building, and he has taken over as the medical director of a camp for kids with cancer, a position once held by the doctor who inspired him. He is also writing chapters in medical textbooks about the family experience of illness. His father almost never speaks of his brother, although his mother will talk about him at length, if invited to. Chanock has found his own way to cope. He definitely has the zeal. I've known enough remarkable and unremarkable doctors to recognize it when I see it.

Those of us who have experienced a loss know when we're supposed to stop talking about it, when the patience of those around us has been stretched thin, and when we're expected to be "over" it. My first brush with this was via a boyfriend in ninth grade, five months after my brother's death. It was my brother's birthday, and I was too quiet. The boyfriend sent a mutual friend over to probe me for what was wrong. I told her. She relayed the information and reappeared within a few minutes with his reply. "He said you should be over that by now."

Granted, adolescents aren't always noted for their sensitivity, but it was a reaction that, unfortunately, isn't limited to children. Jeanann, who was twenty-four when her brother Sam died, said that the first year after his death was torture, but that the second year was almost worse. "I went into a deeper depression then, because it was like, 'The milestones are over, and he's never coming back, and now what am I gonna do?' And by then, even the people who may have been inclined to be sympathetic may be less so. They're ready for you to be done with it. I had a guy I dated, oh, three years after Sam died. At first he was very understanding if I was having a moment. But then he was like, 'You should really be done with this.' I thought, How dare you? I will never be done with this."

Linda, who lost both a brother, Peter, and her identical twin, Paula, went to a support group twenty years after her twin's death. She'd totally repressed the experience. Her brother's death ten years after Paula's was the first one for which she was truly able to grieve. Then both her parents died in close succession. After that, there was no repressing the death of her twin anymore. It was time. She found a support group and went. But she told people that she was there to mourn her father, the most recent of her losses. "I went undercover," she said.

Once, she brought a friend, Peggy, whom I also interviewed for this book. Peggy's younger brother had been murdered more than fifteen years earlier. She said she was still angry, that she felt gypped that she did not have her brother in her life. The man who killed her brother was out of prison, and had a job. She knew this because every once in a while she'd hire a private detective. "I haven't done it for a while because I'm afraid I'm going to find out that he's married and has kids," she said. After the session she attended with Linda, a woman approached her and said, "What are *you* doing here after so many years?" "Everyone thinks, My God, after the first couple of months, get over it," said Peggy.

The idea that it will never end can be unwelcome to someone newly initiated to the loss. I will never forget Britta, a young German woman who came to see me, desperately needing answers, less than a year after her sister had drowned in Turkey. "How long does it go on?" she kept asking, as she shredded Kleenex in her lap. "When is it going to end?" Her husband's patience was running thin. I had no answer for her. I didn't know yet, myself.

There was a time when we didn't try to quantify and qualify grief, a time when expressing pain over a long period of time was considered normal and customary. "Before World War I, grief was understood to be about attachment and continuing bonds," explained Robert Neimeyer, Ph.D., a professor of psychology at the University of Memphis and editor of the journal *Death Studio,* who is one of a handful of people who have been working hard to redefine the experience of loss.

A Victorian widow or widower wore the loss, literally and metaphorically, for years after the death. Those were the days of mourning clothes and lockets that held a lock of the lost one's hair. "It was the model of the broken heart that could never be mended, a recognition of the lifelong impact of loss," said Neimeyer.

World War I changed that. "When the French front opened, all of a sudden these little British villages and towns and big cities, long accustomed to elaborate public displays of emotion, were trying to recover from all of these deaths." With hundreds and thousands of bodies being brought back, the old system completely broke down. "It completely overwhelmed the capacity of the populace to engage in the customary high grief responses." There was time only to draft the next batch of boys.

"Almost overnight," said Neimeyer, "there was a new posture toward loss. It became a patriotic duty to repress one's grieving, and to distance oneself from it. This model of self constraint, rather than self expression, became the approved way of reacting to loss." Meanwhile, Sigmund Freud published his essay "Mourning and Melancholia," which confirmed this take on loss. "He suggested that grieving requires completely letting go," explained Thomas Attig, Ph.D., a philosopher whose specialty is the theory that we continue relationships with those we have lost. "The idea is that you remove emotional capital [energy] from the person who dies. Success in grieving is when the capital is entirely removed."

Some have argued that Freud didn't mean to say that. Whether he did or not, this was the message he conveyed. The stiff upper lip became the model for all grief, an approach that Americans, who were also overwhelmed by the war dead, adopted from the Europeans.

In November 1942, it gained even more scientific validation. That was when approximately one thousand people, many of them young men shortly shipping off for military duty, found their way to the Coconut Grove Nightclub in Boston, Massachusetts. The hot spot of the moment, the club, which favored Polynesian decor, was decorated with colored cloth draped from its walls and ceiling, and braided rope running up poles topped with artificial palm leaves and coconuts. All was well until one fateful moment, when an employee lit a match so that he could see to change a lightbulb.

The decorations went up in flames. The fire spread quickly, and the panicked people inside ran to the doors that provided the club's only means of entrance and exit. But the doors, which were designed to swing inward, proved to be a crucial element in the tragedy. The people pushing to get out became their own impediment. When the fire was finally extinguished, firemen found bodies stacked four and five deep just on the other side of the doors. Four hundred and ninety-two people died.

The fire is famous in part because it led to changes in fire safety codes. From then on, places of assembly had to post occupant-capacity placards. (The Coconut Grove had been overcrowded.) Certain flammable decorations were forbidden. And exit lights identifying escape routes became mandatory, as did doors that opened outward. In the medical realm, the fire offered the first opportunity to try out penicillin, then a new drug.

In psychiatric circles, the fire was made famous by a Boston–based psychiatrist named Eric Lindemann, who studied the survivors and the bereaved to document the experience of loss. Lindemann followed five hundred people who survived the fire, and the bereaved relatives of those who hadn't. It was the first attempt by a scientist to truly quantify and describe the course of grief. Two years later, he published a paper in *The American Journal of Psychiatry* in which he described the symptoms of grief, and coined the term "grief work" to describe the psychological process necessary to healing.

Lindemann endorsed Freud's idea that, to heal, one had to totally let go of the lost person. In addition to supporting that point of view, he listed "symptoms" that accompanied grief, and he added a new dimension to the equation—a time frame. He thought that grief work should be accomplished within a period of four to six weeks. If it lasted longer than that, it was abnormal. "Grief," said Attig, "became an illness with symptoms that needed to be resolved."

To be fair, there were positives in Lindemann's work, too. "He said some fairly useful things about having to engage with your emotions and return to your life," said Attig. "But the strongest legacy of his work was in strengthening the idea that grief was a short-lived problem, an affliction that needed to be gotten over promptly, like a disease."

The next chapter in the study of grief came with the publication of Elisabeth Kübler-Ross's book *On Death and Dying*, in 1969. The book was based on a seminar she'd arranged at the request of four theology students at the Chicago Theological Seminary. Kübler-Ross's students had wanted to understand what fatally ill people were going through as they faced death. Kübler-Ross arranged, with no small difficulty, for them to talk to dying patients themselves. It quickly became clear that these people were desperate to talk about death, and wanted someone to listen.

Kübler-Ross observed that many dying people seemed to go through a five-step process before death: denial and isolation; anger; bargaining; depression; and acceptance. "People were captivated by the five-step model," said Neimeyer. "Her impact on both the public and professional audience was huge. Her book was translated into more languages than the Christian Bible."

But somewhere along the way, her five-step model was applied not only to those who were facing death, but to the loved ones they left behind. Suddenly, grief was presumed to be a five-step process, as well. Once again, grief was an illness that had to be mastered in a defined period of time. And now it had identifiable stages. Kübler-Ross's work reinforced the notion that hanging on to a lost loved one signified a failure.

"The five-step model has straitjacketed people into thinking about their experience in that way. They get told they're stuck in denial, or they need to get angry to move on. Or they haven't reached a stage of acceptance yet, so maybe they need medical help," said Neimeyer. The five-step model remains so pervasive, in fact, that even people who've never read the book can recite it.

It's frustrating for people like Attig and Neimeyer. They are grateful to Kübler-Ross for breaking the long cultural silence on death, but they feel the book is outdated. And it wasn't meant to be applied to grief in the first place. "It's an insult to Kübler-Ross to mindlessly mouth her preliminary ideas, formulated in the mid to late 1960s," said Neimeyer. "It's a poor tribute to any pioneer not to stand on her shoulders and try to see farther."

Neimeyer and Attig propose something quite different from the grief and loss-as-disease model. Their theory is, in fact, a more enhanced version of what the Victorians used to believe: We have a continuing relationship with the dead. The premise that moving on means letting go is wrong.

When I was in high school and in college, I found myself rereading one book over and over again: William Faulkner's *The Sound and the Fury*. It would take me many years to figure out what attracted me to it so much. It tells the story of the Compson family, a dysfunctional clan whose members are struggling, in different ways, with the simultaneous disintegration of their family and the Southern way of life. Two of the family's children, Caddie and Quentin, have a particularly intense relationship. Quentin, in fact, is fairly obsessed with his younger sister, who, in the novel, symbolizes the Old South. Caddie's promiscuity, her refusal to act according to proper code, appalls, threatens, and challenges Quentin.

Ultimately she marries one of her paramours, and Quentin, out of his element up at college in the cold North, feels he has lost her, and his roots, forever. The novel is told in four sections, each from a different character's point of view. Quentin's is full of images of watches and clocks, ticking away. Ultimately, Quentin loads his pockets with stones and jumps from a bridge, putting an end to his torment. Quentin always interested me the most, and I finally realized why. He'd killed himself because all that he had left of Caddie was the pain of losing her, and time—as we are all told—threatened to take even that. ("Time heals.") Quentin killed himself to keep her while he still had her, in the only way that he could.

When I was told that time would heal my pain, and that I was supposed to "get over" my brother's death, in the way Freud decreed, it caused me more panic than comfort. No one wants to be in pain forever, but if the end of pain means the end of the person in our lives, the pain becomes something of which we can grow possessive. If it's pain or nothing, many of us will take the pain.

"I was very afraid to have it feel better, because I didn't want to forget him," said Amber, of James. "The more I heal, the more parts of me will forget him. And I am afraid to forget completely. I'm fearful of healing too much. I want to keep his memory alive." I wanted this, too. The way I stayed attached to my brother was to stay attached to the trauma and grief of his loss, because I thought that that was the only way I could keep him.

I desperately wanted to be happy, to be "normal," but I was stuck: If I lost my connection to my brother, I wouldn't be happy, and I would lose part of myself. But maintaining the connection I had with my brother meant carrying my intact grief. And that also meant that I couldn't be happy. It was the same as Quentin's dilemma, the same as Amber's. What I finally realized is that, somehow, in our cultural embrace of the "get over it" approach to loss, we confused two things—grief over the loss, and the continuing relationship with the lost sibling.

Grief, the day-to-day pain of being confronted with the permanent absence of a person who helped define the parameters of our world, can and will ease over time, if we let it. But we don't ever "get over" the relationship. It isn't lost with the grief. They're two separate things. This is at the heart of what Attig and Neimeyer, and a growing number of others, are saying.

"Suppose a baseball player had something happen to his arm, so he couldn't play anymore," said Attig. "He's still ready to play baseball, mentally. He still wishes he could play. He still imagines what he would do in different situations on the mound. His legs are ready to run the bases. His other hand is ready to catch the ball. He just can't throw anymore. Part of his makeup is still a baseball player. It's the way we are, too. The people we love are rooted deep within us, in our desires, our habits, our motivations, our expectations, our hopes, our dreams, our preferences, our needs. When they die, we're still wired that way."

Just like the baseball player who still wants to play but can't, we want the people to come back and make our lives orderly again, the way we're used to. "It would be stunning if that baseball player, with the ruined arm, suddenly had no desire to play baseball anymore, if he couldn't even imagine what it would be like to play baseball," said Attig. But that's exactly what the "get over it" model proposes as its goal.

It's a goal that is unrealistic and impossible to meet. People die; our sense of connection to them, our love for them, doesn't. The challenge for those of us who have lost loved ones is not to "get over it," said Attig, but rather to find a way to continue having these people in our lives and to love them even though they are not physically present.

"Until you resolve the core issue of what you're going to do with the love you still have for this person, there will be a huge reluctance to move on and engage with the world," said Attig. "The world is there, waiting for you to engage with it again. Why not bring the person with you and appreciate how different you are for having known him? Why not make some difference in your other relationships with other things in the world, in part because of having known him? Why not do that in appreciation of the continuing contribution he's making to your life?"

The best and happiest examples of sibling "carrying" are like the one Meredith and Stephen Chanock have devised—a way to keep their brothers in their lives while still leading their own. What Meredith is doing is about and for Jon, and staying connected to him, but it is also for her—she doesn't want anyone else's sister to go through what she's gone through. Marathon running is also a dynamic activity, something she can keep relating to, almost, but not quite, as one does with relationships with others. It is also a training ground for learning to incorporate into her own identity the things she had depended on Jon to do for her. Marathons are helping her complete her identity—the self without the other—without Jon's presence. She hadn't consciously chosen to take up running for these reasons, but nonetheless, she stumbled upon the perfect activity for her.

One woman I talked with via e-mail was an immunologist who was working on the disease that killed her sister. She'd already been a scientist, but her sister's death had influenced her line of research. Kathleen had been flattened by the wrongness of her sister's death. Janie wasn't supposed to die before their parents. At first Kathleen had been flabbergasted at how little comfort she'd derived from her religious faith, and by how unhelpful her religious community had been when she'd needed them. When I first approached her, she talked of "carrying" Janie by trying to embody some of her traits. Janie had been the giving and quiet one, Kathleen the "hard-ass." She was trying to be more like Janie in order to honor her.

A little later, in a subsequent exchange of e-mails, she had come to a new place. "I realized that the loss was not only real in the physical realm, but also in the symbolic realm," she wrote. "My life up until my sister's death had been orderly, predictable, linear. My sister's death upended all that. My religious 'faith' died a quick and needed death. In its place, slowly and wonderfully, is growing a big and wide and flexible view of spirituality that is much more awesome and mysterious, glorious and profound and fulfilling, then I could ever have imagined." She said that her new spirituality, which was a dynamic and daily presence in her life, was her last gift from and for Janie.

The best solutions are those in which the motivation comes from within, and in which you keep and maintain your own identity. Carrying is about bringing your lost sibling forward, not becoming him or her. To do it consciously requires no small amount of introspective work. Who were you in relation to your sibling, and what did you contribute to her life? What did she contribute to yours? It means defining the self without the other, and then redefining reality to instill that "other" back into your life. Gradually, it becomes easier to let go of the idea that grief is all you have left of the person. The grief isn't your sibling, it's just shaped in her outline. That's how I've come to think of the way I carried my brother for years—my brother in a grief suit. I lost the real person when I repressed his death. It took a leap of faith—that if I mourned there would be something of him left for me, other than the pain—to really begin to let his death go.

I talked to a lot of people who seemed to be at various stages of figuring this out for themselves. One often unconscious mode of solving the dilemma of the absent person was a phenomenon I call "seeking." It's long been known that people pick partners and friends based on the types of relationships they have with their parents. The personalities we grow up with create our taste, in a way, for future relationships, by making certain ways of being feel familiar. It's what that "click" is about, that strange sense of familiarity with someone we've just met, that uncanny resonance.

Siblings can create a "taste" for relationships, too. I think of the sibling relationship as a dialogue that starts at the moment we meet our brothers and sisters, and continues on, with lulls, arguments, and professions of loyalty and love, throughout our lives. To lose a sibling is to have one member of that conversation abruptly stop talking, to be left wanting a response that will not come. The tendency, then, is to find another person who can pick up that sibling's end of the conversation, engaging those parts of us that were most active in the ongoing dialogue we had with our brothers and sisters.

For most people I interviewed, this process had been unconscious. Some had already realized what they'd done by the time we spoke, but others seemed to have the realization dawn on them as we were talking. One woman I interviewed, a writer who'd been overwhelmed and intimidated throughout her life by her overbearing older sister, an actress, admitted during the interview to being slightly relieved when her sister died. The weight of her presence in her life had been, sad to say, heavy. But as we were talking about this issue, a funny look crept across her face. She'd suddenly realized that many of her women friends were overbearing actresses.

One young man I interviewed, who was in his early twenties, always compared the women he dated with his younger sister, who was seventeen when she died. Usually, the women came up lacking. But he kept looking. Jeanann told me that several friends had pointed out that Mike, her new husband, seemed to resemble her brother Sam. "They'll say, 'How tall was your brother?' And I'll tell them. And then they'll ask me what color his eyes were. And I'd think, Oh my God."

Mike has some of Sam's spirit and is mechanically gifted, as Sam was. But she hastens to add that though Sam and Mike share certain characteristics, like body type, height, eye and hair color, the total picture doesn't add up to Sam. Still, she's found the comparisons both amusing and slightly embarrassing. "I sit here and think, 'God, did I subconsciously go about finding someone who would give me the best chances of producing another one?' I don't know. *I don't know.* I don't think that I did that consciously."

Helen Rosen remembered that she'd craved friendships with older, wiser women. "I remember looking at one of my female teachers in high school, who was near Karen's age, and wanting to have a relationship with her and not knowing what that was about. For years, I was trying to find a woman to have a friendship with, who would fill that need." Joanna Fanos said she'd felt the same thing, and still did. "I've always sought out friendships with women."

One of the people who'd recently realized this in his own life was Kinnon, thirty-three, whose sister Gay died in a bicycle accident right after he left for college. He described his relationship with Gay as "typical older-brother, younger-sister stuff. We got along very, very well, and were very, very close when my parents weren't around. But I taunted her and teased her, and I wasn't always the nicest, best big brother. But we had a fairly good relationship. And we had spent some good time together right before I left to go to college."

He thought he'd figured out how Gay's death had affected him, in his fearlessness about changing career directions ("Because why not? Life is short"), the value he placed on the fact that through hardship, one can grow, and his willingness to acknowledge the place of death in our lives, and to talk about it, even when it's uncomfortable for those around him.

But one thing surprised him when he moved back to his hometown: He made a bunch of friends who were not only Gay's age, but onetime friends of hers. But he hadn't known that initially. "I was like, Oh my God, Kinnon. Are you living out something psychologically weird? Are you friends with these people because you're trying to connect with your sister? I can't answer it. What freaks me out is that it was unconscious. I mean, I enjoy those friendships. But I've recognized that in many ways, I sometimes feel more like a mentor, a big brother. The whole thing makes me realize that I'm going to be working through my sister's death, consciously and subconsciously, for the rest of my life."

There was another way many people had tried to keep a connection with their siblings—with psychics. Movies and books that involve some sort of communication with the "other side" are now a staple of every season. Psychics, and the idea of a continued relationship with the dead, came up a lot in my interviews with bereft siblings. Some said they wanted to go to one, or asked if I'd been to one. Some simply said they sensed their siblings around them, or said they talked to them. What was this all about? I believe it's an outward sign that we're chafing at the constraints of the predominant understanding about the aftermath of death: that it permanently severs your relationship—and your sense of relationship—with the dead.

I went to psychics, too. My brother and I used to talk about the paranormal. He often had dreams that he said came true down to the finest detail. I mostly had premonitions. We talked about déjà vu. We talked about death, and ghosts. How could you know what was true, and what you wanted to believe?

The last movie I remember watching with him was something from our paranormal genre: *Blithe Spirit,* a Noel Coward play made into a movie by David Lean in 1945, starring Rex Harrison. Harrison, as Charles Condomine, plays a widower who's just married for the second time, his first wife having died some years earlier, apparently from a bad cold. Unfortunately, shortly thereafter, an eccentric neighbor conjures her up. The result is a really funny movie in which the living and dead relate pretty much as they had before. They fight, make up, throw tantrums, and get on one another's nerves.

After Ted died, I found myself wondering, not a few times, if he was around somewhere. The first time I talked to a psychic was about eleven years after his death. I was living in Chicago, and I'd heard about the psychic from a friend. She worked by phone—you had to send her the check in advance. I don't remember anymore what she told me. But she must have been accurate enough not to turn me off the idea altogether, because a year later, when I moved to New York, I sought out a "specialist": a medium. Psychics profess to tell you what will happen in your future. Mediums profess to have one particular talent: They speak with the dead.

I had to make an appointment three months in advance. I was told to bring a tape recorder and a blank tape to the appointment, as well as a check for $150 and any specific questions I might have. I only had one rather obvious question in mind: Did my brother still exist somewhere, or not? I preferred to think that he did, that he was still part of my life in some way. It was what I felt. But I worried that that was just what I wanted to believe. I wanted proof, or something close to it. Something that took the burden of skepticism off my shoulders. For a while, at least.

On the appointed evening, I took the subway to the Upper West Side and walked to her apartment in a brownstone in the West Seventies. She looked normal enough. Blonde, shoulder-length hair. Jeans. Sweatshirt. Nice apartment. Nice dog. And there were no scary tools of the trade, like Ouija boards and crystal balls, in sight. All good signs, in my book. I sat on the couch and turned on the tape recorder, trying my best to cling to my skepticism. I had decided to tell her nothing about myself beforehand. She faced me in a straight-back chair, her dog at her feet, and closed her eyes.

The first person she described sounded an awful lot like my grandmother, which surprised me. My grandmother, who'd died a few years earlier, had been a character, but not someone with whom

I'd been particularly close. I'd expected to "speak" with my brother. That spirits might have a mind of their own hadn't occurred to me. But I was polite. And she didn't stay long. After Nana, as we used to call her, had trotted on (perhaps still teetering on the high heels she favored), the medium said that she sensed another presence.

Male. A brother. Name begins with a *T.* I was aquiver. She told me he'd died of a disease. That it felt like it was in her blood, she felt it all over her body. She told me that he'd gone by his middle name. It was all true. Then again, she could have done a newspaper search on my last name and found a fistful of old articles about my brother's life and death. But what she said next gave me chills. She said, "He said you were there when he died. He said that you were meant to be there. He said that he waited for you." The only people who knew that I'd been there were my parents and a few doctors. None of that had gone in the papers.

I don't remember what else she told me. I have a tape, buried somewhere in my apartment. But those three sentences have stayed with me all these years. I left that night feeling relieved for the first time since Ted's death. At peace. Secure. Safe. For the first time I could remember, the world didn't feel as if it had gone horribly wrong. He was still there. He didn't have to be entirely gone.

I never called another psychic or medium. I don't talk to my brother. I pass palm readers without a second thought. It has been such a long time since I was driven in that direction, in fact, that I don't even know what I believe about it anymore. But then, and now, I consider that session with the medium a profoundly healing experience. The reason, I think, is obvious—it was the first time I'd found a way to connect with Ted, to find a way to bring him into my world, whether it was real or not. That was what I needed, at that point, to dispel the horrible loss I lived with.

About a year after I originally spoke with Meredith, I e-mailed her to see how she was and to ask if she was still running. She answered that she was planning to run the New York City Marathon in a week and a half. She also told me that, while running the Chicago Marathon the year before, she found out that her father had passed away. Though he'd been ill with bronchitis, it had been a huge shock. She finished the marathon but had taken a break after that. "I decided not to run the NYC Marathon last year, and to give myself a little time to heal, mentally and physically," she wrote.

In happier news, she said she was planning to run a marathon in Australia, and that she'd met someone. When we spoke, she'd talked about the pressure of being the only child left, and being single and childless. She felt bad for her parents, and worried for herself. Loss made her both desire and fear closeness, something that was not uncommon in others I interviewed, as well. She described this man as "special." And his name, she said, was John. It was spelled differently than her brother's, as she pointed out, but a strange coincidence nonetheless. "What makes it even more odd/special (however you see it)," she wrote, "is that our first date was on my brother's birthday."

I don't think I've yet come across a solution as good as Meredith's for carrying my brother. To be truthful, I think I've spent most of the time, until now, simply carrying his death. But I can see it in subtle ways. My brother, for instance, helped to cultivate my ability and desire to read and write. He read to me before I could read. By the time I started first grade, I was chomping at the bit. I wanted to read just as well as he did. He was the one who informed me that I needed to read Jane Austen and Charles Dickens.

From the time he was a small boy, he'd always treated writing as a craft that required toil and thought. In his papers and books, which date back to his elementary school years, I've found complete plays—childish ones, but complete plays, nonetheless—in which he'd written out everything, including the casting and stage direction. (Since his acquaintances were limited to friends and family, I could usually find myself among the cast.) At one point, when he was a teenager, one of his elementary school friends became editor of the high school newspaper and asked Ted to write music reviews. I can still see him hunched over his typewriter, slaving over an article, line by line. It's a posture with which I've since become quite familiar.

And not long ago, while contemplating why I write, I had a revelation—when I write, my brother is my audience. My job, after his illness, had been to observe and to bring him glimpses of the world out of reach. That's what I was doing in Scotland all those years ago. It's what I'm doing right now, as I try to explain as clearly as possible. *See? Do you see?*

Looking back, I've been surprised to see whom I chose as friends. I unconsciously picked people who reinforced the situation in which I'd lived—the silent sibling, repressing emotion, repressing need. That's who I'd been. The relationships would go on and on, until I would find myself feeling very old anger, and end them.

It was an unpleasant pattern. I didn't break it until I claimed the loss and my story, until I refound myself and my brother. In telling my story, I am no longer the girl I once was, standing silently to the side, watching. Not long after I'd claimed my story, I started seeing someone I'd known as an acquaintance for years. I didn't see a resemblance at first. I didn't pick someone like Ted on purpose. He doesn't resemble Ted in any physical way. They do not have the same name.

But he is older than I am, as many people close to me are. He, like my brother, loves books and writing and memorizing poems because he likes the sound of the words. Ted once memorized Edgar Allan Poe's "The Raven" because he loved its cadence. He was prone to bursting out into entire scenes from Shakespeare. This man has the same sort of silly streak my brother had. Sometimes, he teases me mercilessly. Like my brother, he is full of ideas. Let's do this. Let's do that. When I met this person, a piece of me that had been sleeping for a very long time woke up again. It was good to be back.

Chapter Seven

TRAVELS IN TWINLAND

Penny: *What's it like being with someone all the time?*
Blake: *I don't know. I have nothing to compare it to.*
> —Blake Falls, a conjoined twin,
> in the movie TWIN FALLS, IDAHO

It was pure curiosity that got me thinking about twins. I wondered if the same themes that showed up in the sibling-loss interviews would turn up in twin loss. I figured that most people understood that there was often a special closeness in this relationship, and because of that, bereft twins probably at least had their loss acknowledged. But I needed to speak to some bereft twins to find out. My search led me to Dr. Raymond Brandt, the founder of Twinless Twins, a group composed of more than 2,100 people who'd started out in life as an identical or fraternal twin (or even triplets or quadruplets, in rare cases) but had, at some point, because of the death of a twin, found themselves living life as a "singleton."

It was a prickly exchange from the beginning. Brandt and I were like natives of the same country who spoke different dialects.

Brandt was defending a boundary. He asked me if I was a twin. When I told him I wasn't, I felt a slight chill through the phone line. "Well, have you ever known any twins?" he asked, his voice accusing.

It was clear that there was a right and wrong answer to this question. I quickly scanned my memory, and was surprised to realize that there'd been two sets in my childhood neighborhood, though both had been too much older to have been playmates. One, the girl in a pair of boy and girl twins, baby-sat for me. I'd adored her, but I'd always thought of her as just Margaret. I offered up the recollection—instinctively leaving out the fact that I'd never thought of Margaret as a twin. Brandt seemed slightly mollified.

I explained that I was writing a book about sibling loss, and that I might want to do a chapter on twins. Brandt approved of the idea of doing a separate chapter. Contrary to my assumption, he said, people don't "get" twin loss. He explained that twinship was the closest relationship possible, and that the loss of a twin was worse than any other loss. If you weren't a twin, you wouldn't understand.

This was a new wrinkle. I was used to the idea that the loss of a child was the worst loss, and that the loss of a sibling didn't measure up, grief-wise. This was the first time I'd encountered a hierarchy of loss within the realm of siblings.

There was more. Brandt told me that there are levels of loss within twinship, the basic rule of thumb being that the more alike you are, the closer you are, the greater the loss. According to this rule, identical twins, who are genetic copies of each other, suffer the most upon the death of their twin. Next in line are same-sex fraternal twins, who share no more genetic material than siblings born years apart, followed by opposite-sex fraternal twins. I wondered how the fraternal twins felt about this. But I knew that it wasn't wise to ask, at least not of Brandt. He was an identical twin.

• • •

Brandt invited me to attend his organization's annual meeting, which was being held in Fort Mitchell, Kentucky. After a long trip, I pulled up to the Drawbridge Inn, an ungainly building coated in cement stucco and dark brown beams, to make it indistinguishable from a medieval castle. It sat, like a castoff from Busch Gardens, in the V between two intersecting highways. I was feeling vulnerable and uncertain. Brandt's way of framing twin loss as the worst loss—worse, as he'd repeatedly explained to me, than any loss a singleton might feel—had rekindled feelings about the unworthiness of my loss.

The way Brandt kept emphasizing the word "singleton" made me feel as if I had a secret and embarrassing handicap that he felt compelled to announce to the world. In Brandt's eyes, I suspected I did. And there was something about the hierarchy the word implied that left me feeling even more invisible, less entitled to my own story than usual.

On my own turf, I was fine. But in this artificial kingdom in suburban Kentucky, I was confronting what I had faced for years, the message that my own loss was insignificant compared with others'. I was startled and unnerved by how fragile I felt.

"They called us the Zwillings," Brandt had said, when he told me his story. His parents were German immigrants. Zwillings (pronounced "Shwilling") was the German word for "twins." The Zwillings were Raymond and Robert, identical twins, born on May 29, 1929, the third and fourth of eleven children born to Edward and Wilhelmina Brandt in Defiance County, Ohio. "We always dressed alike. That's only natural when all you have to wear is bib overalls." The family had been very poor.

"But even later on when we went to high school and could have had mixed clothing, we never did. The only suit we ever had was identical. The only tie we ever had was identical. This was not intentional behavior on our part, it was just intrinsic to our life.

Our voices were alike. Our personalities were alike. We just never thought of being different. We were simply one person wearing two pairs of shoes."

They slept in the same bed. The elementary schools they attended were rural one-room schoolhouses, so they were never separated there, and even in high school, when they could have been separated, they weren't. (Brandt was adamantly opposed to the more modern practice of separating twins in school.) The only time they were apart was when they worked the fields of the family farm, and even then, he said, they retained an almost mystical mental connection.

"We'd come together in the evening after working and I would begin to say a brand-new thought to my twin, and halfway through he'd finish it. And our siblings would just be aghast. They thought we'd met behind the barn and planned it. But of course, we hadn't."

In the summer of 1949, when they were twenty, Raymond and Robert took jobs working as electrical linemen in Cincinnati. It was a high-risk job. They were often working with hot conductors carrying lethal loads of electricity. But it paid well and they needed the money to go to college. Robert wanted to be a Lutheran pastor. Raymond wanted to be a pediatrician.

On July fifth, they went to work like any other day. "We had always been on the same crew, but that particular morning, the foreman put us on different trucks," recalled Brandt. "At eleven o'clock, I was up on a power pole doing my thing, and all of a sudden I felt this tremendous jolt go through my body." It surprised him, he said, because he wasn't near any conductors at the time. Minutes later, he saw the foreman standing below him, motioning for him to come down. Raymond asked him why. The foreman wouldn't tell him. He motioned again. Raymond understood. "I said, 'My twin is dead, isn't he?'"

He was. Robert had been electrocuted—at exactly the time that Raymond had felt the surge of electricity in his body. Brandt believes that his connection with Robert was so close, he'd felt the jolt of electricity that killed him. In fact, he believed that he'd spared Robert by taking the pain for him. "I believe I spared my twin that tremendous, traumatic electric jolt."

One of their older brothers, who was also working at the Cincinnati job, climbed up and brought Robert down. "Then we packed up, my older brother and I, and drove up to northern Ohio. Our parents had been told by then and were waiting for us." It was at this point in the telling of his story that Brandt began to cry.

"It was extremely painful for me to leave Cincinnati," he explained haltingly, "because I knew that Robert's body was in a morgue. I felt like I was abandoning him. Every mile for two hundred miles, and in those days they were all country roads, I just kept beating on myself for not staying with my twin."

An undertaker who did all the German Lutheran burials went down and retrieved Robert's body and laid him out in a coffin in the parlor of their house. "I can remember one morning getting out of my side of the bed, and I went downstairs and I stood beside his coffin and I wanted to crawl into that coffin with him. I could not bear the thought of him being buried in the ground without me."

Raymond and Robert, who had, until this time, almost never been apart, who didn't know where one ended and the other began, were about to be separated forever. After the funeral, Brandt found himself in a state of deep shock and despair. And it never got any better. "I was eternally grieving. I wasn't noisy about it. I wasn't showy about it. But I was never happy."

It was here that Brandt's story became bitter. In the German Lutheran community, stoicism was the proper response to loss, a state of being Brandt was too distraught to muster. In response, some members of his family shunned him. Shunning was a German social custom used to express displeasure at unacceptable behavior. "It's still practiced by Amish people," he said. "What it means is that they wouldn't acknowledge my presence. It was like they had a dog in the house. It's basically saying, 'You may be with us, but we're not going to talk to you and we're not going to have any social dealings with you.'"

Worst of all, he said, years later, one of his siblings' children had been buried in the one remaining plot in the family cemetery, the one next to Robert. The one that Raymond had always understood would be for him. At the burial, when Raymond realized what had happened, his knees buckled, and his wife had had to help him out of the cemetery. "I told my wife, I don't want most of my family at my funeral. I'm not trying to get even," he said, "but why should they come and shed fake tears?"

Brandt was drafted into the Korean War shortly after Robert's death. He went willingly, halfway hoping to be killed, so that he could join Robert. He nearly was. During one battle, he found himself wounded, with his company in retreat. He remained behind, comforting a dying soldier on his lap, indifferent to his own survival. Brandt was captured and, in violation of the Geneva Convention rule that dictates that prisoners of war are to be removed from the front, put in a secret prison, where the captors passed the time terrorizing their prisoners.

"They were toying with us," he said. "Each day they would cut so many throats. It finally dawned on me that they were doing it in the order in which they'd captured us. I knew, at one point, that the next morning it was going to be me." That night, he said, his twin and Jesus—Brandt was a lifelong Christian—came to him and showed him how to escape. "I heard them say, 'Come with us.'" He did. He escaped, received a medical discharge, and was awarded two Purple Hearts. He escaped, he said, because though he wanted to join Robert, he didn't want Robert, whose presence he sensed, to endure watching him being murdered.

In his telling of his story, Brandt compressed the thirty-five years that followed into a two-minute summary. He got two Ph.D.'s in human engineering ("I was a workaholic"), married, had four sons, and divorced. He didn't have much to say about his first wife, other than that she had never recognized his twinship or understood the importance of Robert's death to him. He also believed that she resented his attachment to Robert. "It offended her," he said. "And I didn't talk about it, because I was trying to be a proper husband." (His second wife, Miriam, was much more solicitous about both his twinship and his loss.)

Relationships, he explained, can be difficult for twins, and for their partners. "When you're born with a twin," he said, "it's like being born with the love of your life." Spouses, he said, don't always appreciate being second. Many twins don't marry, he said. Instead, they live out the rest of their lives in the perfect partnership they were born within, a feature, he said, more common to identical twins than fraternal twins.

Brandt's story picks up in 1985, when, at the age of fifty-six, more than thirty years after Robert's death, he was "reborn" as a twin. "The International Twins Association came to Fort Wayne," he said. "I was recently divorced, and I felt I could finally be open about my twinship. I went in the back door of this Holiday Inn, where it was being held, and I saw hundreds of sets of twins."

A pair of male blond twins from Minnesota caught his eye. "I approached them and I said, 'Hi, I used to be a twin.' And they looked at me, stunned. See, I felt like I had to tell them why I was there because I was by myself and everyone else there had a twin. And so they said, 'What do you mean, you used to be a twin?' And I told them that my twin had been killed. And they said, 'When you are born a twin, you die a twin.' I was, in a sense, reborn."

Brandt had assumed that since his twin was dead, he'd been rendered—like the majority of the population—a singleton. But that automatic transformation had not occurred. From his earliest memory, his identity had been predicated upon Robert's. It was useless to pretend otherwise.

To erase his twinhood, to not acknowledge the part of him that had been shaped by being a twin to Robert, was to lose a vital part of himself. The realization that despite Robert's death he was still a twin, that he was still wired that way and that couldn't and wouldn't change, clarified his loss and his predicament: He had to let himself be who he was, a twin, but learn to function in the world as a singleton. "I tell people," he said, "that losing a twin is like learning to live life all over again as a single-birth person."

This was an enormous revelation in Brandt's life—he'd finally understood his loss and claimed the story his family had denied him. He immediately set about re-forming his identity as a twinless twin. Shortly after the twin meeting, Brandt formed Twinless Twins, an organization that, under Brandt's guidance, became part emergency hotline—Brandt was known to pick up the phone at any hour of the day or night—part support group, and part disseminator of Brandt's own theories on twins and twin loss. His membership grew astronomically after his appearance on a 1995 episode of the Maury Povich show. Almost every twin I interviewed found Brandt as a result of that program.

In forming Twinless Twins, Brandt had also found a way to "carry" Robert. His work with the organization was, by definition, an ongoing acknowledgment of the role Robert had played in his life. And Robert had wanted to be a pastor. In the twinless, Brandt had found a flock, although it consisted of people who needed saving of another kind. In addition to the notion "Once a twin, always a twin," Brandt preached the hierarchy of grief, that no one could understand a twin's loss, that others were jealous of twins, and that the loss would always be excruciatingly painful. He told his twins they would have to learn to live as singletons, that it was their duty to offer support to one another, and that surviving twins should live their lives to bring honor to their lost partners.

Brandt's peculiar mix of compassion, devotion, tendency to pass judgment, and miserliness when it came to other losses made me uneasy. His story, particularly his shunning by some members of the family, was horrifying. His passion for making something positive of his pain, and the time he devoted to helping bereft twins in crisis, was moving. He'd talked more than a few surviving twins through a bad night and several out of suicide. The ones that threatened suicide and were never heard from again haunted him.

He did all this despite three bouts of cancer, a heart condition, and, not surprisingly, an increasing level of physical fragility. He was an exceedingly generous and well-intentioned man. But his need for his loss to be the worst and his belief that all nontwins were jealous of twinship made me uncomfortable.

I wondered if his experience with his family, the horrible shunning, had colored his thinking. And I wondered if his presumptions about the feelings of nontwins didn't actually promote alienation within families and friendships, serving to further isolate grieving twins, rather than helping them to reach out and let others know how to reach out to them.

That first night at the Drawbridge Inn, I had a nightmare. There'd been a mistake. The person who'd had my room before, a foreign man with an accent, wasn't done with it. I heard him rattling his key in the door, coming in, standing by the bed, making noise with his suitcase. I was petrified. The man was angry. He wanted me out of his room, out of his bed. He was screaming in rage. I was Goldilocks, caught in bed. I wanted to scream, too, but I found that I couldn't make a noise. I was voiceless. I woke up in the murky darkness, half expecting to see the man still standing there. My heart was pounding. The screaming was a fading echo inside my head and chest.

I never went back to sleep. I was working on mustering up some sort of semi-clinical objectivity or cool professionalism with which to shield myself from the emotional assault I could sense coming. But it wasn't working. I knew that for me to make myself visible the next day, to keep myself from cowering in the back of the room, was going to take herculean effort. And the truth was, I didn't know if I was up to it.

I felt sick. A familiar stomachache, a gnawing knot, started to make its presence known. Over the years, starting with my brother's death, I'd suffered from chronic stomachaches. For one strange year, the year that I had begun graduate school and started working on my first sibling-loss project, I woke up every night at the time my brother had died, nauseated. I had had every unpleasant and expensive GI test known to man and received a handful of misguided diagnoses and an assortment of drugs, some of which had alarming side effects. None had worked, and eventually the nausea had ebbed away on its own.

I'd long since realized that my stomach was my canary in the coal mine. The aches were my body's way of acknowledging what my conscious mind was too habituated to register—that I was carrying unprocessed sorrow and anxiety. (I found this to be a common trait of surviving siblings.) The worst trigger was travel, which had mystified me until I realized that it was an echo of that day I'd been hustled off the plane to my brother's bedside. Rationally, I knew that my chances of being greeted upon landing with some horrifying shock were slim. But there was a part of me, apparently, that still braced for the unexpected. I've since realized that the travel doesn't even have to be literal. It can be metaphoric—a new situation, a new experience, a new emotion. Being aware of it has helped—I can neutralize the effect by learning something about my "destination."

Bleary and apprehensive, coffeeless, and with map in hand—the hotel was a maze, and its hallways had been given medieval names—I wound my way out to the registration table in front of Yeoman's Hall, the room where the conference was being held. A man stood behind the desk, overseeing the distribution of a box full of folders in a variety of colors, each containing the schedule of events.

"What color?" he said.

I sensed a loaded question. I looked at him blankly, my anxiety level rising a notch.

"What color?" he repeated in a kindly enough fashion.

"Any color," I responded, uneasily.

"You have to choose."

I looked at him, wondering if this was just his perverse way of amusing himself, but there wasn't a trace of guile in his face. In fact, he was all earnestness. Finally, it dawned on me. This was singleton training for bereft twins, a baby step toward making once dual decisions alone.

"Green," I finally said. The man smiled behind his mustache and handed me my folder.

I walked into the hall, a large room with fifteen rows of folding chairs arranged in three neat sections, facing a podium at the front. Cowardice overcame me. I sat down in the last chair of the last row in the left section, near the door, and busied myself with my packet. Inside, there was a schedule indicating that after a few opening comments, we would spend the morning "time-sharing" with Dr. Brandt, a phrase that conjured up an image of beachfront condos. I didn't know what it would entail, but whatever it was, it was lengthy. According to the schedule, we'd be at it from 9:45 to noon, with an hour-and-a-half break for lunch before starting up again from 1:30 to 4:30.

Other items inside the folder: Fund-raising information; a pamphlet entitled "Why Twin Loss Is Uniquely Different," with a quote from Dr. Brandt printed in italics on the cover that read, *"Twin loss is uniquely different from any other loss. Although single birth people don't fully comprehend it, they need to just accept it."* Also a letter from Dr. Brandt about one bereft twin who, despite Brandt's phone ministrations, had committed suicide. "Our team play," he wrote, "is to, in our darkest moment, reach out to another survivor twin. To touch another twin in a way that you wish to be embraced, loved, and cherished. For obvious reasons our family members are handicapped for they are of single birth, they cannot feel our pain."

I braved a look around. There were about fifteen people in the room. Some were seated, waiting. Others were milling around. Some looked happy, others pensive, still others hazy and unfocused.

To my left was a bulletin board upon which people were pinning snapshots of themselves with their twins in happier times, usually as toddlers. I glanced to the front of the room and immediately spotted the man who had to be Dr. Brandt standing in front of the podium. He had a face like a cherub, was perhaps even more diminutive than my five-three, and held himself, in his sober blue suit, with a certain erect dignity. He was hugging people who had lined up to greet him, like a mourner receiving condolences at a funeral.

I got in line. When I introduced myself, he was alternately welcoming and wary. He waved my outstretched hand away and hugged me—"Twins hug," he said—and he made a slight moue of dismay at my apparent youth. He held my hand while he talked to me, and told me he was going to introduce me to the group when he started speaking so that no unsuspecting twins would mistake me for one of their own and unwittingly unburden themselves. I nodded and told him I wouldn't speak to the twins unless they approached me first, thanked him for allowing me to come, and scuttled back to my seat.

Before long, the room was full. People were seated, gazing raptly at Brandt as he opened the session, introduced me, and passed the microphone he was holding to a pretty, slender woman in her thirties with short blonde hair and a tan. She took a deep breath and, in a ragged voice, told the story of her identical twin's death six years earlier. Her twin had gotten into her brand-new Jeep and, while driving on the highway on her way to work, tried to pass a truck. She didn't make it. The truck bounced the Jeep across the road, where it was hit by a car and another truck. She'd been killed instantly. This woman said she'd run around her house when she was told, grabbing pictures of her twin and throwing herself on her bed, where she'd hugged them to herself and cried.

She sat down and passed the microphone. And so it went, for more than two hours. One by one, bereft twins stood up and, in a span of five minutes or so, told the story of their twin's death.

Sometimes Brandt would jump in with a comment or words of comfort. Sometimes he would stand silently, patting their backs as they told their stories. One woman—women far outnumbered men in the group gathered in Yeoman's Hall—stood up and told an intriguing story. She'd been watching TV one afternoon, watching, in fact, Dr. Brandt on the Maury Povich show. The next thing she knew, her fiancé was coaxing her out from behind the couch, where he'd found her huddled in a trancelike state.

She was convinced she'd had a twin. Her parents told her it wasn't true, but even their assurances couldn't convince her she was wrong. Eventually, she'd tracked down her mother's medical records from her pregnancy, and, as it turned out, she'd been right. She'd had a twin brother who had died in utero, his body reabsorbed. Her mother's doctors had never told her parents, assuming, I suppose, that telling them could only bring unnecessary pain. You can see the reasoning: You can't mourn what you never knew you had. Only, in this case, apparently, they'd been wrong.

Her story, like Brandt's phantom sense of electrocution when his brother was killed, speaks to one of many quasi-mystical aspects of the twin relationship, this one in particular being the notion of in utero bonding, which presumes that the twin relationship begins before birth with each twin's innate sense of physical proximity to the other. In fact, several in utero studies have documented varying degrees of twins' awareness of each other before birth, from being quietly entwined to actively kicking, punching, stroking, embracing, and kissing each other, and even, in the case of identical twins, sucking each other's thumbs. Sometimes, the twins appeared to continue the dynamic they'd established in utero after their birth, as well.

And though this woman's remembrance of her twin's presence was unusual, twin pregnancies that result in single births are not. Charles E. Boklage, a geneticist at East Cardina University School of Medicine, estimates that for every set of twins born alive, there are at least six single-born people who are the sole survivor of a twin pregnancy. In fact, in as many as 55 percent of twin conceptions, one twin dies before birth, a phenomenon known as vanishing twin syndrome. In these cases, a genetic abnormality in one twin makes continued development impossible, usually during the first trimester. Or the physical burden of a multiple pregnancy on the mother causes her body to reduce the stress by aborting one fetus. That fetus is then reabsorbed by the mother's body.

Though it's an issue that has never been studied systematically, Brandt believed that these apparent singletons had shared the experience of in utero bonding, and could suffer from a loss they might have never, consciously, known they'd had, just like the woman who told her story at the conference. Twin researcher Nancy Segal, Ph.D., author of *Entwined Lives: Twins and What They Tell Us About Human Behavior* and a fraternal twin herself, writes that she has been approached by people who believe they started out life as a twin, but who lack medical proof. "Common threads to their stories," she writes, "have been lifelong feelings of depression and emptiness, and a sense that 'someone else is out there.'"

Parents of infant twinless twins, she writes, have approached her wondering whether certain traits, such as an excessive need for physical contact and an apparent tendency to search for someone, are signs that their child is suffering from the loss. But twins who were separated at birth and then reunited as adults don't report any of these feelings or sensations, said Segal. In fact, most are shocked to learn they have a twin. Nor, she said, do these twins show an elevated level of depression. Her conclusion, thus far, is that there's just not enough evidence to know the impact of losing a twin in utero.

By noon, when Brandt announced that we were breaking for lunch, all I wanted to do was bolt for my room. Listening to the stories had raised my own sadness over my brother's death. Before I could escape, I was approached by one of the twins, who asked me to lunch. In a normal emotional state, I would have said yes.

But I was barely keeping a grip on myself. I knew that I needed, desperately, to get away. I made a transparent excuse, watched her face fall, and heard Brandt's lecture echo in my head—about non-twins being comparatively ungenerous.

I slunk back to my room, feeling like a heel, and for the better part of the hour lay on the bed with tears running down my face. At one-thirty, I washed my face and went back to Yeoman's Hall. I sat in my seat and waited for the next half to begin. This time, I was hearing some stories for the second time around, because I'd interviewed several of these twins before coming to the conference. One of the people I'd spoken to was Linda, a tall, pretty woman with wavy blonde hair.

Linda and her identical twin, Paula, at twenty-one, had been in the midst of learning to separate and develop as individuals. It's a process that most twins, particularly identical twins, talk about going through at some stage of their lives. Then Paula died. Her death had left Linda without bearings. She no longer had Paula as a guide, someone to be different from. And because they weren't done separating, part of her, Linda said, had died with her sister.

This sounded to me like what I had heard in other sibling interviews—brothers and sisters serving as reference points. As children, said Linda, her and Paula's lives had revolved around each other. Together, they were a self-sufficient little unit. As toddlers, when they started talking, it was in a made-up language all their own. They shared friends. They shared life tasks. If one was good at one thing, explained Linda, the other didn't have to be. "We relied on each other," she said. "We had a shared approach to life." This, too, reminded me of what I'd heard in the other sibling interviews, the way that they distributed traits among themselves.

The fact that others saw Linda and Paula as a unit made it that much harder for them to differentiate themselves from each other. Growing up, they were always referred to as "the twins," just like Raymond and Robert. People couldn't tell them apart, yet couldn't resist labeling them. "One of us got labeled the happy-go-lucky twin, the other one the serious twin," Linda explained. Not only were they struggling to balance like and unlike between themselves, others were casting them in roles, as well.

In high school, they began to feel the need to stretch beyond their labels and their identity as twins. Each began to cultivate her own set of friends. When it came time to apply to college, it was understood that they would go their separate ways. "We never even talked about going to the same school," said Linda. "We needed to get away from one another." When she got to school, she said, "It was like, today, I became an untwin, a not-twin."

But being your own person is harder than it looks. And as the people at the conference said, twins who become twinless need to learn how to handle even some fundamental tasks that siblings learn earlier on—making decisions on such day-to-day tasks as ordering food at a restaurant. That's why twinless twins had to pick their own folder color at the conference.

Virtually every twin I spoke with also said that one had been dominant, the other more of a follower. It sounded like Frances Fuchs Schachter's deidentification theory—that siblings allot roles and tasks in such a way as to reduce friction with one another. Linda, who said she was the less dominant of the two, found it especially challenging. (In fact, there were an enormous number of less-dominants in the crowd at the conference, which underscored the fact that not only is twin loss very difficult to negotiate, but the loss of a dominant twin is, perhaps, even more difficult. I didn't have the opportunity to take a poll on who was the dominant and nondominant twin among the survivors at the conference, but it did make me wonder.)

"There's a lot with twins about who's the leader twin and who's not," said Linda. "And I was *not* the leader twin. I think I got married so early because I was looking to replace Paula." Linda was eighteen when she married for the first time. In retrospect, she said, she had been avoiding living life as an untwin. It had been too hard. She doesn't know if Paula felt the separation as acutely, because they never had the opportunity to go through the entire process and then look back on it together.

The first Thanksgiving after college, Paula decided to spend the holiday with friends in Key West. It would be the first holiday the twins had spent apart. Linda remembers sitting in the passenger seat of a car on Thanksgiving Day, driving down the highway and being overwhelmed by a claustrophobic panic and the urge to jump out of the car. Later she would discover that, at the same moment, Paula was strapped into a four-seater airplane plummeting into the ocean off the Florida Keys. A witness, standing on the back deck of a restaurant, saw the plane go down and verified the time.

I was struck by the similarity to Brandt's story of physically sensing what his twin was experiencing. I'd heard of similar experiences from a few other twins, too. It is yet another example of what seems like a mystical connection between twins, this ability to read each other's thoughts, and to sense pain and emotion that the other is feeling, often from thousands of miles away.

Only two bodies were recovered, one of them Paula's. Linda said she went into shock and stayed there for quite a while. "I moved away immediately afterward. I moved to Hawaii. I tried to move to paradise," she explained. Facing the extent of her loss was more than she could handle. She stayed in Hawaii for nine more years, barely acknowledging Paula's death to herself or anyone else. Then, her older brother, Peter, who'd been her enemy as a child— "he used to bench-press me to the ceiling"—and her protector and buddy as they'd become adults, was killed in a car accident.

She moved home to take over the family business, which her brother had been running. She moved into his house for a time. She even emulated some of his hard partying ways. She grieved, she said. Shortly after her brother's death, her mother and then her father were diagnosed with cancer and died within a year of each other. Their deaths brought her sister's death up anew, and this time Linda was ready to deal with it.

Ultimately, she took a year off from the business just to work on her grief. She'd remarried and had another child. She had a strong urge, she said, to fill the void left by her parents, twin, and brother. And she was doing pretty well. But passing by all those graves in the cemetery was often too much to bear. "Sometimes," she said, "there's really not much that helps the loneliness."

I watched and listened as Linda told the crowd the story of the plane crash, then sat down. And there were more. More than I could take in. We went way past the expected ending time. By six o'clock, we'd made it through everyone, and again, I was barely holding myself together. Brandt concluded the session and we all got up. I went to the bulletin board to look at the pictures, and to introduce myself to Linda, whom I'd only met by phone. She was on her way into Cincinnati for dinner with some others.

Linda invited me to join them, but I declined, pleading emotional exhaustion. Telling the truth this time, I said I was going to go collapse in my room. She nodded. For her, she said, the exhaustion of the emotions was checked, somewhat, by the happiness of being among twins again, if only even for a brief time. "It's my twin fix," she explained.

The next morning, I went to a lecture and a question-and-answer session with Betty Jean Case, a fraternal twin who was a friend of Dr. Brandt's and author of *Living Without Your Twin,* though she was not herself a bereft twin. As I sat in the audience, I heard both fraternal and identical twins voice the issues that their twin's life and death had left them with. They had always been compared, and their identities had often been based on opposing traits.

In this way they, like other siblings, had been interdependent in both visible and invisible ways. While talk of strained relations was only alluded to—in Brandt's view, to not get along with your twin was shameful—some spoke of not always liking what they saw reflected back at them via their twin. At least one twin at the conference was twinless because she and her twin were estranged.

Twins, it seemed, could mirror each other in both good ways and bad. Some spoke about the aching loneliness they'd been left with, the agony of knowing that no one would ever know them that well again. They talked about who each had been in the relationship, the strong one, the quiet one, the student, the athlete. Almost every twin, like every sibling I'd spoken to, referred to the shock of the impossible, the non-sense of the loss.

Twins assumed that, since they'd been born together, they would also die together. No one had felt prepared to handle this different reality. Many said they no longer felt like whole people— a more extreme expression of the amputated limb analogy I, as well as other siblings, had used. As in single-birth sibling-loss stories, comments like "She was my strength" and "He was my conscience" were common.

It reminded me of a line from the movie *Twin Falls, Idaho,* which was written and directed by Michael Polish, and featured him and his identical twin, Mark. In it, they play Blake and Francis Falls, Siamese twins, fused side by side. The question of separation looms over the movie. Francis's heart is failing; Blake's is essentially pumping for two. Only Blake will survive if they are separated. But if they aren't separated, Francis will die and take Blake with him. What is right?

The decision is taken out of their hands. They're separated and Francis dies. Blake survives, but he's left crippled, a metaphor for the psychological impairment after the death of a twin. It's an image that recalls one of Brandt's descriptions of life after the loss of a twin: You have to learn to live life all over again as a singleton. But the line that electrified me was the one delivered by Blake to explain his new state of being after his loss: "The story of me is over."

Twins don't always have a sense of "I" the way that those born alone do. For them, the "I" can be spread over two people. In one of his newsletters, Brandt printed one of his own poems, titled "HeMeWe: Identical Twins Can Be," which spoke to twins' different sense of self: "He is not me, nor is me he?/But yet it feels like we are me and he is we," he'd written. These are the kind of linguistic tongue twisters that bereft twins use all the time to try to understand what it is they're feeling.

Without words to describe the relationship, it is even harder to describe the loss. Language has largely been formed and used by those of single birth, to describe the experience of those of single birth. The only language we have that expresses coupledom relates to romantic attachments. We have no language for people who have defined themselves, from birth, in pairs.

At the conference and in my interviews, the twins, like many siblings, talked about trying to find another person with whom to form that same kind of bond, to share that closeness. They spoke of their disappointment that they never were able to find it. "Twins are used to sharing everything," explained Millie, a woman in her forties whose identical twin, Nellie, drowned when they were young. "I have always wanted to search for that very best friend." When she'd met her husband, she fell in love. "I loved his qualities," she said. "But he wasn't like my twin."

I asked her if that disappointed her. "I was always disappointed by it," she said matter-of-factly. "I still feel disappointed by it." Even the relationship with her daughter, who is named for Nellie, is different. She adores her husband and daughter. But there was simply no replacing the bond. Others who talked of seeking a replacement bond also talked of being disappointed and, on occasion, hurt when their overtures were rebuffed. Still others had a hard time recognizing boundaries, because they had always been so nakedly open with their twins. As a result, they'd end up feeling hurt and misunderstood.

I had intended to stay for the entire conference. That night there was to be a banquet dinner at the hotel to honor Brandt and the fiftieth anniversary of his twin's death—which was one reason this year's conference had been scheduled just outside Cincinnati, where Robert had died. The next morning, the conference was scheduled to end with a balloon release. Every twin would be given a helium balloon upon which to write a message to his or her twin. At the appointed time, they'd gather outside, let them go, and watch them float up to the sky.

I'd heard and seen more than enough. Listening to the stories had called up a lot of my own still-churning feelings about my brother. And I was in the worst possible place for that. Here, amid these bereft twins, the message was what it had always been—that my loss was lesser, that it didn't matter. And yet, it mattered to me. I couldn't face Brandt, so I took the cowardly route. I went to my room, changed my plane reservation, checked out, and left him a note thanking him for letting me attend. Then I climbed into my rental car and fled.

But I continued to interview twins. And of all the twins I spoke with, there was none whose story was more moving than Chloe's.

When I spoke with Chloe, she was living in Colorado but planning to move to Alaska to be a guide at a remote sports camp. Her father was a mountaineer and she'd grown up on a ranch, in Colorado, so she was comfortable in the rugged outdoors. Shortly after we spoke, she e-mailed me to say she was going to be visiting friends in New York City, and did not want to be interviewed on the phone. It would be the first time that she'd told her story, and she wanted to do it in person. At the time, I had no way of knowing what a big step that was for her.

We set up a time to meet, and on the appointed day she came to my apartment. I opened the door to a young, tan, blonde woman who looked like a cross between a model and an athlete, but more petite, and with a much softer edge than either of those comparisons implies. She had the kind of healthy outdoor glow that's rare in New York City, and my first thought when I saw her was that even in the crowded streets of the city, where locals struggle to stand out amid the varied population, she probably had. I made tea, and sat on the couch while she curled herself into an overstuffed chair, the tape recorder on an ottoman between us.

She spent a lot of time circling the subject—something that, in my experience, was unique to the way twins told their stories. While bereft siblings often started their story with the loss, bereft twins circled it, often making two or three approaches before finally bringing themselves to say the impossible, that their twin had died. Chloe had additional reasons to circle. The circumstances of her twin Josh's death four years earlier were still so murky in Chloe's mind—although ruled an apparent suicide, this was based on the account of only one person, whom Chloe had never met—and the shock of his death so profound, that it had taken her a long time to even admit that he was gone. There was no story yet for her to claim, only confusion.

She had a hard time saying words like "death" and "funeral." When she made reference to "my" birthday, later in the conversation, she pointed out that, for her, it was healthy that she could even say that word. It had always been *their* birthday. (Having birthdays alone was a tremendous source of pain and guilt for every surviving twin I interviewed.) "I lived every birthday for Josh," she said. "On April fourteenth, I always wrote 'Joshua's birthday' on my calendar, and we always raced to see who could call the other one first."

It was May 26, four years earlier, after their twenty-third birthday, that it happened. She had a two-week break between the end of the regular school term and summer school, so she set out on the eight-hour drive home to Colorado. "Halfway there, it started to snow. This is Colorado, in the end of May. In Colorado, it's always snow," she said. "I had Christmas music on," she said, laughing a little, "because there's nothing that makes me happier than Christmas music. And I was thinking, Life is so perfect. Wow. Could anything be better? And then I thought, I should be going to see Josh."

Josh was a bona fide cowboy, a drifter, the type who was born in the wrong century. He got up every morning before sunrise, played a game of chess with himself, turning the board around after every move, and was out riding by 5 A.M. He worked ranches all over the West, doing whatever work needed to be done. The places he lived were often so large and remote that there were no phones nearby or shelters to sleep in. The men who worked these ranches often spent the day on a horse and the night on a bedroll.

At the time, he was living in relatively comfortable circumstances in a one-room cabin in Arizona, fifty miles from the nearest town. Chloe had talked with him on the twenty-third. He'd mentioned a woman that was coming to see him, but he told Chloe it wasn't serious. Chloe thought the woman might be married, but she hadn't pressed him. She decided, as she drove, that she'd spend a few days with her parents and then drive down to see Josh.

She got home that night and had dinner with her mother. Her father lived two mountain passes away, on the other side of the family ranch. At ten-thirty, she found herself looking at the clock and saying she had to go. She visited with her father and his new wife, and then took the phone to bed, because she was waiting for a call from her boyfriend who "rodeo-ed" around the country. The phone rang at 2 A.M., and when she answered it she heard a woman's voice on the other end of the line.

"I couldn't understand her. I had no idea what she was saying. I thought maybe my father was cheating on his new wife, because here was this woman calling for him in the middle of the night, asking for him by his first name. I finally said, 'Who is this? Why are you calling so late?' And it was my mother. She'd been crying so hard I couldn't recognize her. And she said, 'Josh shot himself.'" Chloe said she started running, screaming for her father. "I was vomiting. I fell down, I couldn't get up. I just sat there screaming. And I knew. I knew he was gone."

She knew but she couldn't accept it. For the next week, she stayed in her room, refusing to eat or drink. "I sat on the floor the entire seven days. My dad would come in the room and I'd say,

'You're crazy. You're buying into this. Someone is trying to trick us.' I thought I needed to escape my family, because they were crazy."

At the funeral home, while her parents were making arrangements, she continued screaming, banging her fists against the table. "I told the lady who was trying to organize the music that everybody was crazy. And then she started talking about a hearse. And boy, I had never used foul language before, and suddenly, I was using it. I said, 'There is not going to be a hearse,' and a few other colorful words."

Her family made her view Josh's body. Her older brother and father half dragged, half carried her to the coffin, and when they got her there, she squeezed her eyes shut. Finally she looked. People had told her he would look peaceful. He didn't. "I had never seen him look more distraught in his entire life," she said. "And you have to take into consideration that it was a gunshot wound to the head, right here," she said, pointing between her eyes. "So, there was swelling. He didn't even look like himself. He looked like he was saying, 'I need you, Chloe.' That's all I could think. I could hear him screaming, 'Help me!'"

But the worst shock was yet to come. When the death certificate arrived, it said "apparent suicide." An accident would be one thing; a suicide, for a twin, was quite another. Chloe could not believe that Josh would do that to her. Like every other twin I spoke with, they had had a pact. "We would never have left each other. Never. We were brought into this world together, we always knew we were going to leave it together." When she saw "suicide" on the death certificate, she thought he'd broken his lifetime promise. "I can't tell you the feelings of being left behind," she said. "How could he choose to leave me?"

It soon turned out that the facts of the case were unclear, and dependent upon the woman Josh had mentioned to Chloe in their last conversation. According to the woman, she and Josh had driven into town and gone drinking. By the time they left the bar, they were both drunk. When they got back to the cabin, the key to the front door wouldn't work, and they had words. The woman claimed Josh hit her and then, upset with himself, broke into the cabin through a window and shot himself.

Chloe had a number of unanswered questions about the incident as reported by the woman, but she says the woman had disappeared. Chloe vacillated between thinking he killed himself, which made her feel angry and betrayed, and feeling certain that he would never take his life, which made her hungry for more information about what had happened. "To this day," she said, "I don't know what happened. There has been no closure. It just looms, day in and day out."

Meanwhile, Chloe has struggled to function in a world, she said, that has totally changed. At first, she couldn't leave the house. She had four or five people sleep around her in bed at night, because she was so overwhelmed to be without Josh in the world that to be alone scared her beyond all tolerance.

When she went back to school, she felt suicidal. Occasionally, when it got to be too much, she'd go sit on the railroad tracks and wait for a train. Her roommates always came to get her. After that, she, like Brandt and Linda, had tried blocking it out. "For a long time I tried to make myself believe that I never had a twin, that Joshua never existed, because that was my only way to cope. For me to cope," she said, "was not to cope."

On her first birthday without Josh, her friends tried to throw her a surprise birthday party, which enraged her. Chloe threw the cake on the floor. She asked her family and friends not to acknowledge the day in the future. She got busy with a teaching job, signed up for every activity at the school, and spent as little time as possible being idle. "I would get up before sunup and I would go all day until I was exhausted and fall into bed at night and fall straight to sleep, where I didn't have to think about it."

Her relationship with her older brother was never close and is not very good now. Long upset over the exclusiveness of Josh's and Chloe's relationship, she says he was angry rather than welcoming when she turned to him after Josh's death. When she lay sobbing on the floor after viewing Josh's body, she said, he looked down at her and said, "Look at you, you're acting like you don't have another brother." This was a side story within twin stories that I heard a lot. The surviving twins were often angry and hurt by their other siblings' behavior, which they saw as callous and cruel. The other siblings sounded as if they'd long harbored anger over being left out of the twins' relationship.

The worst thing for Chloe was the identity crisis. She didn't recognize herself anymore. When Josh was alive, she felt like a sweet and caring person. A bubbly person. The student in the family. A happy spirit. "I look back at the letters people used to write me when I was in grade school and even into high school, and the things people wrote in my yearbooks. And it was always 'your radiant smile, your soft, tender spirit . . .'" She pauses. "And now I just feel like this wicked thing. This evil, cynical, negative, mean thing."

In fact, she did seem friendly and sensitive, but she was unable to see that. "When you're somebody's hero, and when you have a hero, and they're gone, what do you do?" she said. "I don't have a hero anymore. He was my self-esteem. Most people grow up and they have that self-esteem on their own, but I think my self-esteem came from him." She was slowly, shakily, trying to develop some of her own.

While she says she wants to heal, it's hard to feel like she is leaving Josh behind. Her life now is not the life she expected. With Josh gone, she has tried to keep alive all the things that mark his existence, and his dreams. "I kind of feel like I have to live for two of us now. I try to keep in touch with all of his friends. I was going to take his music—I have all his poetry and songs written out—and I was going to take them to this big national cowboy poets thing. All the stuff he wanted to do."

And though she is scared of what is in front of her, she said she has reasons for trudging forward. Josh has a son. "I try to get him to ride and do all those things as much as I can, because his dad's not here to do it with him. So, that's hard. And it's funny," she said, "little Bowdry started calling me 'Dad' this year. And I said, 'Why are you calling me 'Dad'? You call me Aunt Chloe. You've always called me Aunt Chloe.' And he said, 'Well, Aunt Chloe, I already have a mom and you look just like my dad, so you might as well be my dad.' And that's a huge honor," she said, starting to cry. "But it's hard, too. I was supposed to get to be the aunt."

Alaska is going to be hard, she said, because she's going to have to think about what happened, and she's going to have the time to think about it. "I know that I have to do it, or I'm never going to heal. It's so hard." She wants to heal, but she doesn't want to be without Josh. It is an impossible equation. In fact, it is Quentin Compson's dilemma all over again. The Alaska opportunity had come about, she explained, because once, a couple of years ago, she saw a twin magazine with a picture on the cover of twins on top of Mount McKinley. "Usually, I wouldn't even look at them," she said of the magazines. "When they'd come, I would just pitch them, chuck them right in the trash. I didn't want anything to do with them." The sight of twins who still had each other was too painful.

But this one showed twins in the outdoors. "I thought, Okay, this one I can relate to," she said. It was the story of identical twin brothers, Mike and Marty Phelpps, who'd led their mother, who was blind, to the top of McKinley, in the first-ever ascent of that mountain by a blind person. But what had really held her attention was a twist in the story of these twins. The article was a letter from Mike to Marty, and it was the story of their twinship. It was a memorial of sorts. Several years earlier, the brothers had gone hunting sheep in the Rangal Mountains in Alaska, and only one had returned.

"They'd been dropped off at Bernard Glacier, and the plane wasn't supposed to come back for ten days to pick them up," said

Chloe. "On the morning of day two, there was a huge avalanche.
They were standing fifteen feet apart, and the whole mountain
just collapsed and buried them both." Mike clawed his way out,
assuming Marty was doing the same. But when he got out, there
was no sign of Marty. "Mike went through hell, knowing he had
to leave Marty because he knew he had to get help," said Chloe. It
took him forty-eight hours to attract the attention of a bush plane,
which flew him to a remote lodge. To this day, Marty's body hasn't
been found.

There was something about the desperate loneliness of Mike's
story that spoke to her. Chloe called Information and got his
number, and Mike became her confidante, the only one who
understood her, "the only one I would let understand me." And it
was Mike who'd hooked her up with the lodge she would be
working at in Alaska, the same lodge he'd been flown to after the
avalanche. She wanted to be out in the wilderness, to try to cope
with Josh's death and to create the person she would need to be in
the future in order to make living without Josh okay.

Last year was the first time she celebrated her birthday since
Josh died. She'd gone to visit Mike and his family, planning to
ignore the day, as she had done every year since Josh's death. But
Mike had forced her to sit and open presents. She cried so hard
she couldn't see. She had eaten some of the cake, but wanted to
throw up. She knew what she was doing was healthy but she hated
it. "I said, 'Mike, how could you do this to me?' And he said,
'Because I'm the only one who *can* do this to you.'"

On her trip to Mike's, she had two identical daisies tattooed on
her ankle. She lifted her leg and lowered her sock for me to see.
(Twins, especially bereft twins, seem drawn to anything in twos.
Linda told me she'd made a scrapbook of her life with Paula, just
for herself, and gone mad with little rubber stamps, which she'd
inked up and used decoratively, always in twos, all the way
through it.) "He always gave me daisies. It was our birthday-
month flower, and they grew all over where we grew up," said

Chloe. "And Alaska is full of fields and fields of daisies." In Alaska, she said, she wants to learn to breathe again. "Just breathe."

Brandt, who had long suffered from cancer and heart trouble, died in June 2001, almost two years after I met him. He was buried, far from Robert, in Arlington National Cemetery in Arlington, Virginia, on July 5, the fifty-second anniversary of Robert's death. Another twinless twin took over running the organization. Brandt's second wife, Miriam, told the members of Twinless Twins that his involvement in their lives and in their healing had brought him both joy and solace. Brandt was a profoundly religious man, and had always felt that we met those who had "passed" when we died ourselves. When I heard the news of his death, all I could think was, I hope he got to see Robert.

In the end, I decided that Brandt was partly right. The issues a twin had to face when his or her other half died sounded very much like what I'd experienced and what I'd heard from other siblings. But they were often more intense versions of issues us singletons had to tackle, and potentially more disabling. To me it seemed that, although twins might look like separate people, they really do overlap. Siblings overlap, too, but there's more range in how much. With twins, it sounded as if the overlap could be almost complete.

To be rendered a singleton by the death of the other was not to be immediately reborn as a single-birth person, but to be cleaved in two. To outsiders, twins were perceived as a unit. They'd lost both their inner and outer identities as a twin in the world. It was as if they'd suddenly found themselves in disguise.

And since they were used to being completely, often wordlessly, understood by their twin, they were often baffled when others didn't understand what they were going through. The strained relationship between other siblings sounded more like pain—perhaps years' worth of pain at having been excluded from the twins' relationship, kept at a distance—than jealousy.

• • •

My sojourn into the world of twinless twins at the conference stayed with me, although it took me a while to recognize why I'd been so disturbed. It was how I'd felt. It seemed to me as if I had started to vanish as soon as I arrived. I'd been put on notice that my loss was lesser.

What finally struck me was this: While Brandt had been confident that I could not understand twin loss and had preached this logic to his members, he did not see that he could not understand my loss. As someone who had, from his earliest hours, been a twin, he could not understand my experience as a single-birth person, in a relationship with a nontwin sibling who had been the center of my world.

The simple truth might be to say that every loss is unique. When it comes to our societal understanding of grief, the important question is not whose loss is the worst but what does this loss, your loss, mean to you? The truth is, the worst loss is the one that is happening to you, the one that has picked you up and thrown you down and left you struggling to put your life back together.

Why have we gotten so sidetracked by wondering whose loss is worst? Perhaps it's human nature to want or need our experience to be bigger or better or worse than someone else's. Whatever it is, there is something wrong with it. It only serves to alienate people from one another when they need one another most. And here was where a painful revelation came to me: I'd done it, too. In my self-absorption and anger at my parents for not seeing my loss, I had failed to appreciate theirs. It has been twenty-three years since my brother's death. In that time, my mother, my father, and I had all quietly harbored our own secret pain, separated by the same event that united and defined us.

Chapter Eight

RETURN

"... it's a compound, or multiple,
love story, pure and complicated."
—Buddy Glass, introducing his family story in
FRANNY AND ZOOEY, BY J. D. SALINGER

My parents made this easy. It was they who had set the shroud of
silence on the subject of my brother. They never talked about what
had happened. And they would talk about Ted only on rare occasions, when I was alone with one of them. None of us brought up
my brother when the three of us were together. I didn't even know
if they would talk to me for the book. My mother, at first, greeted
my request with an emphatic *"No!"* Then she relented and said she
would talk to me if I didn't quote her directly. She said she considered what happened to my brother a private matter, and that she
didn't like to air things. It wasn't her way.

There were complications on my end in getting together,
which my mother seemed happy to accommodate. We could do it
later, she said cheerily. Finally I realized that I would need to interview her by phone. When I called her and asked if we could talk

then, she sounded cornered. Frightened. Faint of voice. But she agreed. I explained that because I'd been a child when my brother died, I'd never understood the story from an adult point of view. I wanted to know what happened.

It was interesting, hearing her try to find a way to tell it. She sounded like the version of me who had struggled to type the word "I" and go on. Finally, she began with the night of the bruises. She told me, again, of my brother sitting at the dinner table when she commented on them. Although this time, she said that my father had brought him into the hospital that night, not the next day. It was clear, she said, that something was very wrong. This, according to my brother's records, was September 6, 1972.

The next day, my father met her at the entrance to the hospital. As she walked in he said, "It's aplastic anemia." She almost fell to her knees. She'd known about the disease already; my uncle had once called our house in the middle of a dinner party to ask about a friend's child who'd been diagnosed with it. Then, hearing my father explain the disease had sent only a small chill up her spine. Thank God. Not her child. And then here he was, my father, saying yes, her child. Her whole life, she started to say . . . and then she stopped and corrected herself. *Our* whole life had changed over dinner.

They brought him home two days later. They were going to try to treat him as an outpatient. They were hoping he wouldn't get infected and that he might spontaneously recover, as some people with this disease do. We went out for Chinese food that night, because that's what Ted wanted after his ordeal. It was September 8.

Sometime in the next week, the doctors tested me to see if my bone marrow matched Ted's. My mother told me I hadn't thought much of that. Ted, she said, was very supportive. He comforted me. I had remembered this scene, in a foggy way, but I'd never been sure if it had really happened. What I remember is feeling attacked by adults, while my brother, one of my own kind, had stood by my right side, telling me that it would be okay. Her retelling evoked the physical sense of him standing by my side again.

He started school. His hemoglobin count was low, and he was tired a lot. My mother couldn't remember how much time elapsed between his diagnosis and the next crisis, but I'd read the records. I knew the next one had come on the evening of September 13.

We were sitting in the family room watching TV when Ted said he felt warm. The thermometer confirmed the fever. A neighbor was called to watch me, apparently after I'd gone to bed, and my parents hustled him into the hospital. The decision was made to put him in The Room. In his medical chart from that evening, there is a page with a six-step plan:

1.) Laminar airflow room but without antibiotics
2.) Complete bacteriological work-up (virus, fungal, bacterial)
3.) Chest X-ray
4.) Routine blood work—daily counts
5.) Consider transfusion of platelets and packed red blood cells, when indicated
6.) Skin care to areas of eczema

What it didn't say was step number seven: Wait and hope. For how long, no one knew. The technology behind these rooms was in its infancy. They'd been used to protect leukemia patients from infection while they were undergoing chemotherapy, which could temporarily decimate their immune systems. No one had ever lived in one for longer than a few months. No one whose immune system wouldn't automatically rebound on its own had been harbored there.

Would this be the beginning of a new way to approach aplastic anemia? Nobody knew. It was an experiment, putting Ted in there. A gamble. A way to buy my brother some time. Ted hoped he'd be out for his tenth birthday, a little more than two weeks after he went in, my mother said. Both of us started to cry at the surety of his disappointment. How could he have known that he would spend eight and a half years there, that at the time of his death, he would set the record?

They were open with him, my mother said. He was far too smart not to be. They explained that The Room was to protect him from infection until his bone marrow recovered. But they didn't tell him everything—that he might die if he wasn't in The Room, and that he might die anyway. She cried when she remembered one night, soon after Ted entered The Room, when this had been revealed to him. Ted's doctor had been trying to start an IV on him. My brother was being difficult. To enlist his cooperation, the doctor said that if he didn't get the IV, he might die. At this point in the story, my mother gave voice to what had become a refrain—a horrified, painful refrain—in my own head: He was just a little boy. When I was a child, my brother had seemed big and all-powerful to me. The combined horror of his youth and his illness hadn't registered. It's only now that I can see him as a little boy in extraordinary circumstances. It is an unexpected and new grief.

The first year had been very hard. In my brother's medical notes, I saw a repeated entry entitled "Room adjustment." When I'd first seen it, I thought it meant they'd had to tinker with The Room to get it working just right. When I looked back, I realized that they were referring to my brother's psychological adjustment to The Room. In these notes, he is alternatively hostile, angry, and cheery. My mother remembered the tantrums. The time he'd thrown everything out of The Room. Like what? I'd asked. *Everything,* she'd answered. There was another story about a very bad day in which he was supposed to get a transfusion of platelets. He did not want another IV. He was screaming. Yelling. At one point he'd even pulled his mattress on top of himself.

My mother had left the room to sit in the waiting room. While she sat, the elevator doors had opened and disgorged two women. One was the woman who ran the platelet lab. The other was the one who'd just donated platelets for Ted, aglow with her good deed. She wanted to meet him. My mother just stared. Horrified. *No way,* she'd thought. The woman who'd made the donation was tactfully steered away. The woman who ran the platelet lab never tried to introduce a donor to a recipient again.

There were other incidents. The one for which he was famous had to do with the pills—several medicine cups full, three times a day. He hated them. He didn't want to take them. It was a daily source of strife with the nurses and doctors. His medical charts record the creative tactics he used to delay the inevitable, like refusing to take them without a particular brand of soda that the nurses' station didn't have. One day, he seemed to turn a corner. The pills, all of them, began disappearing every day. This went on for quite a while, and everyone was pleased with his progress. Then, my mother said, something went wrong with The Room and repairmen had to open up the wall. When they did, thousands of pills came spilling out. My brother had carved a hole in the wall, into which he'd been depositing his pills for weeks.

My impression, all these years, had been that my brother was fine, except for his faulty immune system, and that the crisis had been of a low-grade variety. We were just waiting for him to recover. That wasn't right, my mother said. There had been constant life-threatening crises. He had many infections. He got one from someone who'd served his food. I had skipped by the blood counts and the temperature readings. But when I looked again, I saw that he had had skin infections, an ulcer in his mouth, fevers and sore throats. When things went bad, they went bad very quickly, my mother said, sounding shaky at the memory of them. And bad always meant *very* bad.

At first, she thought he might be out in a year. When it became apparent to her that this wasn't going to happen, she focused on figuring out how to make the family work, given the situation. She tried not to have expectations, to live day to day. She tried to make life as good as possible for Ted, and for me, because it was the only way we were going to survive. She was determined not to let us down. Her philosophy was, when you have bad things to deal with, you have a choice about how you're going to deal with them. When Ted had been diagnosed, all she could think about was every mean thing she'd said to him. The guilt had been horrible. She decided she was never again going to do anything with regard to him that she would have regrets about.

She covered the institutional-looking mini-refrigerator in the nonsterile half of the room with contact paper. She put posters and pictures on the wall near the entrance to Ted's half. Because no one had ever lived in these rooms for very long, no one had paid any attention to what it might be like to eat only autoclaved hospital food—food heated to high temperatures to kill all the bacteria in it. Most foods turned to mush under these conditions. The doctor in charge of the department that oversaw my brother's care thought it should stay that way. My mother pressed for experimentation.

She started cooking my brother's favorite foods and bringing them to the ladies who prepared his food in the hospital. They would send a sample off to the lab for testing and freeze the rest. If it came back clean, he could have it. Using this approach, even with prepackaged foods, my mother made sure that Ted had the foods he liked—meat loaf, pepper steak, tuna fish, mayonnaise, meatballs, Pringles potato chips, Tropicana orange juice in little glass bottles, cereal, oranges and grapefruit (because they had a thick rind that protected the fruit from bacteria), Chinese food made by one of the doctor's wives and the rich chocolate cake that was the specialty of another.

My mother made steaks for Ted on a little portable grill. We had had dinner parties, didn't I remember? I hadn't, not until now. Once my mother started talking, I did start to remember some things. I remembered taking the mayonnaise jar out of the refrigerator and opening it carefully at the entrance to his side of the room. He stood just on the other side of the line, dipping a knife into it. I remember this because I loathe mayonnaise and he loved it. Because he never wasted an opportunity to tease me, he used to wave the glop on the knife under my nose before drawing it back inside.

One of the horrors of my brother's situation had been the loss of human touch. No one touched him, as far as I knew, except to start an IV or draw blood, and then with gloves. There were other things that were hard to hear about, like the one time that my father's parents had come down from New York to see Ted. My grandmother was obese. She had a hard time moving around in her apartment, much less out in the world. It had been a big deal to figure out a form of transport with which she'd feel comfortable. The train had been the best option. I remembered going to pick them up. What I hadn't remembered was that my grandmother wouldn't come into the hospital, even though Ted knew she was there. She had decided she couldn't bear to see him that way. Nor did they ever speak on the phone. My brother had withdrawn from her after that, my mother said.

My mother's mother visited, but she was such an eccentric that her visits were a different proposition entirely. She was an aging Southern belle with flaxen hair that she had twisted into a French knot and fastened with an ornate clip at the beauty parlor once a week. She favored flowing dresses that exposed her cleavage or tight pants and tight girdles that gave her the shape of an oil drum. She was, in short, a character, and my brother and I had long since made a game out of luring her into committing amusing acts of eccentricity. Once, my parents went to Europe for a week—their only vacation alone in my memory after Ted got sick—and she came to stay with me and look after Ted. Upon my parents' return, Ted told my mother that he felt sorry for me and he was glad he was in The Room.

The entire conversation with my mother was like this, full of

memories that were so unbearably sad that they left me feeling
seared, and things that were funny or evoked my brother so clearly
that it took my breath away. She told me they talked all the time.
He planned on having a future. He worried how all of this was
going to affect me. He had not started off as a sensitive boy, but he
had become one. And how all the young, scared people on the
ward, patients and children and siblings, gravitated to his room to
talk and hang out. They visited during the day, when I was in
school. He became everything she hoped he would be. She told
me, with great difficulty, about a note she received, after Ted died,
from one of the nurses. The nurse had been on duty during a big
snowstorm. That morning, she walked into my brother's room
and said, "Oh, well, it looks like your mother won't be coming in
today." My brother had turned to her and said, "My mother
always comes in."

My mother said she had not been a strong person, but that she
had learned to be one. She told me, with great pain, that she knew
that she had spent a lot of time on Ted, but that she had tried to do
things for me, like volunteer to be one of the parents on class trips.
It was only then that I realized another aspect of how painful the
idea of my writing this book must have been for her. It would be
a public acknowledgment that my brother had been right to
worry, that I had not been okay. And there was nothing she could
do about it now. This was a new grief to add to the old one,
another loss. A regret she had not anticipated. Hearing about how
Ted's illness had transformed her and given her life a purpose that
occupied almost her every waking moment, I realized the magni-
tude of the chasm that had opened up in her life upon his death.
What else in her life would matter as much as saving her son?

When I told her I felt that by not talking about him, we'd
erased him, she was shocked. She hadn't forgotten him, she said.
She thought of him every day. He was always with her. And
though my father found it too painful to have pictures out, she
had managed to display one, a family portrait taken not long

before Ted's diagnosis, in the foyer of the house, and another, a baby picture of Ted, up in the bedroom. The other pictures she keeps in the upstairs studio, where she paints. It had not occurred to her that she kept him quietly, to herself, and that I did not have the memories she did.

Nobody could understand him, she said. Nobody could understand that she was not mythologizing him when she spoke of him. He *had* been larger-than-life. When she said this, I realized my predicament as a child. My brother had had a real-life obstacle with which to struggle. My parents had had their son to take care of. My struggle had been invisible.

In my mother's view, her toughness, her silence, her strength in holding back the tidal wave of sadness, is the way she pays homage to my brother and his life. That was what I had grown up believing, too. But it hadn't worked for me, and I'd never realized there was any other way to be. I needed the opposite solution. Where my mother was compelled to silence, I was compelled to articulate. Where my mother was driven to stash away memories like treasures in secret drawers, I was drawn to rifle through those drawers. Only, in many cases, the treasures had belonged to her. Until now. She wanted to help, she said. She just wasn't sure what I needed.

I told her that I liked the stories of Ted being bad the best, because they gave me such a strong sense of his presence. They revealed him at his most amusing and quirky. The Ted who rigged an electric game to ring a fire alarm that terrorized the nurses on the floor. And the Ted who persuaded one of his friends to tape a balloon on the back of his door and affix a razor blade to the back of a chair that sat behind the door, at approximately balloon height. The idea was that whoever stepped into the room would jump out of his skin when he heard the pop.

In addition to the many other roles he'd played in my life, Ted had always been a big, taunting pain, a walking, talking punch in the arm. A big brother, really. He'd been ready to gleefully stick a metaphorical pin in me anytime the opportunity arose. And the funny thing was that I had loved him for it, and I love him for it still. These stories brought him back. They were my version of family heirlooms. My mother said that it was his toughness that had helped him survive. She told me that she would probably remember more of those stories, and that she would tell me when she did.

Later, after we'd hung up and I had transcribed the tape of our conversation, I discovered something. Almost all of my sentences, whether they were questions or responses, began with the words "I remember . . ."

I had thought my father would be the difficult one. When my mother would mention Ted's name, he never responded. On the rare occasions in which he had alluded to my brother's illness or death, our conversations had lasted perhaps five minutes. But he surprised me. When I asked him if I could interview him, he said it would be painful, but yes, he would talk to me if I thought it would help.

We set up a time to meet at one of his favorite restaurants in New York City. I beat him there, and I saw him walk in. My father does not move like an unsure man. He has the air of someone who knows he's important. In his thirties, at a time when most oncologists considered the idea of treating patients with drugs tantamount to poisoning, my father and a handful of others had designed a chemotherapy regimen that had proved to be the first drug cure for an adult cancer, Hodgkin's disease. This regimen was the platform from which future regimens for other cancers would spring. Though he claims to be as self-doubting as the next person, you'd never know it to look at him. But when he walked into the restaurant that night, his self-assurance seemed subdued. He, like my mother, seemed resigned.

We said hello, sat down, and ordered, and I fiddled with the tape recorder. He asked me what I wanted to know. I told him what I had told my mother—that I wanted the adult story of what had happened, the story that the medical records could not tell. He looked at me warily. Then he picked up the tape recorder and, because the restaurant was noisy, held it close to his mouth and began to talk.

He told me, in the course of this conversation, that I'd "really opened up a can of worms" when I'd decided to write about Ted's death. It was, as we both knew, an understatement. There had been times when I was interviewing siblings and searching for my own answers that my parents and I had not been speaking to one another. Neither had said it was because I had pried open the lid of a box that he or she had preferred to keep sealed. The superficial explanation was their displeasure that I was seeing a man who was in the midst of a divorce, the same person who so reminded me of Ted. We finally tired of the stalemate. But not before a lot of ugliness had passed between us. When I asked them each if I could interview them, it had been only five months since we'd begun speaking again.

One of the sibling experts I interviewed had once told me how struck she'd been by the fact that parents tended to be very future-oriented with regard to their children. I thought about this once, when, in conversation with my mother, I'd offended her by saying, "Who knew where Ted would have gone to college?" She was sure that he would have gone to William and Mary, where she and my father and I had gone. Unlike me, she had a clear picture of the future my brother would have had, and of what she had lost. One of the tensions left among survivors is that each must build and maintain a truth that he or she can live with, while taking care not to upset someone else's. My probing, I think, had upset my parents' grip on their own stories.

My father remembered the beginning only slightly differently from my mother. In his memory, my brother was in the living room when he first saw the bruises. "I knew right away that it was one of a couple of things. You don't get big bruises all over your body unless you've lost platelets or you have a bleeding disorder

like hemophilia, which he didn't have." He thought it was probably either leukemia or aplastic anemia. "We knew the diagnosis
that night," he said.

How was this awful irony possible? How could the child of a
man who has cured so many other people's children come down
with a rare and lethal blood disorder for which there is little or no
treatment? "We looked for everything," he said. "The dog had
been sick recently; maybe they'd both been exposed to something.
The bird had died. Was there a connection?" His particular nightmare was that, on a family vacation shortly before that September,
my brother had come down with bronchitis and he'd prescribed
an antibiotic for him. One of the potential triggers for aplastic anemia is an antibiotic. It wasn't the antibiotic my father had prescribed. But that hadn't made him feel any better.

"There was a lot of guilt in that for me," he said. "Everyone
spent a lot of time trying to make me appreciate that tetracycline
doesn't cause aplastic anemia. But I worried about it. We never did
figure out what caused it," he said wearily. "And in the end, it didn't
really make any difference. Because knowing what caused it really
didn't help. All we knew was that a certain percentage of people got
better, and a certain percentage didn't. Generally, the more you
know the better. But the real question," he said, "was what was
going to help him? And the answer, at that point, was not much."

Aplastic anemia can be mild to severe. My brother's case was
very severe. Somehow, his bone marrow had been extensively
damaged. There wasn't much to do for it in 1972. Some patients
had recovered after taking androgen hormones. But some patients
recovered on their own, so who was to say what worked? Bone
marrow transplants were in their infancy then. Even when there
was a match, my father remembered, patients bodies on my
brother's ward had rejected the transplants, and their skin had literally fallen off them. Though they had asked me to see if I was a
match, he and my mother had ultimately both agreed they
wouldn't do that to Ted.

And there had been no time to try. Ted's blood counts were severely depressed. He wasn't going to make it on the outside. The doctor who saw my brother suggested putting him in the laminar airflow room to give him a chance to recover. They had had no choice, my father said. It was put him in the room, or let him die. "I think it was a good decision, in the sense that he lived for eight years where he might otherwise not have lived. We gave him whatever chance there was."

My father's burden was twofold: knowing what could go wrong and how hairy the situation really was, and being the chief of the department in which my brother was hospitalized, thereby making him boss and parent. "That was always my dilemma," he said. "It was always hard to separate myself from that." During the time of Ted's illness, in fact, there had been a couple of controversies.

Once, a disgruntled physician who hadn't gotten the promotion she'd wanted had talked to a journalist about how my brother was getting preferential care because of who his father was. It made for a week or so of scandal in the Washington papers. An article in *Science* helped clarify matters. The people at NIH were part of a community, wrote the author, and everyone was working to help this little boy survive his hideous situation. Everyone who read it had understood. There was an investigation. It concluded that my brother wasn't getting preferential care. Among other things, he was the only one with this illness ever to be confined indefinitely to a laminar airflow room. No one was even sure, yet, how much it might help. There was no case to compare it with. But the scandal had been hellish, nonetheless. "It was hard enough without having to go through all of that," my father said.

He said he thinks about my brother every day. He feels guilty about the things that Ted had wanted to do with him and that he had never done. As one of my friends with teenagers said, "You think there is time to do everything later, and then they grow up and they're on to their own lives. You have much less time than you realize." In my father's case, that time had been cut in half, at least with things they had wanted to do outside The Room. He wouldn't tell me what they were. He looked down at his plate and told me that if he did, he would cry.

My father had been surrounded by people who knew his story. One NIH scientist I'd spoken with said my brother's illness, and the irony of it happening to my father, was the stuff of legend in the medical community. I had also been to events where doctors who'd trained at NIH under my father had told me that they used to draw blood from my brother. "You can imagine the interesting sociology of the situation," one well-known breast cancer expert told me. It had been intimidating enough to work on the boss's son. It had been doubling intimidating to work on Ted, who, as my mother was prone to say, "put people through their paces."

My father was oblivious to the stories that followed him. I told him a few, including the one about the breast cancer expert. He was shocked. He knew that doctor well, had for decades. And yet my father did not know he'd met my brother. But the man hadn't hesitated to tell me, when I'd met him and the book had come up in conversation. My father realized he'd encountered Ted's history in small ways—having a question sprung on him while being interviewed on TV on another topic, for instance, and in newspaper interviews.

He, like my mother, remembered a constant state of crisis, including one time in which my brother had developed gangrene on his arm. "We all hoped he'd get better. We all prayed he'd get better. There were times when his counts would improve and it would look like, 'Oh my God . . .' and then they would drift down again. He had a very damaged marrow . . . ," he said, his voice trailing off.

When he read the first article I wrote about my brother's death, he said he had been taken aback. "I was really quite shocked that you actually had thoughts like that. Because we tried to keep you from getting too anxious about what was happening. I don't ever remember talking to you about what might be happening to him.

We just didn't tell you a lot. We wanted you to be happy and encouraged that he was going to get better.

"It was another life," he said. "We had to figure out how to make it work with him being in that room. Your mother had to figure out how to be a mother. We miscalculated with you, I think. We just assumed that if we didn't tell you anything, that that was best. You were only six years old."

My father carried another unique burden: As a scientist, he couldn't hide from the gradual evolution of technology that could have saved my brother if it had come in time. It was aplastic anemia that first gave scientists the inspiration for bone marrow transplants back in the 1960s. The disease appeared to be straightforward—some sort of technical failure that resulted in the obliteration of bone marrow. Scientists reasoned that they could solve the problem by simply transplanting marrow from a healthy donor to a sick one. They tried it with a pair of identical twins—the ideal match—but it didn't work. The patient's immune system rejected the marrow.

The next leap was to try to head off the response of the immune systems before the patients received the transplant. Doctors tried radiation, which was expensive and impractical back then. They tried immunosuppressive drugs. It wasn't long before they realized that patients' blood counts improved during the drug phase prior to the transplant. And this led to a revelation—the lack of bone marrow in these patients was, at least in part, due to the fact that the marrow was being actively destroyed by T lymphocytes, the pit bulls of the immune system, whose job it is to attack foreign pathogens. While T lymphocytes originate from the marrow, too, they live longer than the types of cells they're attacking—up to ten years—so they're abundant even when the marrow gets depleted.

In the eighties, a reasonably successful drug combination had emerged—cyclophosphamide and another chemotherapy drug called ATG. Together, they could improve patients' blood counts by 60 to 80 percent. It was far from a cure. A perfectly matched bone marrow transplant paired with immunosuppressive drugs was still the ideal option. But 70 percent of patients can't find a match. This drug combination, along with blood transfusions and a new category of drugs that helped prod transfused cells into multiplying and lasting longer, became standard treatment.

More recently, Dr. Robert Brodsky, an assistant professor of oncology and medicine at Johns Hopkins University in Baltimore, Maryland, stumbled upon another startlingly effective treatment. He had gone to Johns Hopkins to do the last leg of his training in immunology. Going through some old files, he'd stumbled upon an incomplete study of cyclophosphamide alone. Twenty years earlier, when ATG had become temporarily unavailable, a Hopkins scientist had given ten patients only cyclophosphamide to see if it was adequate in preparing them for transplant. But ATG had quickly become available again, rendering the question irrelevant. The researcher, now long gone, had abandoned the study. Brodsky figured tracking down those ten patients, who were most likely dead, would be a tidy project. He was totally unprepared for what he found.

Seven of the ten were not only alive, but had entirely normal blood counts, and they weren't receiving any other treatment. Brodsky duplicated the trial, this time in twenty patients, and confirmed the earlier study's results. He's repeated the study with the same results several times since. Cyclophosphamide, as it turns out, has a unique quality that makes it an ideal drug to treat autoimmune disorders like aplastic anemia. It wipes out the problematic T cells, but leaves the marrow alone, freeing it to resume production of white and red blood cells.

"At Hopkins, we've almost stopped doing bone marrow transplants for aplastic anemia because the results are so good," said Brodsky. "It's probably one of the most remarkable things I've ever seen. Here are these patients with this horrible, horrible autoimmune disease, and they can be returned to normal. Not long ago, eighty percent of aplastic anemia patients were dead within a few years. Now, when people come in," he said, "we quote them a cure rate of seventy-five to eighty percent."

These days, a patient overly disposed with aplastic anemia might get any of these treatments or even a stem cell or cord blood transplant. None would be confined to a laminar airflow room for any length of time. Ted had gotten a little bit of all of these treatments, but stem cells and cord blood, in their earliest and crudest forms. But their quality hadn't been good, and no one had yet learned to administer them well. He'd get a little bit of something, get a little blip in his counts, but also have a reaction that made it impossible to continue. The most devastating things, my father said, were the chelation agents. Chelation is a process by which iron can be stripped from the blood. In Ted's day, they'd known that all the iron in his transfusions would eventually cause trouble. They knew, in fact, just how many transfusions would occur before that damage began to happen. And unlike now, there was no drug to make the transfused cells last longer, thus reducing the number of transfusions he had to have.

My brother, my father said, should have been getting chelation agents all along. But it was the same story as with the other technologies—it was new and doctors didn't know how to use it. "I think he got a week of it," my father said. But it had been too little, too late. It was the iron overload that had killed him, not aplastic anemia. "With iron chelators, it's possible that he wouldn't have had trouble with iron, and his blood counts might have gotten high enough for him to come out of the room and make it the next five years. But I don't think he could have stayed in that room another five years," he said, shaking his head. These days, a pamphlet on iron chelation therapy is in the standard packet the Aplastic Anemia and MDS International Foundation, Inc., sends out to new patients.

My father never felt like the same doctor after Ted died. In the patients who looked to him, the famous oncologist, so expectantly, he saw the hopeful face of the son he could not save. It was then that I understood how perversely painful it must have been for him when people approached him to thank him for saving their son, daughter, father, mother, husband, wife. It happened all the time, in all kinds of settings. It occurred to me that it was probably hardest when it was unexpected, out of the medical setting. One moment he is buying toothpaste at the drugstore, the next, an innocent thank-you brings the entire sad eight years back to him.

He didn't know if it was right or wrong not to talk about my brother, only that it was hard for him. "Is it the right thing to bring it up?" he said. "Is it bad not to remember him?" I didn't have any answer for him, only for me. "We survived," he said. "Has life gone back to normal? No, and it never will. What choice do you have? You could blow your brains out," he said. "But I choose not to do that. I've done the best I can."

I turned off the tape when we were having coffee. We got the check. My father turned to me and asked if I wanted to talk again. "This isn't that bad," he said. He looked relieved. I told him that maybe we could have another conversation another time. We walked out of the restaurant, hugged silently, and walked off in opposite directions. In the end, there were just no more words. It was sad. But I walked off that night feeling, for the first time, that this had happened not just to me and not just to them, but to us.

On a rainy day in May, nearly twenty-three years after Ted's death, I went back to the National Institutes of Health to see The Room. In my mind's eye, it had remained vacant and unchanged since Ted left it so long ago. I saw the walls, still painted the same pale green. I saw the speckled linoleum tiles. The big yellow chair with the metal arms. The black rolling footstool that was often my seat. I heard the laminar airflow filters roaring in the background, saw the breeze tickle the plastic curtain. I saw everything but my brother.

I wanted to see The Room with adult eyes. I'd put it off and put it off. I expected it to be brutal, and I was scared. What if someone was in it? What if I got hysterical and made a spectacle of myself? Though I've come to make different choices as an adult about how I handle emotion, the knee-jerk fear of exposing myself is still there, just like the scar Ted left on my cheek when he pushed me into the fireplace when I was five.

It had changed, of course. All of it. What hasn't, in twenty-three years? The turn into NIH from the main road looked the same. The parking lot was on the left, the monastery on the right. But there the familiarity stopped. Midway down the lane, a police officer wearing a red vest and wielding a yellow flag stood in the center of the street and waved me off the road to a makeshift, canvas-covered inspection area. When I pulled in, one policeman checked my trunk and waved a bomb-sniffing wand over my steering wheel. Another scanned my driver's license. All because of September 11. The NIH, the hub of all federally funded health and medical research, is a national treasure, and the government is taking no chances.

After the policeman let me pass, I turned left and took the same turnoff we'd always taken, which brought the big glass-fronted face of the building up on our right. But instead of the familiar glass facade, I saw yet another rising up, part of an addition, I later learned, that will be bigger than the original hospital itself.

In the lobby, guards scanned my ID once again. Then, like a stranger knocking on the door of her childhood home, I waited to be escorted into the hospital I'd once roamed with impunity. I was waiting for Stephen Chanock, the doctor whose brother had died the same week Ted had. Chanock came bounding into the lobby looking like all the doctors I remember from my childhood—in his element and in a perpetual but good-natured hurry.

In the lobby, I was given a visitor's badge and ushered unceremoniously through a metal detector, feeling like a celebrity unrecognized at Cannes. Which is to say, I was slightly crestfallen that my entitlement to the place apparently wasn't as evident to everyone else as it was to me. This place belonged to me more than to the security guards who now police it. I'd put in time here. I knew the place, the old place, at least, with all the intimacy with which I knew the house in which I'd grown up.

Chanock led me through hallways that were amalgams of the old hospital and the new. For ten paces I'd recognize a stretch of old dark green tile, an embossed metal door, and then we'd pass through a foreign section, all museum-white and carpeted. We went up in the old elevators, which, in my childhood, had been manned by a fleet of elevator operators in wine-colored uniforms, all of whom I'd known by name. When the elevators got out of synch and opened between floors, as they often did, those of us waiting would see only pairs of legs. It had been my game to try to identify the elevator operator by his or her shoes. But the operators were a distant memory now. Chanock punched the button for the thirteenth floor.

There were two patient wings—east and west—on each floor. Chanock was sure that Ted had been on 13 West. The east corridor, he explained, had been used only for overflow patients as far back as he could remember. I can't remember all the streets in the neighborhood in which I grew up, but I knew which hallway my brother was on: east. I followed Chanock down the west corridor anyway, thinking, No harm in looking.

At the far end, we stood outside a room and paused, getting lost in conversation about people we knew in common. While we were standing there, a small boy, bald and wearing a hospital gown and a surgical mask, walked out of the room pushing an IV pole, waving casually at us as he passed. We waved back, and Chanock made a reference to how much laminar airflow rooms had changed.

It was only then that I realized that we had been standing outside a new laminar airflow room, and that the little boy who'd just ventured down the hallway was its occupant. The first rooms, created in the late sixties, had been bubbles with beds in them. My

brother, explained Chanock, had lived in the second incarnation—
a sterile room protected by plastic curtains and a steady stream of
positive air pressure that blew potential pathogens out a door-
sized opening in the curtain. In Ted's day, the technology that sus-
tained The Room had been state-of-the-art, no more than four
years old. He had been one of the first to occupy one.

The room before us had a tiny alcove in its entryway, a space
large enough to allow an adult to don a sterile gown and mask.
There was a door between the alcove and the main room. But that
was the only thing that made this room noticeably different from
any other. No barrier divided the patient from the outside world.
Its walls, Chanock explained, were embedded with Hepa filters,
the same thing many of us have purchased, in smaller form, to sit
in a corner of the living room and drag dust mites and cat dander
from the air.

What's more, as this boy had just demonstrated, those confined to these rooms had the freedom, with minor precautions
like the wearing of surgical masks, to leave them. My brother
almost never left The Room. On the few occasions on which he
did, he wore a Nassau space suit. It had a backpacklike air pump
that reversed the airflow and kept bacteria out. The "helmet" was
made of green fabric, like the rest of the suit, with a clear plastic
mask in the front so he could see.

It was hard for him to go out in it. People stared. Once, we got
on the elevator to go down and a nurse stepped on, stuck her face
into his, and said, "What is *that*?"

Sometimes my parents took him to drive-in movies. We all
went to some rock concerts at the Capital Centre, a big arena in
the Washington area. The man who owned it, Abe Pollin, loaned
us a sky suite so that Ted wouldn't be too exposed to stares. But
the people in the adjoining sky suites stared.

The only time Ted wasn't stared at was when we went to a *Star
Trek* convention. On that occasion, when my brother walked into
the elevator, a boy about his age made the Spock hand sign for

"peace" and said, "Nice costume, man." My brother nodded and made the hand sign back, with his gloved hands. In the early days of the suit, he came home a couple of times. But he stopped doing that. It was too hard for him to be home and then have to leave.

In a segment of our conversation that had left me, quite literally, speechless, Chanock told me that the laminar airflow rooms had been a trend. Since my brother's day, he explained, researchers had discovered that the problem wasn't so much the pathogens in the environment, as much as the fungi and bacteria patients carried in their own bodies.

Now doctors try to clean out the patient rather than the environment. They might put someone in one of the rooms for a little bit as a precaution, while they administer treatment, but long-term stays are considered too onerous, "as you know," he said. I was shocked when that little boy, waving, casually walked out of his room. I wondered whether my brother might have been able to do so, too. My brother's biggest challenge had been The Room. Could he have avoided it? My father doesn't think so. But we'll never be sure.

Chanock and I walked over to the east corridor. When we opened the door, I immediately recognized the proportions of the hallway. The nurses' station was in the same place. But I saw carpeting instead of the familiar tiles, and pastel peach walls, not the pale green walls I remembered.

As we walked down the corridor, I caught a familiar odor. An aroma that *feels* wet. Betadine. A purplish brown antiseptic that stains the skin tea-brown. A few feet later it was the astringent smell of alcohol invading my nostrils. I told Chanock that I could remember the baked smell of the autoclave, a big metal vault with a round metal door and a round metal wheel to spin it shut. Everything that went into my brother's room—food, clothes, toys, medical instruments—had to be packed in plastic and autoclaved. Chanock joked that he could arrange for me to smell it again, if I wanted. That autoclave was there, dinosaur that it was.

The funny thing was, I liked the smells. When I started writing this book, I began to have flashbacks. My therapist had told me, long ago, that she believed that I suffered from post-traumatic stress disorder. I'd had social workers tell me this was impossible, because the general idea with PTSD is that it happens as a result of a sudden trauma. A car accident, yes. An eight-and-a-half-year illness, no. But what they failed to understand is that children are kept in the dark in these cases. I had never been kept apprised of my brother's condition. I didn't know that he was going to die until I walked in The Room and saw it happen. He might as well have been hit by a car in front of me.

PTSD explained the numbness, the sense of a Plexiglas wall between me and anyone with whom I interacted. Even some of the frozen quality of my grief. I'd known that flashbacks were supposed to be part of it. But I grew up on Hollywood flashbacks— an ex-military man hears a car misfire, and then we see what he sees, a war scene punctuated by the pop of gunfire.

Mine weren't like that. I later learned that the kind I was having were more typical. It wasn't scenes that came up, but looming emotions—fear, anxiety, and sadness. The triggers were often sensory. One day, while cleaning out the debris underneath the bathroom sink, I happened upon an ancient first aid kit. When I opened it, the smell of rubber and powder emanating from the surgical gloves inside sent me into near hysteria. Anytime anything had to be passed into my brother's room, sterile gloves had been a necessity. There'd always been several boxes in the nonsterile side of The Room.

When Christmas rolled around, the aroma of roasting chestnuts from street vendors brought back the smell of the autoclave, and with it a deep sorrow that began in my stomach and crept up my chest and back. I tried to avoid the street corners where the vendors sat with their carts, packing chestnuts into tiny wax-paper bags. But the wind often carried the aroma far beyond the carts. The sight of the clear plastic rain hoods that New York City mothers drape over their children's strollers made me nauseated. The children looked encased to me, trapped and semi-obscured behind the plastic sheeting.

The sight of IVs or bleeping heart monitors in TV shows and movies filled me with an anxiety so great I felt as if my brain, my head, would shatter. Sometimes, but not often, my brother's face— close up, real, not a distant image—would flash before my eyes.

I had feared that something like this would happen when I went back to NIH, where the chance of encountering the smell of Betadine and alcohol was greater than the chance of not smelling them. But nothing of the kind had happened. In fact, the smells filled me with nostalgia. Strangely, considering the struggle that transpired here, it was the smell of home. It made me think of the overstuffed-closet analogy my therapist had used to explain my distress in our first session. At the time, she'd told me that I'd stashed so many memories, so much pain in a closet in my mind that the door could no longer close and things were falling out at random. Working on the book, opening the door a bit wider and examining the past, piece by piece, had eventually given me a chance to reestablish some equilibrium. The flashbacks, in a way, had been more orderly than that random tumbling.

We walked down to the end of the corridor. I knew that the last two doors on the right, before the storage room, were those that once belonged to my brother. They had stood side by side, two laminar airflow rooms, connected by an accordion door in their nonsterile halves. When the hospital personnel needed to do maintenance work on one room, or when they just wanted to give him a change of scenery, they'd shift him to the other.

I have no memory of the first time I saw him in The Room. Maybe it was my age. Six is an age when our brains are just beginning to master the capacity to file memories in such a way that we can retrieve them later at will. Maybe it was the shock of seeing him through the sheet of plastic and not being able to touch him. Or his distress—I cannot imagine a scenario in which he is not distressed—at being trapped on the other side, at having us turn and leave him there when visiting hours were over.

You entered The Room through a vast metal door painted a sickly green that made a slight *whoop* sound when you broke the airlock created by the incessant rush of air inside. It was shaped like a rectangle, like any hospital room, except for one enormous difference—a clear plastic curtain that divided the room in half ten feet from the door.

On this day, the doors to both rooms were open. Gone were the plastic curtains, the built-in bookcase, the sink hanging off the wall on the nonsterile side, the squirrel's tails sent by a Louisiana cousin taped to the mirror over the now absent sink. The little closets off the entrance to each room, which used to house enormous rolling garbage cans and supplies, had been turned into bathrooms. They were clean and modern and pleasant, these rooms. They bore no resemblance whatsoever to those I remembered.

I didn't know whether to be disappointed or relieved. I'd been uneasy about coming back, afraid of having to cope with overwhelming emotion. But I'd also expected more. Somehow, despite the fact that twenty-three years had passed, I thought The Room would be there, unchanged. I figured that the basic framework would be recognizable. But it had been erased. I stood there, waiting for some emotion, some residue of my brother's life and death, to creep into my skin. Nothing happened. Chanock stood agreeably waiting. I stalled. Nothing.

The Room and the ward were like those benign grassy meadows where a gruesome battle is said to have taken place, where people have died on the very spot you stand holding a camera and a guidebook. Once, a tragedy had unfolded here. But there was no trace of the story now. All that it told me, this room, was that while I had spent twenty-three years with my gaze turned backward, life, for most everyone else, for most everything else, had moved on. The Room, or rather its ghost, had nothing to tell.

It was not the place where this story resided. The place it really lived was in the hearts and minds of its survivors, myself, my parents. When I was a teenager, I'd found one of the journals someone had given my brother in my mother's bedside drawer. It was oversized, heavy, with a tooled-leather cover and thick paper. People had always told him he should write about his experience. He never did. Once I'd asked him why. "I have to live it," he said. "Why should I write it?"

When I found this journal, I hoped that he'd changed his mind. I debated about whether I had the right to read it, and then, without having arrived at an answer, in direct opposition to my leave-my-stuff-alone, little-sister training, I opened it. It was empty. Pristine. I was disappointed. But I think, now, that I understand. My brother kept himself sane by focusing on the future, focusing on getting out. To write about it was to dwell where other people dwelt when they thought about his story, and he had no interest in that.

My brother had a story he chose not to tell. My parents each have a story, which, for the most part, they choose not to tell. It doesn't matter. Now I have a story, and it's mine.

RESOURCES

BOOKS

MEMOIRS

For a long time, the experience of losing a sibling could only be found hidden in fiction. In Jane Eyre, for example, Charlotte Brontë's portrait of the long-suffering Helen Burns, who dies as a result of tuberculosis contracted in a stringent boarding school, is based on the death of her older sisters, Maria and Elizabeth, in similar circumstances. The death of Beth, in Lousia May Alcott's *Little Women,* describes the death of Alcott's younger sister, Lizzie, from scarlet fever. With the emergence of memoir, bereft siblings have found a more direct way to explore their loss, one that affords the opportunity to find, tell, and claim their stories. The following are among the most compelling I've come across.

Bereft: A Sister's Story, by Jane Bernstein
    Bernstein was seventeen when her older sister, Laura, was stabbed to death. Twenty years later, when she discovers she still needs to mourn, she reexamines her childhood, learns the details of her sister's death, grieves, and in the form of this memoir, claims the story. "My sister: I adore my sister," she writes, describing their early relationship. "That we sometimes bite and scratch each other, fierce as animals, is irrelevant. I adore her slavishly, and do everything she asks. She says, 'Eat fish food,' I do, without question. I eat fish food; I run outside naked; I stand in the center of our living room at a family gathering and call, 'Fat lady, fat lady!' to a sullen, obese aunt because Laura says. . . . I am a happy slave."

The Road to Coorain, by Jill Ker Conway

The death of Conway's older brother, Bob, in a traffic accident is only one event in this memoir, but it's clear that, for Conway, it was a defining one. "He had been like the sun in my universe," she writes, "and most of my aspirations at school and in my daily life had centered on winning his approval. . . . I realized I would always be trying to live out his life for him."

The Boy on the Green Bicycle, by Margaret Diehl

Diehl was nine when her older brother, Jimmy, fourteen, was hit and killed by a car while riding the bicycle he'd just gotten for his birthday. Diehl, now in her forties, writes from the perspective of the child she was when Jimmy died. She captures the confusion and pain of children confronted with overwhelming loss. When I spoke with her, Diehl told me that writing the book had unfrozen her. "Now I'm an adult and Jimmy seems like a little boy," she said.

Phoenix: A Brother's Life, by J. D. Dolan

As a child, J. D. Dolan worshiped his older brother, John, but their relationship grew complicated and estranged in adulthood, especially as J.D. became the successful one. When John was burned over 90 percent of his body in a power plant accident, the possibility of reconciliation was taken away. "I said, 'Hi, John, it's Jay,'" writes Dolan, of seeing his brother in the burn unit. "Saying 'Hi' to my brother after what he'd gone through, and after the years of silence between us, felt terrifically inadequate. I tried to say 'I'm sorry' and I tried to say 'I love you,' but what came out was more whimpering."

Hilary and Jackie (originally *A Genius in the Family*), by Hilary and Piers du Pré

Famed cellist Jacqueline du Pré died of multiple sclerosis in 1987 at age forty-two. In this book, her two surviving siblings, Hilary, her elder by three years, and Piers, her younger by three, take turns writing about their lives with and without their sister. This approach shows how each member of a family can experience the family, and his or her relationships within it, very differently. "By retracing our lives through this story," they write, in one of their few tandem statements, "we hope we will be able to create an honest portrait of Jackie, the sister we knew behind the public image; and in doing so, rediscover the sister we lost. . . ." (The book was made into the movie *Hilary and Jackie* in 1998.)

Shot in the Heart, by Mikal Gilmore

Gilmore is the youngest brother of Gary Gilmore, who became famous when he requested death at his trial for the murder of two men in 1976. At the time of his trial, in 1977, the Supreme Court had recently made it possible for courts to punish criminals with the death penalty. But as Mikal Gilmore writes, "The country didn't have much taste for legal bloodshed." That is, until Gary Gilmore paved the way for a resurgence of the penalty, making him the first man to be killed by capital punishment in a decade. There are many aspects of sibling relationships hidden between the lines in this book—the way siblings in the same family can live separate lives, estrangement, the longing for a relationship, loss, and guilt for surviving.

The Seeing Glass: A Memoir, by Jacquelin Gorman

Gorman tells the story of a frightening period in her life in which she lost her sight and didn't know if she would regain it. One crisis often raises the specter of past ones, and that's what happens for Gorman. In her blindness, she is flooded with memories of her older brother, Robin, who was autistic, and who was killed in a car accident years earlier. Gorman slowly goes about rediscovering the story of Robin's life and death, and sees it all clearly for the first time. "In my blindness, I found my brother again," she writes.

Visions of Gerard, by Jack Kerouac

Kerouac's older brother, Gerard, died from a congenital heart defect when he was nine. Kerouac was four at the time. ". . . for the first four years of my life, while he lived . . . I was Gerard, the world was his face . . ." This book speaks to the experience of those who were very young when they lost an older sibling and have fragmented memories, as well as to those whose lost sibling became a sainted ghost in the family.

My Brother, Jamaica Kincaid

Kincaid's younger brother, Devon, with whom she had an ambivalent relationship, died of AIDS in 1996. Her memoir, like Dolan's, captures the difficulties inherent in coping with the death of someone with whom you had a troubled relationship. "I said that nothing good could ever come of his being so ill, but all the same I wanted to thank him for making me realize that I loved him . . . ," she writes.

Under a Wing: A Memoir, by Reeve Lindbergh

Lindbergh is the youngest of the five surviving children of the aviator Charles Lindbergh and the writer Anne Morrow Lindbergh. Her memoir is about growing up amid that fame, which included the notoriety surrounding the kidnapping and death of the oldest Lindbergh child, Charles. The sections that address her older brother's death speak to growing up with the ghost of a sibling you have never known. "The kidnapping was not part of my daily life," she writes, "but it was a moving shadow in the background of my experience, nonetheless, another piece of the past that was and was not mine."

Name All the Animals, by Alison Smith

Smith's older brother, Roy, died in a car accident when they were teenagers, propelling her family into a prolonged state of shock. Smith's memoir paints an apt portrait of the often different coping styles within the same family, and grief so overwhelming that it separates rather than unites. Years later, in the form of this memoir, Smith delves back into her past to find the story of her brother's death and to understand the impact it had on her life.

The Million Dollar Mermaid, by Esther Williams

Esther Williams was just eight when her older brother, Stanton, died at age sixteen. It was Stanton's acting talent that had brought them from Dodge City, Kansas, to Hollywood. He was going to make the family rich. After his death, their parents fell apart. "They had pinned so much hope and expectation on him," she writes, "that his sudden death left them without a reason to live." Out of the four siblings left behind, it was Williams who stepped in to fill the void. Williams, famous for her glamorous swimming roles in films like *Bathing Beauty* and *Million Dollar Mermaid,* became MGM's top female box office star, and forever after took care of her parents. But her past haunted her in ways she would not fully understand until she was an adult with three children of her own and her life was falling apart.

The Lost Boy, by Thomas Wolfe

The Lost Boy is a novella about the death of Wolfe's older brother Grover, who died of typhoid fever contracted at the 1904 World's Fair in St. Louis. Grover was twelve, Wolfe four at the time. Wolfe, like many who lost siblings young and have few or no memories of them, felt compelled to search for Grover. He collected stories of other family members who remembered him and his death, and he went back to the house where it happened. Grover's death is briefly addressed in Wolfe's most famous and highly autobiographical novel, *Look Homeward, Angel.* Twins may nod their heads at the strange mannerism that Ben, Grover's fraternal twin, develops after Grover's death: continually making comments to an invisible companion.

BOOKS ABOUT SIBLINGS

Since the 1980s, a slow but steady trickle of nonfiction books have explored the nature of the sibling relationship. The following books are among the best.

The Sibling Bond, by Stephen P. Bank and Michael D. Kahn

This is the third edition of the book. The first, published in 1982, brought attention to what had long been a neglected subject. The book covers many themes in sibling relationships, from loyalty and identity to incest and abuse, and there's one chapter on sibling survivors. It's a fairly reader-friendly book, though a little on the academic side.

Original Kin: The Search for Connection Among Adult Sisters and Brothers, by Marian Sandmaier

It was Sandmaier's curiosity about her own adult sibling relationships, the longing for a deeper connection with her siblings, and the loss of one brother that compelled her to delve into this topic. It is a reader-friendly book that addresses what we do and don't know about the psychology of siblings. Sandmaier uses interviews with siblings on the nature of their relationships with one another to explore these topics.

Sibling Relationships Across the Life Span, by Victor Cicirelli

This is an academic book, the aim of which is to lay out, in brief, the major themes of sibling relationships. It is much heavier on science than on examples, and is best for those who simply want to get a sense of the breadth of sibling research to date.

Born to Rebel: Birth Order, Family Dynamics, and Creative Lives, by Frank Sulloway

Sulloway's belief is that birth order can decree whether you become a conventional or a revolutionary thinker. He uses a number of famous sibling pairs—like Charles Darwin and his older brother, Erasmus—to make his point. Many were critical of the case Sulloway makes when this book came out. Whether you do or do not agree with Sulloway's main thesis, he does cover an array of interesting birth order research, and to see the family unit analyzed from a Darwinian perspective is fascinating.

The Accidental Bond: How Sibling Connections Influence Adult Relationships, by Susan Scarf Merrell

Scarf Merrell uses the stories of siblings, punctuated with scientific research, to explore the sibling relationship.

Separate Lives: Why Siblings Are So Different, by Judy Dunn and Robert Plomin

This book, written for a popular audience, puts forth Dunn and Plomin's ideas about why siblings in the same family, who share DNA, can wind up so different from one another. Their theory: An enormous number of unshared aspects of life, hidden within the intimacy of family, shape us into people very different from our brothers and sisters.

Brothers and Sisters, by Judy Dunn

One of Dunn's early books. This is an interesting look at the subtle ways in which young siblings find connection. Dunn has an eye for the amusing, and she shares it with the reader via anecdotal descriptions of the siblings she observed.

Books About Sibling Loss

Books about sibling loss are rarer than books about the sibling relationship. Most of them were written by and for academics, many of
whom lost siblings themselves and wanted to explore the meaning of
the loss in their lives.

Shadows in the Sun: The Experiences of Sibling Bereavement in Childhood,
by Betty Davies

Davies, a nurse, spent a lot of time working on pediatric oncology
wards, which meant she had a bird's-eye view of the families who
went through the crisis of a childhood-cancer diagnosis. The siblings
particularly caught her eye. This book is the sum of those observations, and might be helpful to those looking to see if others shared
their experiences and outcomes. It also offers a snapshot of the study
of sibling loss as well as the emerging study of grief. As in Rosen's
book, below, it might be helpful for parents searching to understand
the experience of their surviving children.

Sibling Loss, by Joanna Fanos

Fanos, a research psychologist, lost her older sister, Judy, to cystic
fibrosis. This book is based on the experiences of siblings who survived brothers and sisters with the disease. Although the mode of
death is specific in this book, the feelings these surviving siblings give
voice to will be recognizable to most survivors. Her book offers a very
complete overview of the scientific literature on sibling loss.

Sibling Bereavement: Helping Children Cope with Loss, by Ann Farrant

Like Helen Rosen, Farrant, a British journalist, came to this subject the hard way. She lost her oldest daughter, Rosamund, who was
three and a half, and was completely unaware of the effect this had on
her surviving daughter, Lucy, who was younger than two at the time.
When Lucy turned fifteen, a series of events triggered her long-suppressed grief, and Farrant was forced to confront the impact
Rosamund's death had had on her younger daughter. The book is
divided into chapters by themes, such as "Dead Sibling Fantasies" and
"The Scapegoat," and is full of quotes from surviving siblings.

Unspoken Grief: Coping with Childhood Sibling Loss, by Helen Rosen

This was the first book to appear on sibling loss, and it's a perceptive one, most likely because Rosen, a psychotherapist, is a sibling survivor herself. It documents the family experience so common to those who lose siblings while young—the silence surrounding the lost sibling, and the erroneous perception that the brothers and sisters who survive are unaffected by the loss. This would be a helpful book for people who find comfort in others' shared experiences, and for parents who have lost a child but still have remaining children to parent. It's out of print, but can be found via online services that procure out-of-print books.

CHILDREN'S BOOKS THAT ADDRESS SIBLING LOSS

There are a number of fictional books for children that have taken on the subject of sibling loss. These might be useful for children who have experienced such loss, and for adults who lost siblings as children and want or need to reconnect with what they felt at the time.

Something for Joey, by Richard E. Peck

The true story of rising football player John Cappelletti, who scored touchdowns in honor of his younger brother, Joey, who had leukemia.

My Daniel, by Pam Conrad

An old woman looks back on her childhood to the time she lived out her dead brother's dream—finding a dinosaur fossil that would help them save the family farm.

Mary by Myself, by Jane Denitz Smith

A ten-year-old girl struggles with the death of her baby sister and the impact of the loss on her family.

When I Was Older, by Garret Freymann-Weyr

Sophie was thirteen when her eight-year-old brother, Erhart, died of leukemia. Two years have passed, and she's having a hard time letting herself grow older and away from her brother.

The Other Shepards, by Adele Griffin

Geneva and Holland Shepard have lived with the ghost of their three older siblings, who were killed in a car accident before they were born, all of their short lives. In this novel, they embark on a quest to find a place in their lives for the siblings they never met.

ORGANIZATIONS/WEBSITES

The Sibling Connection
www.stlouiscounseling.net

A website created and maintained by St. Louis–based therapist Pleasant White, who specializes in treating those who have experienced sibling loss. It's an expansive site addressed to people who lost siblings at all ages. It includes a list of books and films with sibling-loss themes, a message board, a list of academic articles on sibling loss, and a variety of information about grief.

The Compassionate Friends
PO Box 3696
Oak Brook, IL 60522-3696
Phone (toll-free): (877) 969-0010
Fax: (630) 990-0246
www.compassionatefriends.org

A national support group started for and by parents who've lost children, this group began offering sibling support groups for all ages in the 1980s. There are online resources for siblings on the website, and a page—www.compassionatefriends.org/states.shtml—that lists support groups in each state. For those who can't find a group in their state, there's an online message board for bereft siblings.

Twinless Twins Support Group
PO Box 980481
Ypsilanti, MI 48198-0481
(888) 205-8962
www.twinlesstwins.org

Twinless Twins is a support group for people of all ages who have lost a twin, lost a twin in utero, are estranged from their twin, or are the lone survivor of a multiple pregnancy. One of their express missions is to heal by helping other bereft twins. Many twinless twins correspond via phone, e-mail, and mail. They have an annual meeting in a different state each year. Many of the bereft twins I interviewed considered this organization a lifeline.

The Dougy Center
Phone: (503) 775-5683
Fax: (503) 777-3097
E-mail: help@dougy.org
www.grievingchild.org

This center emerged in 1982, specifically to help children cope with loss of all kinds. It offers support groups for children, often divided by type of death and age at loss. Although the center is based in Seattle, its website offers a state-by-state list of other centers that have been trained to help children cope with their grief.

SELECTED BIBLIOGRAPHY

Alcott, Louisa May. *Little Women*. New York: Tor, 1994.

Aries, Philippe. *Centuries of Childhood: A Social History of Family Life*. New York: Vintage Books, 1962.

Atkinson, Kate. *Behind the Scenes at the Museum*. New York: Picador USA, 1995.

Attig, Thomas. *The Heart of Grief: Death and the Search for Lasting Love*. Oxford: Oxford University Press, 2000.

———. *How We Grieve: Relearning the World*. Oxford: Oxford University Press, 1996.

Bank, Stephen, and Michael Kahn. "Freudian Siblings." *The Psychoanalytic Review* 67, no. 4 (1980): 493–504.

———. *The Sibling Bond*. New York: Basic Books, 2003, 1997, 1982.

———. "Sisterhood-Brotherhood Is Powerful: Sibling Sub-Systems and Family Therapy." *Family Process* 14, no. 3 (1975): 311–37.

Banks, Russel. *Affliction*. New York: HarperPerennial, 1989.

Bernstein, Jane. *Bereft: A Sister's Story*. New York: Farrar, Straus and Giroux, 2000.

Black, Evan Imber. *The Secret Life of Families: Making Decisions About Secrets*. New York: Bantam Books, 1999.

Blum, Deborah. *Love at Goon Park: Harry Harlow and the Science of Affection*. New York: Perseus Publishing, 2002.

Boss, Pauline. *Ambiguous Loss: Learning to Live With Unresolved Grief*. Cambridge: Harvard University Press, 1999.

Bottome, Phyllis. *Alfred Adler: A Portrait from Life*. New York: Vanguard Press, 1957.

Bowlby, John. *Attachment*. New York: Basic Books, 1969.

———. *Loss*. New York: Basic Books, 1980.

———. *A Secure Base*. New York: Basic Books, 1988.

———. *Separation*. New York: Basic Books, 1973.

Breger, Louis. *Freud: Darkness in the Midst of Vision.* New York: John Wiley & Sons, Inc., 2000.

Brontë, Charlotte. *Jane Eyre.* New York: Pocket Books, 1973.

Christ, Grace Hyslop. *Healing Children's Grief: Surviving a Parent's Death from Cancer.* New York: Oxford University Press, 2000.

Cicirelli, Victor G. *Sibling Relationships Across the Life Span.* New York: Plenum Press, 1995.

Colonna, A. B., and L. Newman. "Psychoanalytic Literature on Siblings." *Psychoanalytic Study of the Child* 38 (1983): 285–310.

Conrad, Pam. *My Daniel.* New York: Harper Trophy, 1989.

Conway, Jill Ker. *The Road to Coorain.* New York: Vintage Books, 1990.

Cunningham, Hugh. *Children and Childhood in Western Society Since 1500.* London: Longman, 1995.

Davies, Betty. *Shadows in the Sun: The Experiences of Sibling Bereavement in Childhood.* Philadelphia: Brunner/Mazel, 1999.

Denitz Smith, Jane. *Mary by Myself.* New York: HarperCollins, 1994.

Diehl, Margaret. *The Boy on the Green Bicycle.* New York: Soho Press, Inc., 1999.

Doka, Kenneth J., and Joyce D. Davidson. *Living with Grief: Who We Are, How We Grieve.* Philadelphia: Brunner/Mazel, 1998.

Dolan, J. D. *Phoenix: A Brother's Life.* New York: Alfred A. Knopf, 2000.

Donald, David Herbert. *A Life of Thomas Wolfe.* New York: Fawcett-Columbine, 1987.

Donnelly, Katherine Fair. *Recovering from the Loss of a Sibling.* iUniverse.com, 2000.

Dunbar, J. *J. M. Barrie: The Man Behind the Image.* Boston: Houghton-Mifflin, 1970.

Dunn, Judy, and Frits Boer. *Children's Sibling Relationships: Developmental and Clinical Issues.* New Jersey: Lawrence Erlbaum Associates, 1992.

Dunn, Judy, and Robert Plomin. *Separate Lives: Why Siblings Are So Different.* New York: Basic Books, 1990.

———. *Sisters and Brothers: The Developing Child.* Cambridge: Harvard University Press, 1985.

Du Pré, Hilary, and Piers du Pré. *Hilary and Jackie.* New York: Ballantine Books, 1997.

Faber, Adele, and Elaine Mazlish. *Siblings Without Rivalry.* New York: Avon Books, 1998.

Fanos, Joanna H. *Sibling Loss.* New Jersey: Lawrence Erlbaum Associates, 1996.

Farrant, Ann. *Sibling Bereavement: Helping Children Cope with Loss.* London: Cassell, 1998.

Fass, Paula S., and Mary Ann Mason. *Childhood in America.* New York: New York University Press, 2000.

Flook, Maria. *My Sister Life.* New York: Broadway Books, 1998.

Frame, Janet. *An Autobiography.* New York: George Braziller, Inc., 1991.

Frankfort, Tamara. "Going the Distance." *Real Simple,* September 2000.

Freeman, Lucy. *The Story of Anna O.* New York: Walker and Company, 1972.

Freymann-Weyr, Garret. *When I Was Older.* New York: Puffin Books, 2000.

Gay, Peter. *Freud: A Life for Our Time.* New York: W. W. Norton & Company, 1998.

Gerin, Winifred. *Charlotte Brontë.* Oxford: Oxford University Press, 1987.

Gilmore, Mikal. *Shot in the Heart.* New York: Anchor Books, 1994.

Gordon, Lyndall. *Charlotte Brontë: A Passionate Life.* New York: W. W. Norton and Company, 1994.

Gorman, Jacquelin. *The Seeing Glass: A Memoir.* New York: Riverhead Books, 1997.

Gray, Loren. *Alfred Adler: The Forgotten Prophet.* Connecticut: Praeger Publishers, 1998.

Griffin, Adele. *The Other Shepards.* New York: Hyperion, 1998.

Guest, Judith. *Ordinary People.* New York: Penguin, 1976.

Harris, Judith Rich. *The Nurture Assumption: Why Children Turn Out the Way They Do.* New York: Touchstone Books, 1999.

Johnson, Linck C. *Thoreau's Complex Weave: The Writing of a Week on the Concord and Merrimack Rivers.* Charlottesville: The University Press of Virginia, 1986.

Kahn, Michael. *Basic Freud: Psychoanalytic Thought for the 21st Century.* New York: Basic Books, 2002.

Karen, Robert. *Becoming Attached.* New York: Oxford University Press, 1998.

Kerouac, Jack. *Visions of Gerard.* New York: Penguin Books, 1991.

Kincaid, Jamaica. *My Brother.* New York: Farrar, Straus and Giroux, 1997.

Klass, D., et al. *Continuing Bonds: New Understandings of Grief.* Philadelphia: Taylor and Francis, 1996.

Kowal, Amanda, and Laurie Kramer. "Children's Understanding of Parental Differential Treatment." *Child Development* 68, no. 1 (1997): 113–26.

Kramer, Laurie, and John M. Gottman. "Becoming a Sibling: 'With a Little Help from My Friends.'" *Developmental Psychology* 28, no. 4 (1992): 685–99.

Kramer, Laurie, and Dawn Ramsburg. "Advice Given to Parents on Welcoming a Second Child: A Critical Review." *Family Relations* 51 (2002): 2–14.

Kramer, Laurie, et al. "Parental Responses to Sibling Conflict: The Effects of Developmental and Parent Gender." *Child Development* 70, no. 6 (1999): 1401–14.

Kris, M., and S. Ritvo. "Parents and Siblings: Their Mutual Influences." *Psychoanalytic Study of the Child* 38 (1983): 311–24.

Kübler-Ross, Elisabeth. *On Death and Dying: What the Dying Have to Teach Doctors, Nurses, Clergy and Their Own Families.* New York: The MacMillan Company, 1969.

Leman, Kevin. *The New Birth Order Book: Why You Are the Way You Are.* Michigan: Fleming H. Revell, 1998.

Lindbergh, Reeve. *Under a Wing: A Memoir.* New York: Simon & Schuster, 1998.

Mansfield, Stephanie. "Youth in the Glass Cubicle Dies." *The Washington Post,* May 29, 1980, A-1.

McCurry, Anne. *Letters to Sara: The Agony of Adult Sibling Loss.* 1stBooks Library, 2001.

Merrell, Lisa Scarf. *The Accidental Bond: How Sibling Connections Influence Adult Relationships.* New York: Ballantine, 1995.

Mitchell, Stephen A., and Margaret J. Black. *Freud and Beyond: A History of Modern Psychoanalytic Thought.* New York: Basic Books, 1995.

Murphy, Lisa O. "Siblings and the New Baby: Changing Perspectives." *Journal of Pediatric Nursing* 8 (1993): 277–88.

Neimeyer, Robert A., et al. *Meaning Reconstruction and the Experience of Loss.* Washington, D.C.: The American Psychological Association, 2001.

Nowell, Elizabeth. *Thomas Wolfe: A Biography.* New York: Doubleday and Company, Inc., 1960.

Peck, Richard E. *Something for Joey.* New York: Bantam Books, 1978.

Perozynski, Lisa, and Laurie Kramer. "Parental Beliefs About Managing Sibling Conflict." *Developmental Psychology* 35, no. 2 (1999): 489–99.

Plomin, Robert, and Denise Daniels. "Why Are Children in the Same Family So Different from One Another?" *Behavioral and Brain Sciences* 10 (1987): 1–60.

Pollock, George H. "Bertha Pappenheim's Pathological Mourning:

Possible Effects of Childhood Sibling Loss." *Journal of the American Psychoanalytic Association* 20, no. 3 (1972): 476–93.

————. "Childhood Parent and Sibling Loss in Adult Patients: A Comparative Study." *Archives of General Psychiatry* 7 (1962): 295–305.

————. "Childhood Sibling Loss: A Family Tragedy." *Annals of Psychoanalysis* 14 (1978): 5–34.

————. "On Siblings, Childhood Sibling Loss, and Creativity." *Annual of Psychoanalysis 6 (1978): 443–82.*

Richardson, Robert D. *Henry Thoreau: A Life of the Mind.* Berkeley: University of California Press, 1986.

Roberts, Cokie. *We Are Our Mothers' Daughters.* New York: Perennial, 2000.

Rosen, Helen. "Prohibitions Against Mourning in Childhood Sibling Loss." Omega 15, no. 4 (1984–1985): 307–16.

————. Unspoken Grief: Coping with Childhood Sibling Loss. *Massachusetts: Lexington Books, 1986.*

Rosen, Helen, and Harriette Cohen. "Children's Reactions to Sibling Loss." *Clinical Social Work Journal* 9, no. 3 (1981): 211–19.

Salinger, J. D. *The Catcher in the Rye.* New York: Little Brown Books, 1991.

————. *Franny and Zooey.* New York: Bantam Books, 1962.

————. *Nine Stories.* New York: Bantam Books, 1986.

Sandmaier, Marian. *Original Kin: The Search for Connection Among Adult Sisters and Brothers.* New York: Plume, 1995.

Saxton, Martha. *Louisa May: A Modern Biography of Louisa May Alcott.* Boston: Houghton Mifflin Company, 1977.

Schachter, Frances Fuchs, et al. "Sibling Deidentification." *Developmental Psychology* 12, no. 5 (1976): 418–27.

Segal, Nancy L. *Entwined Lives: Twins and What They Tell Us About Human Behavior.* New York: Plume, 2000.

Sipes, Nancy J., and Janna S. Sipes. *Dancing Naked in Front of the Fridge.* Vancouver: FairWinds Press, 1998.

Storr, Anthony. *Freud.* Oxford: Oxford University Press, 1989.

Stroebe, M., et al. *Handbook of Bereavement: Theory, Research and Intervention.* Cambridge: Cambridge University Press, 1999.

Styron, William. *Lie Down in Darkness.* New York: Vintage Books, 1951.

Sulloway, Frank J. *Born to Rebel: Birth Order, Family Dynamics, and Creative Lives.* New York: Vintage Books, 1997.

Sutton-Smith, B., and B. G. Rosenberg. *The Sibling.* New York: Holt, Rinehart and Winston, Inc., 1970.

Trapido, Barbara. *The Travelling Hornplayer.* New York: Penguin, 1998.

Tresniowski, Alex, and Lyndon Stambler. "Relentless." *People,* September 17, 1999.

Vonnegut, Kurt. *Slapstick.* New York: Dell, 1976.

Weisel, Elie. *The Accident.* New York: Bantam Books, 1990.

Williams, Esther. *The Million Dollar Mermaid.* New York: Simon & Schuster, 1999.

Wolfe, Thomas. *Look Homeward, Angel.* New York: Scribner, 1995.

———. *The Lost Boy.* Chapel Hill: University of North Carolina Press, 1992.

Wright, Lawrence. *Twins and What They Tell Us About Who We Are.* New York: John Wiley & Sons, Inc., 1997.

ACKNOWLEDGMENTS

This book is the product of collaboration, and there are so many to whom I'm grateful. Joanna Fanos, Helen Rosen, and Betty Davies, who have spent much of their lives studying the impact of sibling loss on surviving siblings, shared their time, their perspective, and their stories. Judy Dunn, the undisputed queen of sibling research, took the time to help me understand, despite the inconvenience of transatlantic time zones. Jerry Rothman, who died suddenly while I was writing the book, was a gentle source of guidance. Founder of the Rothman Center for Grief Recovery, which later became the Center for Grief Recovery Institute, he was a sibling survivor himself. Pauline Boss, whose theory of ambiguous loss, author of the wonderful book by the same name was a revelation, also gave generously of her time, as did Robert Neimeyer, Thomas Attig, Laurie Kramer, Victoria Hilkevich, Victor Cicirelli, and Hildy Ross. The Writers Room, a haven for New York writers, provided invaluable peace and quiet within which to work.

I'm enormously grateful to my agent, Angela Miller, whose wisdom and support were essential. Janee Albert offered invaluable insight and moral support when I was ready to unlock the door to the past and take stock of what lay within. Jane Rosenman, then of Scribner, recognized the need for a book like this one, and Nan Graham, a stoic supporter of it, ushered it through the transition from one editor to another. I owe a particular debt of gratitude to Mindy Werner, who intuitively understood what I was trying to do and helped make the book immeasurably better, and to Beth Wareham, a fellow survivor.

It seems only right to thank the teachers who propelled me along this path. Fred Tippens, my unforgettable high school English teacher, now gone, told me, many years ago, that I could be a writer. And Barbara Culliton, another survivor, convinced me that my brother's death was part of my life story, too. Her encouragement, many years ago, was the seed of this book.

Two writers' groups helped me at different stages of the book. The Columbia University Research and Writers' Group, especially Mindy Fullilove, Grace and Adolph Christ, Leslie Green, and Alice Fox, helped guide me when I was doing the interviewing, and the members of my other writers' group, Isabel Davis, Victoria Sullivan, Nancy Wartik, and Wesley Clark, cheered me on while I was writing.

Stephen Chanock, an oncologist at the National Institutes of Health, whose brother, Foster, died the same week Ted did, remains my connection to the scene of my brother's illness and death, and graciously offered to help whenever asked. His commitment to his work in the same hospital in which our brothers died is an inspiring example of transcendence.

I'd also like to acknowledge a number of people from the years of Ted's illness, some of whom I'm no longer in touch with, but I carry within always: Phil Pizzo, one of the few complete doctors in the world; his wife, Peggy, the only one to recognize my plight during those early days, and their daughters, Cara and Tracy; David Poplack, another one of those complete physicians, and his wife, June; my buddy George Washington, a male nurse on my brother's ward, and Dorie Marshall, a nurse who took especially good care of Ted; Marc Cherry, who began as Ted's guitar teacher and became part of the family; Norm and Madeleine, two DJs my brother was in the habit of chatting with via phone, who eventually became part of the inner circle; my godparents, Jean and George Canellos and their sons, Peter, George, and Andrew, and Ted's godparents, Annemarie and Eric Fredrickson and their daughters, Annette and Marie Louise; Bob and Barbara Young, and their daughters, Becky and Kathy; Ted's friend Charlie Levy, and David Chambers, who died young, too, and his family, whose misfortune it was to share our experience; Ted's tutors, Charlene Bath and Helen Mays; and so many others I can't remember or can no longer name. Together, they made the world on Ted's ward, 13 East, rich and unique. And, in nourishing Ted's spirituality, creativity, and humanity, they allowed us to keep him with us as long as we could.

The most enormous thank-you must go to the bereft siblings who shared their stories and, in doing so, helped me find my own. Without their generosity, this book would not exist. Jeanann Pock Dodson, Linda Pountney, and Kathleen Cox Jokela, in particular, served as touchstones throughout the process.

I'd like to express my gratitude (and apologies) to my family and friends, who tolerated my absence, and absentmindedness, for three years.

I need to thank my fellow survivors, my parents. We are still there for one another, no matter what we have weathered, together and apart. Despite my effort to describe the depth of their pain, I know that I fell short. There are no words for the courage it took for them to finally tell the story of their own loss. And finally, I'd like to thank my husband, Paul Raeburn, who has been the most extraordinary source of support, comfort, wisdom, and love throughout. His presence in my life is the reward of reaching past pain to the life that exists beyond it.

ABOUT THE AUTHOR

Elizabeth DeVita-Raeburn has been an editor at *American Health* and *Harper's Bazaar* and has contributed to magazines such as *New York, Self, Glamour,* and *InStyle.* She earned her undergraduate degree at the College of William and Mary in Virginia and holds a master's degree in fine arts from Johns Hopkins University as well as a master's degree in public health from Columbia University. She lives in New York City with her husband, the writer Paul Raeburn.